The
Strategy of
Corporate
Financing

The Strategy of Corporate Financing

edited by
G. Scott Hutchison

Senior Associate Editor,
The Harvard Business Review

Presidents Publishing House, Inc.
New York
1971

Book designed by *GEORGE H. BUEHLER*

Library of Congress Catalog No. 74-148495

ISBN 0-87856-004-1

FIRST PRINTING

CONTENTS

Three Case Examples—Concluding Note—
Floor Discussion

PREFACE

"The greatest genius will never be worth much if he pretends to draw exclusively from his own resources."

When Goethe made this statement, he was not relating it in terms of a business context. Nevertheless, it does permit one to draw an analogy to the contemporary business executive— whether he is the top policy maker, financial officer, treasurer, controller, or vice president in charge of corporate growth— who bears the responsibility of providing creative and innovative financial approaches to meet the pressing demand for corporate funds.

Goethe's observation is equally analogous to commercial and investment bankers, lawyers and accountants, and other financial advisors, who are involved in the development of capital sources or who must provide expert advice based on financial data.

For many reasons, companies often require new funds from the capital markets, stockholders, and outside investors—for acquisitions and mergers, new marketing ventures, research and development, expansion of plant and facilities, and even to solve real estate problems.

Raising these needed funds is a significant undertaking, particularly so in our current economic environment which has resulted in the intense competition for available capital bringing about a tightening of the supply. Yet the sophisticated manager recognizes the need to give up as little corporate equity—that is, to avoid drawing "exclusively from his own resources"—as possible in order to maintain his company's cash flow position, earnings, ownership, and ability to raise additional funds at some still future date.

What is required in this short-supply situation are new financing instruments, new financing techniques, and creative financial men. This brings us to the purpose of this book. Namely, to provide insight for management on the sources, costs, and uses of standard and innovative financing techniques and methods.

In an economic environment when the competition for capital is as great as it is today, no compilation of discussions on "new" financial instruments and approaches can expect to remain new for very long. But a careful selection of discussions that reflect the most-up-to-date financial, legal, and accounting thought relating to corporate finance can be of considerable value to the manager charged with providing his company with sound financial management.

Out of nearly 40 discussions on corporate financing, I have chosen 21 which give a well-rounded picture of a wide variety of problems faced by companies when raising new capital. Individual chapters focus on such critical areas as public equity financing, commercial paper, warrants, convertibles, current trends in the public markets, recent accounting developments, sources of venture capital, cash flows, alternative sources of capital, and many other areas crucial to the financial management of a business organization.

The chapters that comprise this volume are based on material presented in a series of informal management lectures in New York City by Corporate Seminars, Inc.

In all, the 21 authors represent a distinguished panel of experts. These men are drawn from the business, financial, and academic communities, and each is an authority or innovator in his respective field. As outsiders, they offer points of view not tied to corporate policy commitments or the past, but sensitive to the needs of today's capital markets and the objectives of sophisticated business executives.

Understandably, in a book of this kind that relates the experiences and expertise of practitioners, there are both convergent and divergent views on the various approaches to and sources of capital funds, as well as some topic repetition which can scarcely be avoided. These chapters are neither offered as a complete treatment of the complex financing subject, nor do they reflect the entire content of the seminar workshops in which they were presented. However, they are representative of today's finest thinking on innovative equity and debt financing techniques.

I extend special acknowledgement and appreciation to Miss Catherine E. Ferrick, who typed the original manuscripts and revised drafts of the entire contents of this book.

G. Scott Hutchison
March 1971

*The
Strategy of
Corporate
Financing*

Chapter 1

THE SOURCES
OF VENTURE
CAPITAL

Robert D. Stillman

Venture capital has been important to America ever since Queen Isabella staked Christopher Columbus to a voyage to the New World—or to fall off the edge of the old one, if that be his fate. As the economy developed, the emphasis of new ventures changed from trading to basic industry, to transportation and mining, to consumer goods and to high technology. But the combination of the entrepreneurial spirit and risk-oriented capital has remained a fundamental strength of American enterprise.

Venture capital is money made available on a debt or

Mr. Stillman is a Partner of Payson & Trask, which invests its own funds in closely held companies. He also serves as a director of a number of these businesses.

equity basis to companies or projects which have a limited history, and which consequently involve a high degree of risk. The number and diversity of venture situations has grown steadily through the years; fortunately, so has the amount of available venture capital and the variety of sources which supply it. The wealthy individuals investing at the recommendation of investment bankers or promoters have been supplemented by a wide range of organizations and agencies which are actively interested in locating, evaluating and investing in venture opportunities.

As a result, money is available today for any venture which can satisfy a few basic objectives—and available from a variety of sources with differing styles, goals, predilections and organizations. In today's environment, the trick in venture financing is to match a particular venture with the right source of money.

This chapter deals with the sources of venture capital—the various approaches they take and the way each can service the needs of particular ventures. Following this is a discussion of how an entrepreneur can contact capital sources, a suggestion of the elements of an effective presentation, and an indication of some criteria by which ventures are judged.

At the outset, it should be emphasized that, despite their wide diversity, virtually all venture investors have three cardinal objectives in seeking investment opportunities: respectability, profitability, and liquidity.

1. The venture must meet the investor's standards of respectability, a highly subjective test. For most investors, not only must a venture be legal and honest, but it must meet whatever particular criteria they may use to determine that the project is one with which the investor would be proud to be associated.

2. The venture must offer an opportunity for profit or capital appreciation that is commensurate with its risk.

3. There must be some means by which paper profits or appreciation can be converted to a liquid or marketable state.

These objectives seem pretty obvious. Yet, many businessmen who complain most bitterly about the shortage of venture capital base their conclusions on unsuccessful attempts to raise money for (a) projects which inherently are not likely to produce significant profits if successful, (b) companies which the dominant owner wishes to control indefinitely, or (c) ventures with such modest potential or such a high initial valuation that extraordinary appreciation is all but impossible for any shareholders other than the promoters themselves.

Identifying the Money Man

There are six general classes of venture capital sources which might irreverently be called:

1. The Gamblers
2. The Gunslingers
3. The Mutual Funds
4. The Institutional Investors
5. The Veterans
6. The Old Guard

The Gamblers

These are the individuals or organizations that have the courage, foresight, or poor judgment to invest in very new and very speculative companies, often with little knowledge of the field, but with an instinctive "feel" for potential profit. They range from the wealthy individual willing to gamble on a friend or on an exciting technology to the sophisticated professional investor who recognizes the immense potential of investing at a very early stage in a venture. They are sometimes shrewd judges of people, and sometimes incredibly naive.

Some accept it as axiomatic that participation in a technical company or in one in a currently fashionable field is bound to succeed. The more realistic recognize the hazards, but they are willing to chance them in order to "hit a hot deal." They calm whatever doubts they have by recognizing that the money they are gambling has come from unexpected profits from high-flyers in their regular open-market portfolios.

Since they are motivated by friendship or a dream of tremendous potential gain, the gamblers provide the all-important initial capital for a business without taking such a substantial share of the ownership that the entrepreneur's position is hopelessly diluted. They typically, however, are not prepared to help the company in planning, direction, or arranging later financing. While many "gamblers" fail, the occasional spectacular success assures a continuing supply of this kind of capital.

The Gunslingers

These are the venture investors who are motivated primarily by the potential stock market performance of a company in which they might invest. Heavily influenced by the psychology of the performance funds and the new issue market, they evaluate a venture principally in terms of its public market appeal, rather than its inherent commercial strength.

This type of investor seems to be handing his check over to the company management with one hand and writing the SEC prospectus with the other. A significant segment of this category is the public market itself, when companies which are barely in existence raise money directly. The gunslinger,[1] like the gambler, is rarely interested in making, or able to make, a contribution to the management of a venture company, but can be most helpful in bringing the company's stock to the public on some basis.

The size and enthusiasm of the gunslinger segment of venture capital is of course a direct function of the state of the stock market. In a "hot market" they flourish, whereas in a period of marked retraction they are hard to find.

An early public offering is often appealing to a young com-

---

1. "The Gunslinger" is a term used by Adam Smith in *The Money Game* (New York, Random House, Inc., 1967).

pany, particularly when a high price is placed on the stock by the underwriter. However, the hazards of this approach are considerable. The creation of "paper millionaires" among management members often warps their collective judgment and incentive. A high early public valuation reduces the attractiveness of subsequent management stock options which must be granted at the market price. Management is forced to spend time with shareholders, and it is pressured to look to the near-term stock price rather than the long-range growth of the business. And an unfair price—either too high or too low—as often exists in small issues can make subsequent financing difficult if not impossible.

The Mutual Funds

Over the years since 1947, there have been a great number and diversity of publicly owned venture capital organizations. These include both regulated investment funds and Small Business Investment Companies (SBIC's)[2] which have public ownership. In addition, some of the broad-based mutual fund management companies have established special funds for high investment in stocks with little or no marketability.

There is no way to generalize on the operations of these funds. Some have been run in a manner which is referred to later on in this chapter as the "old guard" syndrome. Others have specialized in individual areas of high technology, oftentimes attempting to invest in a relatively large number of companies with the expectation that the occasional success will outweigh a number of disappointing investments. Some are prepared to devote a considerable amount of time and support to companies in which they participate, whereas others wish to avoid the expenditure of time which this involves. In general, however, these funds have a primary interest in high technology, relatively glamorous areas.

---

2. Licensed by the U.S. government under the Small Business Investment Act, these organizations are able to borrow funds from the government for venture investing, subject to the rules and regulations of the Act and the Small Business Administration.

The Institutional Investors

The most striking and important recent development in venture investing is the entry of large financial institutions, such as insurance companies, banks, and pension funds. These institutions invest either directly, or through limited partnerships or specialized venture investing organizations which provide professional management to this activity.

Since these institutions are accustomed to investing large amounts of capital, they tend to set aside venture capital pools of considerable size. Consequently, they well may become significant venture capital investors. It is too early to determine, however, whether they will be able to fit into their investment portfolios a group of venture investments which are not marketable, involve high risk, and may not appreciate in value for a number of years, even if successful. Similarly, it remains to be seen whether the amount of capital set aside by these investors for ventures will be influenced strongly by swings in the public securities markets.

The Veterans

This class of venturers represents varying degrees of direct management experience in venture situations. Newest of these is a group of venturing firms which have been established by successful entrepreneurs who have grown wealthy from the sale of their businesses to large companies. Another group of veterans is made up of large companies whose managements believe they can evaluate and work with smaller companies as minority equity partners.

On the one hand, the veterans often offer a venture close support and assistance in management. With their specific experience in small-company management or in specific business areas, these investors can be potent contributors.

On the other hand, many successful entrepreneurs are simply unable to work effectively in a situation where they do not hold a controlling interest, or where their role is merely to advise and suggest rather than to direct. Similarly, executives of successful large companies do not always understand the peculiar environment and problems of the small business.

The Old Guard

There are a number of family and individual venturing firms which commenced operation shortly after World War II, and whose operations have developed a distinctive style. This reflects the fact that they have historically seen themselves as "partners" with the management with which they participate. They are likely to invest on a straight equity basis, or if they are lending money to do so with a minimum number of restrictive covenants. They expect to spend enough time in ventures they participate in to make a meaningful contribution and to base their position with a venture company primarily on their personal relationship with management.

The old guard firms tend to be less willing than others to invest in brand new ventures or to participate in companies which depend for success on a later ability to sell stock to the public at high prices.

It should be apparent that an entrepreneur has a wide range of choice in selecting a capital partner. In view of this fact, it is of fundamental importance that the businessman evaluate his own objectives, strengths, and weaknesses to determine the significant characteristics he is looking for in an investor in his business.

Contacting the Sources

Let us now turn to the ways in which an entrepreneur can come in contact with sources of venture capital. The first thing he should realize is that venture sources are just as interested in finding good investment opportunities as he is in securing financing. Consequently, he need not anticipate a cold-shouldered response from reluctant capitalists waiting to be wooed.

Rather, he can expect a fair hearing almost wherever he goes for money.

One approach is to use a professional broker, or finder. All of the investment banking houses, as well as being potential underwriters of new issues, have officers who are involved primarily in private placements. If they are impressed with a project, for a fee they will advise on the form of financing, help prepare a description of the venture, and search for the capital. Similarly, many of the larger banks have officers who provide various corporate services, including advice on sources of equity financing.

Many entrepreneurs, however, approach professional capital sources directly. They perhaps desire to save a finder's fee, or feel they can present their story best in person, or are unable to interest an intermediary of acceptable quality.

An entrepreneur may know of wealthy people in his community who are apt to take a flyer on a new business, or he might contact investors who are known to have participated in similar ventures in his field. He might also contact one or more of the well-known SBIC's or old guard venturing firms, which could steer him to other investors if his project did not suit their specific objectives.

As we have seen, the objectives of investors vary. A presentation to a gambler, for instance, must offer a convincing argument that the company may have spectacular growth. A gunslinger will be looking for public market acceptance of such a venture. The veteran usually concentrates in specific market areas. The old guard looks for long-term growth of a business which it can assist as well as invest in. Since selling stock is like selling anything else, the seller had best recognize what the customer wants.

Critical Investor Elements

For most investors, however, the elements of a venture which invariably are critical are management, market and product potential, financial need, and the potential reward to the investor. To a reasonable degree, then, each of these eight conditions should exist:

 1. The product line or industry of the company should be large enough to enable it to grow to considerable size if successful.
 2. The specific initial products or services of the company should be good enough relative to competition to give the company an immediate place in its field.
 3. The management must have the breadth of ability to operate and control a successful commercial operation.
 4. The management must have the desire, drive, and sophistication to build a company of meaningful size, rather than being content with modest success.
 5. The management must have sufficient breadth and flexibility to deal with adversity, and to develop and pursue alternate plans if the original ones fail.
 6. The key strength of the company, whether it is a technical position, marketing organization, specialized manufacturing ability, or whatever, must be truly impressive to the venture capital source.
 7. The financial requirements of the business as it grows should not be so large as to constantly outstrip its ability to generate or raise new money on reasonable terms.
 8. The potential rewards for the investor must be attractive relative to the risk involved and to his alternate investment opportunities.

In making its presentation to investors, the company should give evidence of its understanding of its field, its plans for the future, and its reasons for expecting to succeed. Any experienced venture investor recognizes that plans change, and often dramatically. This is no excuse, however, for not having a specific plan at any one time. The investor wants to evaluate the clarity and credibility of that plan, both for what it tells of the venture and how it reflects on management's ability.

The original presentation made by a company should cover a clear description of the business, its objectives, its history, its technology and markets, its organization, its plans for the future, its strengths and weaknesses, and its proposed financing. The management should present past financial data, and projected profit-and-loss statements, balance sheets, and cash flow forecasts for several years into the future.

In Summary

Venture capital is available today from a wide variety of investors. An individual venture is apt to appeal more to one than another. If the venture offers an investor respectability, profitability, and liquidity, however, it should be possible for any worthwhile project to find capital for growth.

Chapter 2

THE COST
OF CAPITAL

George N. Morris

The topic of the cost of capital generates a great deal of heat, confusion, and smoke in my firm. Sophisticated attempts have been made to define the concept, but they appear in terms that no one understands.

Most of the executives whom we deal with are partially aware of the various levels of costs in the capital they raise, know what their costs of capital are, and also know how to determine them. But we find an abysmal ignorance that I am sure is not confined to corporations alone, as to how the costs of capital can be applied in a practical way to finance a company's growth.

Mr. Morris is a General Partner of Hornblower & Weeks-Hemphill, Noyes, and serves as the firm's administrative director of the Corporate Finance Department.

I shall *first* review the various types of capital and how in a fairly simple way they can be costed out; and *second*, list what we consider management transgressions which lead to particular data either not being used, or being used in ways that are not in the interest of the common stockholder of the affected company.

Earnings Measurement

Let us define the cost of capital. This is difficult because, regarding the cost of common stock, in many cases no one is being paid for the use of funds raised by the sale of common stock. In other words, there is no clear yardstick for measuring the cost of debt capital. Thus we have to invent a method of equating this cost. Hornblower—and I know of no serious disagreement with our method—relates the cost of capital to its effect on the owners of the company.

In other words, we eliminate the company completely, and we look at what happens to the stockholders. We say that the cost of capital must be appraised by the effect various decisions have on the stockholders' value in the marketplace, or in the potential marketplace. This value is most often gauged, as far as the industrial corporation is concerned, by looking at the per-share earnings, since earnings are what determine the prices of almost all industrial stocks.

Of course, this is not as true for public utilities, where dividends are more of a factor. In addition, other companies are appraised, particularly in a bull market, by different factors such as times sales or times net worth.

A company that does not know its cost of capital is a company that does not know what return it must make on funds raised in the marketplace, or even through retained earnings.

A company that earns money must retain some. And a company certainly ought to know at what rate it must put out funds in order to keep the stock from declining in value. Thus no matter what one does—whether he owns a corner gas station or General Motors—the problem is the same—namely, the employment of assets and the rate of return that those assets must earn, which can only be measured in terms of what the capital actually costs.

Levels of Capital

I shall run fairly quickly through the various types of debt equity, which I call levels of capital, and in so doing I shall also illustrate my points with a hypothetical example of an A-rated industrial company. I shall discuss kinds of equity in terms of a normal market price for the company's stock of, say, 15 to 20 times earnings.

Straight Debt

The cheapest possible way for a company to obtain capital almost always is by the raising of straight debt through short-term liabilities, such as borrowing on 90-day notes from the bank.

The long-term market is not difficult to understand. It essentially consists of two parts: the private long-term debt market, and the public. Peculiarly enough, the buyers of privately placed debt and publicly placed debt are in many ways more similar than they are dissimilar, and their market is largely institutional.

Bonds, in recent years have not held much attraction for the individual investor. Thus in going public with a bond issue, one is generally talking about selling to small institutions. Conversely, when a company does a private issue, it is generally selling to large institutions. There are a number of differences between the two markets.

The public market normally has a lower interest rate. Let us say that our A-rated industrial company today can go to market at somewhere around 7.10% to 7.15%.

However, if we could go to market at 7.80% to 7.85%, we could then talk to the large institutions.

Thus for going private, we would pay the difference between, say, 7.15% and 7.80%, for which we would get a number of advantages. Although the terms are somewhat more repressive, if we want to use that word, they are easily changed.

For example, before I joined Hornblower, I was with the investment department of an insurance company in Massachusetts. Our department probably spent 35% of its time changing loan agreements, and the other 65% writing new ones. The 35% of the time we spent rewriting the loan agreements was always to our detriment. In other words and without exception, we were always changing a term to the advantage of the borrower. But in every case the borrower had a valid, legitimate reason.

We always equated our interests with that of the long-term interests of the company and its stockholders. As a result, we usually met any reasonable request; and, in my opinion, we also complied with many unreasonable requests to the advantage of the borrower.

Thus there is a major advantage to paying the extra 50 basis points or so in going private.

A major disadvantage today in private or big institution money is simply that it is not available until six, twelve, or eighteen months down the line, because of their advance commitments.

There is also a lower cost when one does a private issue. The broker, such as ourselves, or any major investment banker, operates on a much lower fee—generally 50% or less of what the public bond rate would be. In addition, there are no tremendous accounting, legal, and printing expenses associated with a public issue.

There is another kind of debt equity, which is called off-balance sheet financing, where one has a lease as typified by the industrial revenue bond. (I think of such things as leases and industrial revenue bonds as merely other forms of long-term debt.) Since the industrial revenue bond issue is now limited to a $5 million maximum, the costs of the legal work, printing, and various other factors involved, plus the higher underwriting spread that the investment banker charges because it is a public offering for most companies, rule this out as a really viable or economical way of financing. There may be exceptions but, of the ones we have reviewed lately, we have opted in the direction of going other routes simply because we believe that in most cases a $5 million industrial revenue bond issue, even at a lower percentage interest cost, makes no sense when you add in all those other expenses.

The rule for costing out the expense of debt is simply to use the interest rate.

Preferred Stock

The next level of capital, in terms of cost, is the straight preferred stock. This is a seldom used vehicle today with the single exception of the convertible preferred, which is favored by people taking over other companies. The reason for this is the obvious one that the convertible preferred with a vote counts under the Internal Revenue Code as a tax-free reorganization. Consequently, one can avoid or postpone capital gains tax for the selling company.

If it were not for these convertibles, there would be few preferred issues these days, with the exception of the public utilities.

In general, the actual cost of a preferred stock for most companies is two times the dividend yield that they must pay. Of course, these have to be adjusted for the costs of flotation; thus for every $100 you receive, you may have had to obligate yourself, say, for $110 to cover expenses, the underwriting spread, and so on.

The dividend rate often is somewhat less than the debenture rate on the same company. This may sound odd, because everyone knows that preferred stock is not as good an instrument as a bond in the hands of the investor. The difference is a tax difference. The same treatment you get with your corporate subsidiaries of an 85% exclusion of the dividend, the investor—if he is a taxable corporation—also receives when he buys your preferred. Therefore, there is a definite advantage to him, which means that everything weighed, you can probably sell a preferred for a somewhat lower yield than you can sell debentures or notes.

Common Stock

It is in the area of common stock that we run into the most heat and confusion about the cost of capital.

I remember reading an article a number of years ago in which the author maintained that dividends paid under common stock determine the cost of the capital raised. I would have liked to ask that author: when the company in question falls on such hard times that it has to pass up its dividend completely, does this suddenly mean that all of its capital becomes free?

Of course, it does not mean this at all. The company could presumably go out and sell the common stock at that point, if there were a market for it, and completely dilute its earnings by bringing in new stockholders all the time.

Let me give you an illustration of this dilution problem. About two years ago, my firm underwrote an issue for a large company in the electronic and data processing fields. The company's financial vice president used an analogy that I thought was quite good.

Several of the company executives and I were discussing the various ways in which this money could be raised, one of which was common stock. When this was mentioned, they smiled; then the financial vice president told me about "Ed's million dollar porch."

Some time earlier, Ed, who was one of the officers in the company, had sold some of the stock in order to build a porch. The stock had subsequently gone up 50 times or something like that, and the cost of that porch was mounting every day. At that particular point, it was around $1 million.

This is a back-woods way of illustrating the problem when you sell common stock.

When you sell convertible preferreds, the charge—that is, the interest or dividend—is fixed. No matter how high the earnings of your company go, the charge does not get any larger.

But when you sell common stock, as the earnings in your growing company get larger, the divisor has been increased; therefore, the cost in terms of lost per-share earnings increases as the earnings increase. And this is what the problem of selling stock is basically all about.

Assuming you pay 50% tax, here is a simple rule that we use at Hornblower to determine the cost of common stock: divide the price/earnings ratio into 200. This is the interest rate that you can afford to pay on long-term or short-term debt, and have the same net effect on per-share earnings as if you sold your stock at the market price.

Of course, you can adjust it for the costs of selling the stock and selling bonds. But by dividing the P/E into 200, you will find that there is a rather astounding cost of using equity: 10% in the case of a company selling at 20 times; 20% in the case of a company selling at 10 times.

Convertible Bonds

Now we get down to equity kickers, which are, particularly in today's market, being demanded by the institutions almost before they want to read any information you might send them about a prospective offering. The stock market just loves to get convertible bonds. Basically, there are two types. One is the convertible bond issue, the other is the debenture issue with warrants, and both are really much the same.

One of the large accounting firms has argued that companies are well advised not to sell convertible bonds; they are better advised to sell debentures with warrants. The accounting firm's reasoning was purely on the basis of taxes. The companies, it said, could amortize the difference.

It is true that a warrant issue is better than a debenture issue which is convertible. But the real reason why a warrant issue is better relates to the number of shares into which the security converts, or into which the warrants are exercisable. If the cost of common stock is high, obviously a bond that converts into common stock has a somewhat similar cost. I know of no company that expects its convertible bonds to be paid off; rather, they expect them to be converted. And, when they are converted, the effect is the same as if the company had sold the stock in the first place, except that it has had a few years' reprieve.

However, under the new accounting rules, even this reprieve is eliminated, so that the difference between a convertible bond issue and a common stock issue is very small; whereas between a convertible and a straight bond, the difference is very large.

The debenture issue with warrants is a far better package for most companies, because the warrants are exercisable into a much smaller amount of stock than the convertibles are convertible into. Consequently, the long-term dilution and the long-term costs are less.

This is an important point to remember, particularly in view of the tremendous desire on the part of both companies and the buyers of their securities to go into the convertible bond market today.

Committing to a Financing

How do you go about planning your program when you desire to raise some money? What do you do? What procedures do you follow?

We think the best and most sensible way to go about a program for raising funds is to start with a projection of where you are going to go before raising the funds.

At Hornblower, we run it on a computer. We use a program that does a regression analysis of a company's previous 5 or 10 years, and then projects it out on a probability basis. Acknowledging that a 100% probability is unrealistic, the program projects a compromise somewhere within the range of probabilities that you are willing to work with, and our computer shows you what the next 5 or 10 or whatever number of years are statistically going to look like.

Incidentally, it is interesting to note that many companies which allege they are going to maintain or establish a 10% to 15% annual growth rate find that this kind of statistical regression analysis does not bear it out at all.

Where do you go from there? First, you must make a number of assumptions. Whatever it is that you are going to invest your money in, you must make assumptions as to the return you can expect. If you are going to build a new plant, where will your cost change? Where will you find your new markets? What will the economics be?

Superimpose these assumptions on top of your projections. Then, vary this new projection for the different ways in which capital can be raised. The amount of money you are raising and the return you expect to get have some effect on the cost of capital, and this should be looked at before you make a final commitment.

The point of all this is that you can in some measure analyze the future. You may say, of course, that you cannot look at the future because it is a guess, but remember, every time you are committed to a financing, you are committing to some pattern in the future. When you sell bonds or sell stock, or take whatever action you anticipate taking, you are committing yourself. You ought to know what that commitment is and what the future is that you are banking on before the financing is finalized.

Typical Management Mistakes

In this closing section, I would like to share with you some of the mistakes we see corporations repeatedly make.

One thing we notice is that there are many conventions in our business. There are the conventions of the balance sheet ratios, which tell people how much debt they should have. Then, there is that awful convention of not wanting to have more debt than two or three lenders whom you know very well think you ought to have. I do not quite know the rationale behind this, but it seems to me to give the balance sheet policies over to somebody other than the chief financial officer of your company.

Stockholder Neglect

I have noticed that the larger the company, the more its officers are bound by these conventions, and I think I know the reason why. On the one hand, management that owns or substantially owns a good part of a company tends to look at the company the way it should—that is, from the standpoint of the common stockholders.

On the other hand, management that is a hired management and has very little stake in the company tends to adjust its financings in accordance with what it thinks other people will think of it. We had a very peculiar example of this a year or so ago when a large company asked us—along with several other investment bankers—for proposals on a financing. This company had some problems. Its earnings, although good that year, were not so good as its previous year.

Since the stock was selling at around 15 times, we felt that the best deal for this company's common stockholders was to place privately a promissory note on which the interest was variable, on a running formula from 7% to 9%. Thus it was 7% if the company earned at a certain level, and the lenders shared up to an additional 2% on additional earnings.

There is a market for this kind of paper. It is a little unusual. There are not many of them done. But we compared this with what the company's future per-share earnings would look like if it went the conventional route of convertible bonds. There was such a tremendous difference between the two that comparison was ridiculous. Yet the management of this company elected to do a convertible bond issue. In doing this, of course, management's main reason was to keep a high interest rate off its balance sheet.

But look at it this way: the stockholder, for this clean and conventional balance sheet, was paying a tremendous price. I do not think it was the proper step for the company to take, even though it was the conventional step. I could think of no better way to illustrate the central position of the stockholder to management than to discuss a situation in which this position was ignored.

Shortsighted Thinking

Another area that I shall mention is the almost inane reliance in some cases on bank borrowings: "Well, I know my banker; he is a wonderful fellow. We go golfing together. We whoop it up once in a while. Besides, I have never had to pay him back."

Some six or seven years ago, I talked with a company management that had the rather enviable position of having an inventory consisting largely of precious metals. The entire inventory and working capital were financed by bank loans.

When I learned about this, I said, "I don't think this is right. You ought to have some provision for not putting all your eggs in one basket, and for not being subject to the changes which are quite volatile in the short-term money markets, because your need for this short-term working capital is not a short-term need."

And that exposes another management misconception: working capital is often considered a short-term need, because it is above the line and is liquidated in six months. The fact is that working capital is still long term, because you cannot do without it.

This management was very happy because it had a great inventory of precious metals. It had no compensating balances, and it felt it was in solid.

Two years later, the crunch came. The friendly little old banker thought the loans were a little too much and insisted, I am sure, that the company do a public offering to pay them off.

For some reason, management committed the next sin of going on a convertible debenture, when its stock was 14 times earnings. This was an unwise decision; that company would have saved immensely had it gone long term initially, and funded a substantial portion of its bank loans. As it was, the interest rates had to be enormously high.

I should like to mention the little use that has been made of straight preferred stock. Depending on how you look at it, this can be second cheapest way to finance the average company, but its use is entirely out of fashion and not because the investment banking business does not like to sell preferred stocks. We have recommended them, but no one has bought them—that is, none of our corporate clients. However, there is an institutional demand for them.

I have seen countless companies go to a convertible bond issue or sell common stock at a low multiple and completely ignore the fact that they could have had funds, particularly a number of years ago, at 4½% or 5%, which was a lot cheaper than their common stocks were then selling.

Being Fashionable

Another area of frequent corporate mistakes is in what I call being fashionable. For example, when the convertible bond market is supposedly a good market, everyone wants to sell convertible bonds. However, many companies might do better to sell straight debt, because of the interest they have to pay, and not create all those new stockholders to share in their future corporate growth. This is not so true if your company is not going to grow.

Another mistake we often see is the sale of primary stock —that is, stock sold for the company's account—for the real purpose of setting up a market which the owners can look at and enjoy in the company's shares. This is fine. There is considerable value in having a market, and many people are obviously taking advantage of going public.

But you should analyze the establishment of, let us say, a

250,000- or 300,000-share market, which is about the minimum for a reasonable market, by weighing the prospects of selling your own stock versus selling the primary stock to generate funds for the corporation. In many cases, you would find it much better to sell your own stock, because you would wind up with more capital than if you sold primary stock.

Often, it is difficult to get all the owners of the business to sell the same percentage of stock. Under these circumstances, selling a primary issue has the same effect as forcing each one to sell the same percentage as the other fellow. But, then the corporation often has the problem of how to use the funds. Let us say that they are invested in short-term commercial paper or put into one short-term market or another. Once again, the consequence is the kind of dilution that is not favorable to the common stockholder. Moreover, this is a mistake often made by the common stockholder himself.

Having Surplus Cash

Finally, in thinking about the cost of common stock—and particularly if the company is in the lower range of price/earnings ratios—and the higher this cost looks when analyzed, there is another side to the coin, namely, that the investment of corporate funds in one's own shares has the same return as that high cost of selling them.

Many companies either have large cash accounts, or have invested in marketable securities of one kind or another. I am not talking about companies that have problems with Uncle Sam, but rather those that have an obvious surplus of liquid assets.

To most managers of those companies, this surplus means the stamp of success: "Look what I have been able to do. This business is so profitable that I have a lot of excess money to put into short-term 'governments' or 'municipals.'"

To the investment banker, such a surplus may mean something altogether different. He may deduce that something is wrong with a company which has so limited a choice of investments that it has to place its money in such a way. (I am not talking about keeping a reserve for a rainy day, but about moneys held far in excess of that.) The banker may also conclude that if a company cannot put the funds to work in its own business, it should invest them in somebody else's business, because it is otherwise denying its stockholders the use of those funds.

A company should be very careful about such a situation. Many companies with large amounts of surplus cash also have broad markets. They do not need half the securities they have in the market. Yet, they continue to sit on the surplus cash or pay it out in dividends, where it gets taxed away from the common stockholder.

It is best under those circumstances for the company to buy up its own stock. Existing stockholders benefit because they have an increase in per-share earnings by the elimination of the retired shares; often, there is even an increase in the multiple when it becomes known that the company is at last going to take positive action.

As a result of such action, the company will show an increase in its capital value on which it has paid no income tax, as would be the case with a dividend, and on which there is an increased value for its holdings.

In conclusion, I should like to emphasize again that the ultimate function of management is really a fiduciary function —that is, to raise and use capital in such a way as to maximize benefits to the company's stockholders.

Floor Discussion

Question: Would you please expand on the rule of thumb that the cost of a preferred stock is two times the dividend rate?

Morris: Let's say you raised $1 million with a 5% debenture, and $1 million with a 5% preferred, to make it very simple. The $1 million raised with the 5% preferred has to have twice the return that the $1 million raised by the 5% debenture does in order to cover the higher cost because the preferred dividend is not deductible in most cases.

Therefore, in order to have $1 to pay that 5% dividend, you have to earn $2; whereas, in order to pay the 5% debenture interest, you only have to have $1. So we just multiply by two. Of course, if your tax rate is other than 50%, then you have to use a different number.

Question: Do I understand you to say that the higher your P/E ratio is, the lower the interest rate should be on any debt issue?

Morris: No sir. What I am saying is that the higher the P/E, the lower the cost of selling stock for raising money. We compare the cost of financing by equating everything in terms of interest. Assuming that you pay 50% tax, you divide your P/E ratio into 200. Thus, if your ratio is 33 times earnings, you divide the 33 into 200, and you get 6%.

If you went out and borrowed at 6%—let's assume you earned nothing on the assets you borrowed on—your per-share earnings would be exactly the same as those of a man who went out and sold stock at 33 times.

That is the basic test we use; of course, it is very simplified, but it is extremely accurate in most cases. When we talk about dividing the P/E into 200, we are making one assumption—namely, that the price of a stock in the marketplace will decline to exactly that point at which the new number of shares is still the same multiplier.

Let me put it a little differently: when you file a registration statement to sell common stock, the market generally will take the new number of shares into consideration, and divide the old earnings by the new number of shares. Thus, if you are going to double your number of shares, say, on the basis that you were earning $1, the market is going to be looking at $.50.

Therefore, that 33 divided into 200 is based on the theory that the price of your common stock, as a result of circulating the prospectus, will decline to exactly that price at which it is still the same multiplier times the now reduced earnings.

In fact, this may not happen. We filed a fairly large primary offering at $25, and stock went up to $32. When you file a convertible debenture, the stock does not generally decline in price; whereas, when you file a primary stock offering, it generally does. So that is an advantage.

Question: Are you saying, then, that if you have a high multiple of, say, 35 or more and you are thinking of raising money, it may be preferable to have a convertible debenture debt with warrants?

Morris: No sir. Debt with warrants is preferable to convertibles with warrants. What I meant to say was that you should look favorably on a high P/E stock issue. Better than selling stock by itself is selling convertibles because they convert at 10% to 15% over the market.

Better yet is selling debentures with warrants, because the warrants entitle the holder to a fewer number of these high-priced shares than does the convertibles. Most warrant issues call for 40% to 50% of the amount of stock that the convert calls for.

Question: How do you explain the market psychology that prices do not decline when you issue a convertible debenture?

Morris: I think there are two reasons for this. One is that the dilution is off in the future, and the investment market is pretty much like most of us are: when something is a couple of years away, we don't worry about it so much.

Second, the funds that have been raised by the issue itself will have had time to be employed, presumably at a favorable rate of return. In such a case, when the dilution occurs, you are going to have higher earnings. You are going to be benefiting from the new plant, new inventories, working capital, or whatever it is.

Question: In a privately placed convertible note, is it usual to have to convert lower than the market, as opposed to the 10% to 15% premium in the public market?

Morris: I would say, "No." At least, in our own experience, we are able to get pretty much what the market puts on these things—10% to 15%. In the case of the notes I was referring to previously, where they wanted to do a straight debt issue, we talked them into doing a convertible. We did it at 15%.

The big problem you encounter in the private placement market is that they want the conversion, but they also want the coupon. Where you get by with a 5% coupon in the public market, you go to some of the trustee plans and they want 7¾% and the conversion, which is not a very exciting prospect for the borrower.

Question: Are warrant premiums generally comparable to convertible premiums?

Morris: I would say, "Yes," in like companies.

Question: In private placement?

Morris: In private placements and in the public. One problem why warrants are not used as extensively as they should be is that in the past—going back five or ten years— companies which issued bonds with warrants were usually the ones that could not sell straight bonds. In many cases—this is probably what you are referring to—the warrants back in those days were exercisable at anywhere from 10% to 15% on the under side of the market price.

Chapter 3

CURRENT TRENDS IN THE PUBLIC MARKETPLACES

Ramon M. Brinkman

The rather difficult times that the nation's brokerage houses have seen since late 1968 are characterized by an emerging Wall Street phenomenon, namely a definite trend toward consolidation of medium and smaller firms into larger firms; or an amalgamation of medium sized firms, in both cases to try to maintain or increase a share of the market. This is true not only in New York on Wall Street, but is happening on the West Coast and in many other parts of the country as well.

This trend may well continue until there are only about half the number of firms that now exist. The reason is quite evident.

Mr. Brinkman is Vice President of Frank's Nursery Sales, Inc. He was Vice President of the Corporation Finance Department of Bache & Company when he delivered the address from which this chapter is adapted.

With the tremendous financial and paper backlog problems that we have had in the "street" for the last two years or so, and with the change over to computerized bookkeeping entries, we have been forced as an industry to consolidate in order to cover higher fixed costs of operation in the brokerage part of the business.

Diversification Movement

We seem also to be seeing some blurring of product and service lines from the various houses on the street, both from internal and external forces. In fact, I suggest that we are going to have to change our way of doing business to concentrate more on the marketing program, or sales appeal, to the average investor. If we do not, either one of two things is apt to happen:

1. The volume discount will reduce commissions on large trades to the point where such transactions will not cover the loss leader, if you will, in the smaller trades.

2. Or, if commissions on large trades do not come down, the institutions will have to obtain memberships on the various stock exchanges in order to protect their stockholders and to do the most efficient job they can in getting orders for their stockholders.

Either of these developments will cause the street to be more concerned with the smaller stockholder and obviously, at the same time, there will have to be some permanent adjustment in the commission structure regarding the 100- or 200- share buyer.†

---

†*Editor's note:* On April 6, 1970, the New York Stock Exchange member firms imposed a surcharge of $15 on all trades of 1,000 shares or less to bolster sagging revenues. But even before that some firms, including large houses, had raised the commission rate from the minimum $6. Most set a minimum of $15, but charged as much as $20, and some tacked the surcharge onto those higher rates. The SEC reacted by pressuring for a rollback and refunding to customers of the broker's previous increase. The surcharge

Along with this fusing of services and product, the brokers will also probably look toward other avenues for additional revenue, such as real estate which, if structured properly, is a good form of investment for American citizens. There are already some well-established real estate and leasing departments being operated in the "street;" this is one area where Wall Street will probably continue to make inroads—simply because of its capability of raising large sums of capital.

Another Wall Street trend of the last decade, which in my judgment will accelerate over the next five years, is the diminishing of the traditional raising of capital by one type of firm, and the retail being done by another type of firm. I think this situation will cease to be so clearly defined. The so-called retail firms, such as my own company, are getting more and more into the corporate end of the business—that is, the public offerings, tapping of the public capital markets, and in the merger and acquisition business.

Sources of Capital

Let us focus now on the raising of capital primarily in the public marketplace. I want to compare today's market with 1962 and, to a lesser degree, with 1966.

In June 1962, after the market had broken dramatically in May, the new issue equity market virtually disappeared, and remained nonexistent until about January 1967. That is not true today. Despite the long bear market, there exists a clearly defined new issue equity market looking for quality issues of companies of substantial size—that is, at least a net worth in the $5 million or higher range. In addition, there has to be a record of earnings and some relationship between earnings and market value, or between book value and market value.

---

was due to expire July 2, 1970, but the New York Stock Exchange asked for and was granted an extension by the SEC to remain in effect until a new basic commission structure is implemented.

Convertible Issues

There is not as buoyant a market today for the company going back to the "well" in the equity market for a second or third time. The investor has shown a far greater interest in initial public offerings than in existing markets for securities of the company trying to raise additional capital. In those cases in which the company is seeking to raise additional equity capital, the approach has generally been that if the company cannot sell stock, it should disguise the debt and sell it in some other way.

This brings us to the convertible market, which is useful to the company that is already public. A convertible bond issue is marketable today if the company management is realistic about the premium on the exercise price and the coupon. Thus, in September 1969, the average company with a good growth trend could probably sell a convertible issue somewhere around 6.50% or 6.75% coupon, with a premium exercise price of somewhere between 8% and 12%.

Top management should think a while before it goes ahead on a convertible bond issue, because raising capital does cost money, although the convertible debenture is nothing more than a promise to pay and does not restrict the company's capital structure. It can be quite expensive to float a convertible issue, say, at 6.50% or 6.75% coupon, and if the premium is little —if indeed anything—above the market price.

Other Market Areas

Another means by which some companies in the past few years have tried to raise capital, and which is virtually nonexistent today, is the so-called letter stock market. (I shall differentiate here between executives issuing new stock to raise money for the company itself and those individuals who have transacted a merger with other companies, received stock in payment, and placed it in an institution.)

Before the disastrous 1969 bear market, we had some success placing letter stock for individuals at discount. It did not require a registration statement because a letter of investment was given by the purchaser. However, today the only type of letter stock, which is really a form of private placement, we can talk about to institutions is that which will raise new money for corporate expansion. Here, the seller has to be prepared to talk about a substantial discount. If that discount fades, say, over the next 12 months, he must come up with additional shares in order to make the total value the same at the time the institution wants to sell as it was when the institution originally bought it.

Suffice to say, this again is a very expensive way to raise money. In this era of tight money, which has been with us since about 1966, one thing is clear: when we talk to clients or prospective clients, they want to be sure that the would-be borrower has realistically projected his financial planning for at least three years out. There has been too little hard financial planning. Everybody says, "You can't guess that far ahead." That is true. No company can be 100% accurate, but it can certainly sense some parameters. It should know if it is going to need some capital 18 to 24 months from now and start making firm plans to raise that capital. This also is meaningful for the commercial banker who in the past has only had to supply companies with funds to make up seasonal inventories or fluctuating receivables.

Permanent capital should be supplied either through the private placement market or the public market, in terms of debt securities (20-year maturities) or equity capital.

Dividend Values

Most companies, and let us exclude the *Fortune* top 300 or 400, are not getting the value in the marketplace for any dividends they pay. In many cases, dividends are being omitted or reduced by various companies. This comes on top of our experience within the last year or so in which nobody has been buying a stock for, say, a 1% or 2% yield when they could buy Treasuries for 8% or more. My suggestion is that when the financial manager reviews his total situation of dividends, if he is not really providing the yield to his stockholders, then he should talk it over with his bankers to find out whether the company is in fact getting any value.

The company that trades in the marketplace with a 1%, 1.50%, or 2% yield on its stock, especially in today's market when most stocks are still near the lower end of their price ranges for the last 12 months, would probably not suffer badly if it eliminated its dividend outright. The value of that dividend in the aggregate to the company can be substantial, and I cannot see that most such companies get appreciable value out of paying a small dividend, particularly when it does not return any sizeable yield value to the stockholders.

Floor Discussion

Question: What about substituting stock for cash in relation to your discussion of dividends?

Brinkman: Theoretically, there is no justification for a stock dividend. I think you have one or two alternatives. Because of the tax structure and the taxability of the stock dividend, you either come through every few years with a hefty dividend, like 25%, 50%, or 100%, or you maintain for a long period of time a steady 3% or 4%. You don't really get any mileage out of small stock dividends unless you have a record of ten years for them.

In the marketplace, there are investors who seek out companies which pay 2% or 3% stock dividends every year. They get their cash by selling the dividend and taking the capital gains. But you have to have a long record before you get any additional value for your stock. I personally prefer the other method of hoping that your price will increase to the point where, if your earnings double, your stock will double. This assumes that you're in the right industry and that the market at the time is good.

Question: I recall you mentioning the era of tight money, but I don't recall you making any predictions.

Brinkman: I intimated that sooner or later there is going to be a firming up of the market.

Question: Won't profits decline because of deescalation?

Brinkman: Absolutely, that's why the stock market has taken such a prolonged slump for the last year. People are now realizing that inflation per se, if it's on a 1% or 2% annual basis, is helpful in the stock market. However, if inflation has an annual 5% or 6% rate, this actually works to the detriment of companies because most of their assets are fixed. This means that the replacement costs will go so high that they've got to increase earnings, and quite likely add some external capital, in order to generate the replacement of assets when it comes time to do so. In brief, the investor can live with a 1% or 2% annual rate; the investor cannot live with a 5% or 6% annual rate.

Question: Where does this mysterious figure, almost 5% or 6%, come from?

Brinkman: It's no magic number. Rather, it's just a magnitude. An annual rate of increase of 1% or 2% is obviously of much lesser magnitude than one of 5% or 6%. Therefore, I don't know that it is magic. You are probably thinking of one class of citizenry who are investors. Our federal fathers who are satisfied with 1% or 2% are thinking of the working class.

Question: What do you envision would be the chances for success in the new issue market with an electronics company just really getting started?

Brinkman: We haven't had one in registration. If an underwriter picks a good solid management, which has at least gotten off the ground with some seed money and it is in a product area that has a fantastic growth rate—I say "fantastic" advisedly, like an annual growth rate of 50%, not 10%—then, I think the chances of success are good.

By the way, in regard to the new issue market, in our business there are several declining steps of sensitivity: the New York Stock Exchange is the least sensitive to movement, the American next, then over the counter, and finally the new issue market. Thus the new issue market is really the most sensitive in this whole thing called markets.

Question: On dividend policy—let's take for example a company that has about a 50% payout over a long period of time and has recently gotten into a growth position—now as an alternative to cutting the cash dividend, what other means might be used to actually reduce the cash program, but still keep the stockholders happy?

Brinkman: Someone once used a rather unique device. He eliminated the cash dividend and in lieu of that he issued warrants. That made up not only for the dividend, but through a period of time it more than made up for any cash dividends the stockholders would have otherwise received over the next five years.

Question: How about offering another class of stock in exchange?

Brinkman: Again, you have the other device of calling your common in and swapping it for preferred. Generally, though, I think you'll find that there are not too many investors who want preferred stock in exchange for common stock. You just don't get the yield in exchange for capital appreciation potential. If investors are really interested in maximizing their yield interest, it's not going to be from preferred stock.

Chapter 4

IMPACT OF RECENT ACCOUNTING DEVELOPMENTS

W. D. Sprague

You may question the relevance of accounting to a subject such as financing corporate growth, and I would be the first to agree that accounting, as such, has never created a dollar of real earnings or a dollar of real capital. On the other hand, certain changes in the accounting rules—either announced or in prospect—may have a significant impact on financing corporate growth by reason of the fact that these new rules change some of our traditional methods of reporting. In some cases, they may result in reporting more information; and, in others, they prohibit the reporting of earnings on bases heretofore considered acceptable.

As a businessman, you should know something of the gen-

Mr. Sprague is a Partner of Arthur Andersen & Co., an international firm of accountants and auditors. He has had wide experience in the financial problems of many industries.

eral nature by which accounting rules evolve. The accounting profession does not develop new rules in a vacuum. As a matter of fact, accountants have been poor innovators. They tend to respond to pressures rather than to innovate, and this is probably one of their principal shortcomings.

But today, accountants are responding to new situations, new requirements, and some new abuses. Thus I think you should know more about these new circumstances in order to understand the accounting responses.

New Financial Problems

More and more, we are confronted with such factors as a widespread ownership of securities and continuing increases in the number of shares traded, number of companies with public ownership, volume of financial reports and analyses, and levels of speculative activity.

These circumstances have provided a climate for new kinds of financial activity including the spate of mergers, acquisitions, and take-over bids; the emergence of conglomerates; new concepts of capitalization; and other techniques designed to expand the recognition of corporate resources and values. And all of these pose new problems for the accountants in discharging their responsibility for the fair reporting of financial information.

Per-Share Earnings

One of the end products of this new climate has been the emergence of per-share earnings as the single most important financial fact utilized by millions of stockholders. The concept of per-share earnings is simple and easy to deal with, and can be understood (at least superficially) by the unsophisticated.

It provides, through the price/earnings ratio, a quick means of arriving at a probable value to be placed on securities in the marketplace. But it also has many disabilities. It cannot reflect the quality or character of earnings. A single per-share earnings figure cannot indicate the potential dilution which may exist.

A comparative per-share earnings figure may indicate a trend that does not always correspond to the actual total dollar earnings of the company. And finally, the excessive emphasis on per-share earnings may permit certain financial maneuvers (e.g., through selective poolings) that may be misleading to investors.

EPS in Income Statement

How has the accounting profession responded to this new situation? First, the per-share earnings figure has been made an integral part of the statement of income through the requirement in Accounting Principles Board Opinion #15. It requires per-share earnings to be shown at the bottom of the income account and to be covered by the auditor's opinion.

This is new. You may not have realized that previously the per-share earnings figure had not been subjected to the auditor's opinion. It had usually been given in the president's letter, in the financial highlights, or in the text of the company's annual report, and covered by the financial press and investment services. And while the auditor has sometimes been unhappy about what he may have considered to be a misleading per-share earnings figure, there really was little he could do about it, unless he was prepared to resign the engagement.

The latitude which has existed in describing per-share earnings as being (a) before or after a certain special item, (b) based on a number of shares outstanding prior to a particular issuance, or (c) with or without certain subsidiaries, may have been factual but not necessarily meaningful to the average investor. Thus the per-share earnings figures are now under the discipline of the accountant's opinion and they are subject to certain related requirements which I shall shortly discuss.

EPS and Unusual Items. The second response by the accounting profession has been that companies must now report earnings and per-share earnings both before and after unusual or extraordinary items. This requirement flows from the new guidelines set forth in Accounting Principles Board Opinion #9 which, in effect, resolved the old question of whether unusual items should be included in income or handled as direct charges and credits to surplus.

And this question had to be resolved before per-share earnings figures could achieve a reasonably reliable status as a financial indicator. The decision was arbitrary, but at least it gives us more consistent reporting.

Surplus for all practical purposes is pretty much closed, except for a very limited type of transaction which clearly relates to a prior year and would have been recorded in the prior year if the facts had been sufficiently established at that time. Certainly, for 90% of the cases, extraordinary and unusual items are now shown as such at the bottom of the income account, and the per-share earnings and the net income are reported on a before and after basis.

Admittedly, this is cumbersome, but the basic figures are at least available on a consistent basis. This change may seem restrictive to those who prefer to exercise free choice in this area but, to the extent that it improves the confidence of investors in financial reporting, it is beneficial in the long run.

Potential Dilution. Finally, on this question of reporting per-share earnings, the profession has dealt with the question of potential dilution. Here, again, it is necessary to review some of the developments which gave rise to the problem.

A favorite technique in recent times has been to issue convertible securities, either debentures or preference stocks, which offer attractive fixed income yields, but which still have a "piece of the action" in that they are convertible to common stock. This has usually had the effect of increasing the per-share earnings attributable to the outstanding common.

While this technique is not new, its widespread use has prompted the profession to promulgate certain rules that provide for more complete reporting of possible dilution effects, and in terms of per-share earnings on the face of the income account.

This requirement of Accounting Principles Board Opinion #9, which calls for a fully diluted figure in addition to the primary per-share earnings figure, is not particularly controversial. It merely provides a ready-made calculation to show the ultimate dilution. This is something that the analysts normally do anyway, but which may be a bit difficult for the average investor. I suppose there can hardly be valid objection to this, so long as the figures are clearly labeled as pro forma and contingent on the happening of future conversions.

However, this accounting opinion went a little further; it also stated that the primary per-share earnings should be calculated on the basis of outstanding common shares plus any other class of security which clearly derives a major portion of its value from conversion rights or common stock characteristics. Such securities are considered to be *residual* as opposed to *senior* securities. (The term "residual" has now been replaced with "common stock equivalent.") This requirement touched off considerable controversy. Questions arose as to how to establish the date on which a senior security becomes a residual security and vice versa.

One of the most difficult problems, as you can imagine, had to do with how to determine a common stock equivalent—even at date of issuance, let alone at a later date. Originally, the thinking was that the solution might be to determine a so-called "investment value"—that is, the value at which a convertible would sell in the marketplace if it did not have the conversion feature—and then to set up a rule of thumb such as 150% of this investment value as the test of when a security was selling predominantly on the basis of its common stock characteristics.

This approach ran into all kinds of difficulties and was eventually dropped. The final opinion utilizes a simple test that relates the cash yield to two thirds of the prime bank rate at the date of issuance only, not later. Date of issuance determination is made once and for all time.

If the cash yield is anything less than two thirds of the bank prime rate, then that security is deemed to be a common stock equivalent and it is included along with common stock outstanding in the calculation of the primary per-share earnings.

The requirement for determination of the common stock equivalent resolves a troublesome problem in a simple and straightforward manner, it is not too difficult to live with, and it still includes in the primary calculation those securities which, at date of issuance, are clearly in the common stock category but under a different name.

Earnings of Conglomerates

It has been suggested that investors and the marketplace need more detailed information about the relative contributions of various lines of business to the overall earnings of diversified companies; moreover, that the prospects of a conglomerate enterprise are not measured simply by a figure which reports total profitability. This is another way of saying, of course, that earnings have different qualities, involve different risks, different growth potentials, and so forth.

In 1967, the Accounting Principles Board encouraged diversified companies to make voluntary disclosures in their financial reporting as to segments of the business. In June 1968, the Financial Executives Institute issued its study on "Financial Reporting by Diversified Companies," which concluded that considerable flexibility of choice should be permitted and that a rule of thumb of 15% contribution to revenues or income should be established as a condition precedent to disclosure of the results of operations of segments of the business.

Then, in September 1968, the SEC released a proposal to amend the requirements for reporting under the 1933 and 1934 Securities Acts, and to require disclosure of segmented operating results of similar or related products or services if they accounted for 10% or more of total sales or total net income. These proposals also required similar disclosures for revenues and earnings from foreign sources, from government procurement, and from any single customer.

Later, SEC Release #4988 came out in somewhat milder form and provided for some discretionary treatment. This is now a part of the regulations governing an S-1, an S-7, and a Form 10 registration. It does not apply to the annual report on Form 10-K at present. The SEC has somewhat backed off being definitive as to what it considers a product line or a segment of a business. To date, the Commission has pretty much left that to the judgment and discretion of the individual reporting company.

There is, of course, a danger here in that changes in this direction might be extended to individual products within industry classifications or lines of business. This could easily involve the disclosure of information, such as advertising expenditures by products, that might be detrimental to the interests of the company. It appears that little would be gained from this more extensive disclosure other than to publicize information that is meaningless outside of management circles.

Thus, on the conglomerate scene, I think we just have to wait and see; certainly, the accounting profession as such has made no firm requirement. The type of reporting now required by the SEC will be in the nonfinancial statement section of a registration statement. Although the accounting profession has no direct responsibility for the corporate figures that are given, undoubtedly we may be asked to assist our clients in trying to develop whatever type of presentation they decide is appropriate.

'Pooling of Interests'

This is an extremely controversial area and one that has been subject to some abuse in mergers and acquisitions. It originated about a dozen years ago, when the accounting profession approved a relatively simple concept known as "pooling of interests" to govern certain kinds of acquisition transactions that were consummated with an exchange of common stocks.

For example, let us say that your company owns a store on the northeast corner of an intersection and that my company owns a store on the southwest corner. Then, we decide to form a combined company in which we each hold 50% of the stock, and we go about our business as usual. Why should we have a new accountability? Why should our combined earnings be any different than they were before?

This was known as a joining of two continuing streams of business operations, and the concept made sense, I think, so long as it was limited to those situations in which a real pooling of interests had taken place. Certain safeguards were provided, such as similarity of size and lines of business, and continuity of management and stock ownership.

However, erosion set in almost immediately and poolings soon came to be utilized for almost any acquisition involving the issuance of stock. Many obvious purchases were accounted for as poolings. And yet, the same transaction, in which cash was utilized, had to be treated as a purchase—with the usual revaluation of the assets acquired, with the attendant good will problems, and with no restatement of prior years' results. In a few instances, the restatement of prior years' results in poolings has actually been used to cover or reverse an unfortunate earnings trend.

For example, assume that Company A has a 20% decline in earnings this year, and Company B has a 20% increase. Now, if you have an exchange of stock—in effect, a pooling—you restate the prior year and you will show the same earnings for each year—assuming comparable size. This would be perfectly legitimate under the pooling rules as they now exist, but it gives some of us pause from the point of view of proper financial reporting.

Pressure for Change. As a result of all this some accounting authorities, financial analysts, bankers, and the like are calling for the abolition of the pooling concept. Others want a return to the original strict requirements whereby you had to have comparable size, complete continuity of management and stock ownership, and so forth. Still others want to return to purchase accounting with a requirement that all excess costs, including good will, be amortized by charges to future income.

Consequently, this whole question has been under extensive and on-going examination by the Accounting Principles Board. One result was the release of a research study on "Accounting for Good Will" in 1968. This was not a pronouncement and it did not involve any change in the rules. It was merely a research study which concluded that the concept of pooling was not valid, and that practically all business combinations should be treated as purchases.

This study also proposed a rather novel approach to the good will problem. It suggested that good will (a) be recognized as in the past, (b) be computed on the basis of the value of the stock given, and (c) be charged off immediately to stockholders' equity with complete disclosure in the financial statements.

The net result of this approach was that only the tangible assets (or intangibles like patents, trademarks, and so on) would be revalued on a fair value basis and any good will would be clearly shown as a deduction in the stockholders' equity section of the balance sheet. No restatement of prior years' results would be permitted.

One can begin to understand just how scattered the thinking on pooling is currently when you realize that after this research study came out, it was reviewed by an advisory committee of seven people, and six of the seven dissented on one ground or another from the study's conclusions; moreover, no two of the six dissenters agreed as to their objections.

It is quite apparent that the question of "pooling" vs. "purchases" must deal with the basic concept of good will. Some people think that good will is the amount paid for excess earning power over and above a so-called normal return on tangible property. Originally, it was considered logical to amortize good will over a reasonable period of years during which the purchaser expected to realize this excess earning power.

But with the blessings of the SEC, this idea fell by the

wayside some years back because somebody posed the question: Why amortize good will when it shows no sign of losing its value, and may in fact be increasing in value?

Thus it became accepted practice to record good will in purchases, but allow it to remain unamortized so long as no loss of value was apparent; and, in practice, there usually is no apparent loss of value.

Looking at the present situation, we see amounts for good will on balance sheets that are really meaningless figures. They do not represent a current valuation of earning power but rather some historical estimate of the marketplace that existed at a particular moment in time.

If the purchase which gave rise to the good will had occurred a month earlier, or a month later, the figure might have been entirely different. Thus it really has no significance except as a measure of the value of the stockholders' equity given up at a particular moment in time and in a particular transaction.

Much more difficult to rationalize is the prospect of a purchaser possibly acquiring an IBM or a Xerox and recording good will on the basis of the aggregate value placed on such a company's shares in the marketplace at a given date. This would certainly be a meaningless figure as a continuing asset value, and almost unthinkable as a charge against future earnings of the business.

How can we really defend the notion that the earnings of a business are changed simply because of a change in the ownership of its stock? Nevertheless, that is exactly what happens with good will amortization.

The Accounting Principles Board has not yet acted on this research study and, as I mentioned earlier, opinions are divided. However, I think most people who are concerned with the problem agree that something has to be done about poolings. Certainly, the resolution of this problem could have important effects on the kinds of business combinations that are being formed almost daily under the existing ground rules.

My guess is that poolings will sooner or later be outlawed

or severely restricted. Most likely, a compromise will be reached on the good will question which will set it up as an asset and require amortization over a rather long period of years, possibly up to a maximum of 40 years. Thus the charge to earnings in any given year in most cases will not be particularly significant, and yet the principle of amortizing it through income will be established.

Valuing Underlying Equities

In the case of oil, timber, mineral, and other natural resource assets, the historical cost basis in today's inflationary economy has become a meaningless gross understatement of real values.

As a result, the securities of some of these companies in the marketplace may not be receiving proper valuation and this may make them highly vulnerable to take-over bids.

People who are sophisticated and know something about underlying values can see an immense spread between book values and real values in some of these companies. Even though many accountants are still reluctant to get away from historical costs, there are persuasive arguments for doing so. Accounting limitations have forced some companies to consider other means of segregating these natural resources so that they can be valued more realistically and attract a more appropriate P/E ratio.

One possibility is to spin them off to stockholders. For example, let us say that you have a large company with a natural resource division involving oil, timber, minerals, or the like. You might be in a position to spin-off this group of assets, and thereby achieve a more direct and appropriate evaluation in the marketplace for the securities represented.

Another possibility is to form a separate subsidiary to hold these natural resources. Then, you could market a minority interest of those securities and allow them to be traded independently in order to establish a separate valuation for the underlying properties.

There has been no serious proposal to change historical

cost, although the subject of price level accounting is always on the agenda of the Accounting Principles Board. However, it is conceivable that we might arrive at some kind of discovery value accounting in these areas. In the meantime, the devices I have referred to, such as spin-offs, separate subsidiaries, and so forth, may be the only practical solutions. But this is an area that needs much more research and study.

Extension of the Equity Method of Accounting. A somewhat related problem has to do with the basis of stating investments in companies where there is less than a 50% ownership. The traditional practice has permitted consolidation of a company where there is ownership or control of more than 50% of the stock; or, if the management does not want to consolidate, it is permissible in certain circumstances to carry the stock at underlying equity. In any event, the undistributed share of the underlying earnings is picked up.

In regard to investments that have less than 50% ownership, there has been a reluctance to permit recognition of underlying book value (underlying earnings), except as dividends are declared. This subject is now being actively considered by the Accounting Principles Board. The majority apparently now favors permitting companies to adopt the equity basis; to pick up their share of undistributed earnings of companies in which they own as little as 10% of the outstanding stock. This is the so-called "equity method" of accounting.

There are still some accountants who feel that this is not appropriate except in limited situations where there is a true joint venture—that is, where three or four companies go together and, in effect, form a partnership or joint venture. In such cases, the entity has all of the earmarks of a partnership, but utilizes the corporate form for legal, tax, or other reasons.

Obviously, any extension of the equity concept below the 50% level will result in the recognition of additional values in the reporting of earnings. This may have important implications for the conglomerates or companies that may be holding blocks of stock after an unsuccessful tender offer. In such situations, the money is tied up, possibly with serious declines in the market value of the stock, and with no way to reflect any income (except through the dividend route which might not be too helpful).

If this provision should be adopted, it would mean that a company which happened to hold 15% of another could immediately begin to report its own share of the underlying earnings of that company.

This equity method of accounting is one to watch, and I think it is entirely possible that soon you may be able to pick up your equity in the underlying earnings of the companies in which you have more than 10% of the stock.

Conclusion

There are several important areas in which accounting changes may affect business decisions that involve financing corporate growth. Three of these are largely resolved:

1. Per-share earnings have to be included in the income account and covered by the auditors' opinion.

2. Net income must be shown before and after any unusual or nonrecurring items.

3. Because of the complexity of capital structures today, per-share earnings must be presented both as a primary figure (including common stock equivalents) and as a fully diluted figure.

Then we have certain other important areas under study which may involve even more significant changes in the accounting rules. Consider:

1. The reporting of results of operations by divisions or product lines in a conglomerate. At least, this is going to be an SEC requirement in registration statements.

2. Some solution to the pooling problem, which may substantially eliminate the different results from the pooling and the purchase treatments, and may also require a long-term amortization of good will.

3. Some further study of the historical cost basis of carrying assets where they are grossly undervalued in relation to their fair value.

4. Possible extension of the equity method of accounting to pick up the equity and undistributed earnings of companies in which you do not have control.

Some of these changes may not be popular in all circles and I am sure that not all of them will be the ideal or ultimate answers. On balance, they are designed to provide more meaningful and consistent information for investors, to forestall criticism, and to prevent some of the abuses that were permitted under the old ground rules.

Unless we make changes like these, the courts, the legislators, the regulatory bodies, and the public itself may demand even more drastic answers. And the objective of the Accounting Principles Board, I think, is to foster such reasonable changes as will enhance credibility and thus contribute to the free operation of the securities markets which are so essential to corporate growth and expansion.

Floor Discussion

Question: What is your crystal ball guess on the tax requirement or allowance for amortization of good will in the future?

Sprague: Tax-wise, I have no crystal ball. I have no indication that there is going to be any different thinking in the Treasury Department than there has been in the past. There is no deduction for amortization of good will at present. And nothing that has been released by the Accounting Principles Board has dealt with that aspect of it.

However, if you ever want to make a case for amortizing good will with the Treasury Department, you're certainly in a better position if you're doing it accounting-wise. Because if you're going to take the position that there's no diminution in value in good will, and that therefore you don't have to amortize it, it puts you in a somewhat inconsistent position to go to the Treasury Department and say you should have a deduction for it.

Question: Shouldn't there be some amortization of good will?

Sprague: This is an area of great compromise. Some people feel very strongly that good will is a cost that has to be charged against income sometime. Because those people feel this so strongly, as a matter of principle, it may be that the people who feel the other way, in order to get some meeting of the minds, will be willing to go to a stretched out amortization on the theory that it will not affect the per-share earnings enough to cause distortion.

Our firm prefers to charge it off against stockholders equity and get rid of it, but to also tell everybody about it. We say to the stockholders, "Your board and your management gave up 'x' million shares of stock, having a value in the marketplace of so much, and here's the amount that's being deducted from your equity on the balance sheet. But it won't affect your future earnings; they are going to be the same as though the two companies were simply being added together."

Question: Would you comment on the computation of the shares outstanding and the computation of the per-share earnings?

Sprague: In the past, there have been a number of methods. Some companies have used shares outstanding at the end of the year, some a monthly average, and some average beginning and end. But it seems to me the average outstanding during the year is probably the most practical answer, and I believe that is the recommended treatment.

Question: Hasn't there been some movement in the past

to provide for the reporting of underground reserves, say, in the case of oil companies?

Sprague: That is true in the case of SEC filings. They have prescribed procedures for disclosing and expertising estimates of underground reserves.

But this is a very difficult thing for the average investor to come to grips with. If he is an oil man, or otherwise knowledgeable in the field, it means something to him. He is a sophisticated analyst.

But many people feel it falls far short of achieving a proper and fair valuation in the marketplace for the securities of the company which may have billions under the ground but very few dollars in the balance sheet.

Question: Don't the oil companies resist this anyway from a competitive standpoint?

Sprague: They do. But, unfortunately from their point of view, if they want to register with the SEC, they have little choice, at least at this time. But it may be several years before they do it again. It is only required in connection with registration statements.

Question: If someone writes off good will liberally, to what extent does the Internal Revenue Service object?

Sprague: It normally has no status with the Internal Revenue Service. I am no tax expert, but I think you will find in most cases that purchased good will, unless it can be attached to the basis of tangible property, is not a deductible item. So the IRS in the average good will situation is not concerned.

Question: Would you give some examples of residuals that have the characteristics of common stock at the time of issuance, and also examples of convertibles that do not?

Sprague: I think the benchmark that is being talked about in the Accounting Principles Board deliberations is that a security comes out at somewhere around 150% of its so-called investment value. This has one problem: Who determines the investment value?

One answer is you go to your investment banker and ask

him. An alternative and arbitrary approach being considered, which would avoid this investment value problem, relates it to the prime rate. In other words, if you were selling convertibles with a coupon of 60% of the prime rate, or some similar percentage, that would be the definition of a residual with common stock characteristics.

In general, if it is selling at a level that is due to its conversion rights or other common stock characteristics, such as sharing in the dividends, then it is deemed to be a residual security —as opposed to a senior security which has a prior claim against the earnings applicable to the common.

This is a very involved area, and you can get all shades of opinion as to what should, or should not, be residual. Fortunately, the indications are that the whole matter is going to be swept aside except for those which are clearly residual at the date of issuance.

Question: So a preference stock with a nominal rate approximating prime rate would not be included?

Sprague: I would think that is right.

Question: How do you define extraordinary nonrecurring expense? Is it measured in terms of its relationship to profit before tax?

Sprague: I think most accountants measure it in relation to the final reported net income. In other words, if we have an unusual or a nonrecurring item, and the net effect of that item, including its tax effect, say, is 20% of the net income for the year, I think most people would say that is clearly an extraordinary or unusual item which should be segregated.

As the percentage goes down, you get into gray areas. Some people have more liberal measures of materiality than others.

I think most people are concerned when it is something as high as 15%; some are concerned at 10%; and others are not. Thus this is really a judgment area between a company and its outside auditors as to how big an item has to be before it materially affects, say, an investment decision.

Question: If you had nonrecurring income and expense items of substantial proportion, would you have to state your per-share earnings in three ways or just two ways? Would you net out those expenses and income?

Sprague: If you mean where the nonrecurring items went in two directions, I think you would be inclined to take a rather practical view in most cases and deal with the net amount. What you are trying to do in the final analysis is to tell the reader something that may change his decision making.

If you have one plus and one minus, then the final net earnings figure is still a fair representation of what the company has done for the year, whether you do or don't spell out the details.

Question: I have received some interesting proposals like increasing the working capital by selling and leasing back certain property. Each proposal unequivocally stated that I was going to end up with a clean balance sheet. Is that possible?

Sprague: You mean without recording the leaseback?

Question: Right. I seem to recall reading somewhere, perhaps in the Accounting Principles Board opinion, something to the effect that this may not be the case. Would you comment?

Sprague: I think the general rule on whether or not a company has to report its so-called obligation with an offsetting asset right, if you will, usually turns on whether this leaseback is tantamount to ownership. There are certain rule of thumb tests. For example:

If the lease runs for the entire life of the asset or the property, or if it gives you the right to buy in at a ridiculous figure which is not a fair value figure, then it becomes reasonably apparent in substance that you still have the right of ownership. If that is the case, it ought to be reported as a right to use an asset and as an obligation.

On the other hand, if you sell a piece of property or an asset that has a life expectancy of, say, 25 years and you lease it back for 10, and maybe you have a clause in the lease that gives you the right to purchase it on a negotiated basis for fair value, it is hard to sustain the position that you have all the incidence of ownership, because you don't.

In that case, you simply have a lease, and you would not report any balance-sheet items.

Question: If the pooling concept is discarded in favor of purchase, will this necessarily obviate tax-free reorganizations? If they are going to be treated as purchases from an accounting standpoint, how will the Internal Revenue Service view this?

Sprague: My understanding is this would be two separate and distinct questions. I don't believe that the accounting treatment would be a factor in the IRS determination.

Question: Assuming that good will has been built up through advertising and sales promotion, in the broad sense, aren't you really charging income twice because the advertising and promotion in the first place was charged to income?

Sprague: That is a very good point. And that's one reason why our thinking leans in the direction that good will should never go through an income account. Maybe it's a proper disclosure or charge against stockholders' equity, but not against the stream of earnings.

Question: Has the SEC relaxed its attitude on writing good will off—I believe you said over ten-years—and is there any indication as to the direction it may take?

Sprague: Actually, the SEC hasn't required the amortization of good will for some time now. I think it did have a ten-year rule of thumb at one time, but that's out, provided the company can assume the burden of proof that there hasn't been any diminution in good will.

Thus you can let it sit there with no amortization presently. I don't think the SEC is entirely happy with that. My guess is that if the accounting profession were to come out with some kind of an amortization requirement, the SEC would undoubtedly support it; particularly, if it were over a relatively long period of time.

In regard to the other part of your question about independence, the SEC continues to take the view pretty much that it would like to see the accounting profession make the rules which it would then support so long as the SEC felt that we were in the ballpark.

Question: What about negative good will, or the so-called bargain purchase? How would this work, if we changed the rules on it?

Sprague: Presently, I think most accountants feel that there rarely is a true bargain purchase. In other words, there's usually something "in the wood" such as an overvalued property account, obsolescence in the inventory, lines of business that they ought to be getting out of, or something.

The natural tendency on the part of the accountants is to take the negative good will and set it up as a reserve waiting for things to come out of the woodwork; then, when they do, there is a place to get rid of it.

If nothing happens—that is, if you have a true bargain purchase—the practical answer usually is to amortize it back to income. In a situation where you have a positive good will sitting on the asset side without amortization, and another transaction with negative good will sitting on the right hand side, you might well say it's inconsistent not to offset them. But not necessarily, because they are two separate transactions. One may have been a true bargain purchase, or there may have been some uncertainties and questions which have or have not come to light, so you carry it as a reserve and perhaps get rid of it over a period of years.

Chapter 5

THE STOCK MARKET AND INTEREST RATE OUTLOOK

Walter R. Good

There is an axiom that I find useful in looking at what has been happening in the securities market in the past year or so. It states simply that "good news is bad news and bad news is good news."

Although this axiom oversimplifies, it has a certain amount of truth in it. After a few words of explanation, I shall try to apply it to the situation that we find ourselves in now and, in a cautious way, offer my outlook on the stock and bond markets.

Mr. Good is Manager of Brown Brothers Harriman & Co., where he is in charge of investment research for this leading private banking firm.

Historical Shift

First, I would like to discuss what I mean by "good news is bad news and bad news is good news." If we were to glance at the Dow Jones Industrial Average from the 1920's to about 1950, we would quickly see that it reflected a very cyclical view of the economy. People were often more concerned with picking the business cycle than with long-term growth, because the cycle was the dominant factor in determining whether business could prosper.

I call this the world of Graham and Dodd, after a book familiar to the securities business whose authors were Benjamin Graham and David L. Dodd.[1] It was first issued in 1934, and has been the most successful book in its field. Its assumptions and its approach were largely based on a highly cyclical view of the economy. It was very successful in interpreting this kind of a world, and although later editions have changed, some of the earlier assumptions no longer hold. All one has to do is look at the Dow-Jones average of that period to be impressed with the vast difference from the postwar investment world, which has been characterized by steadier growth and less pronounced cyclical swings.

This sharp contrast between the investment world postwar and prewar ties in closely with the second part of the problem —namely, that many of our patterns of thought were largely formed in that earlier period or else handed down to us by education or tradition. For example, many went to school, as I did, in the early postwar period and took courses from professors who had learned from the experience of this earlier period.

What I am getting at is that many of the developments that were good news in the world of Graham and Dodd are bad news today and vice versa. We really have to look at each new development as it relates to the stock or bond market and ask our-

---

1. See Benjamin Graham and David L. Dodd *Security Analysis* (New York, Whittlesey House, McGraw-Hill Book Company, Inc.).

selves if it may not have the opposite impact on investing under today's conditions than had formerly been the case.

Management by Government

In today's managed economy, one might argue that the recent decline in the stock market (through September 1969) was related—in large degree—to good news as measured by traditional standards, such as too much boom in the economy; conversely, more bad news as measured by past standards, such as too little growth in the economy, would have been helpful.

With the emphasis on change in the kind of investment world we live in—that is, less business cycle, more management by government—the risks in investment, rather than being greatly reduced, may have merely changed their shape. The big investment risk used to be associated with a downturn in the economy; typically, in pre-World War II, the holder of a diversified group of common stocks could lose 50% of his money from peak to trough of the cyclical swing in the stock market. In the 1950's and 1960's, from peak to trough, a similar stockholder could lose about 25% of his money at most, and the trough was rather short lived. Moreover, the market generally went on to new highs quickly so that in the long run it was seemingly a small risk, at least gauged by our postwar history through mid-year 1969, to be invested in stocks.

Stock Index. Let me give an example of one recent development which suggests that risk has changed, not disappeared. *Exhibit I* is an index whereby stocks are divided into four major groups. The first group is *Utilities and Banks*, which by past standards were considered to be defensive—that is, if the economy went down, these companies would not be affected much by the adverse conditions. The second group comprises *Basic Companies*, which are largely the blue chips. Many of these are somewhat cyclical—the kind of companies that are in the Dow-Jones—but there are about three times as many stocks in this index as in the DJIA.

Then there are the growth companies which are represented by the third and fourth categories: *Quality Growth* and *Other Growth*. In the Quality Growth group are companies that are characterized by consistent sales and earnings growth; and, because of the competitive position and basic strength of each company, such growth is generally expected to continue into the future.

For the Other Growth stocks, sales and earning progress may be even faster but is less assured; for these stocks, the record has been less consistent, which usually has something to do with the nature of the company and its business.

By way of explanation, *Exhibit I* shows two 24-week periods, or approximately six months. The bar graph on the bottom covers approximately the six months ending July 25, 1969. The bar graph on the top covers the previous six months in which not much happened to the general market, and there was little variation in the averages of the four groups.

When the market went down, however, stocks did not behave according to the traditional thinking that defensive stocks will not drop as much as others. Actually, the Utilities and Banks group, which traditionally has been defensive, dropped as much as the Basic Companies. Among the growth companies, the one area largely unaffected was that of the high price/earnings ratio Quality Growth companies. By past standards, such high price/earnings ratio stocks should have been vulnerable in a bear market.

Bond Pattern. The point I have been trying to make is that the risk, although changed in character, is still great in investment, and I shall illustrate this a bit more dramatically by looking at what happened to high quality bonds in the five-year period ending in 1969. By traditional thinking, high quality bonds ought to be "safe" and stocks ought to be more risky. I am not suggesting that this pattern has been permanently reversed. But let us look at the index shown in *Exhibit II*, which relates 20-year state and local bonds to the Value Line index of 1,400 common stocks weighted equally. In this index, General Motors does not have more weight than, say Perkin-Elmer,

Exhibit I. Illustration of How Stock Investment Risk Changed Shape

24 Weeks ended February 6, 1969

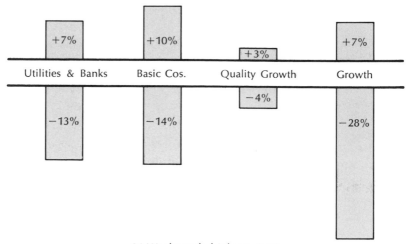

24 Weeks ended July 25, 1969

Exhibit II. Example of How Bond Investment Risk Changed Shape

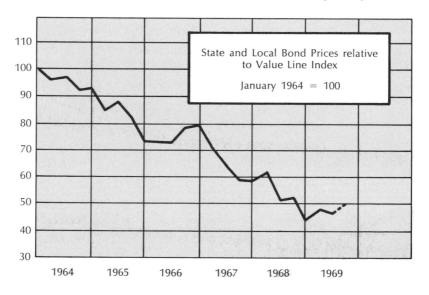

which is a much smaller company. This index gives us roughly the kind of results that the average investor, who could select from any stock in the New York Stock Exchange, might have had if he just invested at random.

What happened in this five-year period was that the index of state and local bonds—all good quality bonds—declined about a third. The Value Line index, even with the 1969 decline in the stock market, was up about a third; thus, the investor who held bonds would have lost about half of his money relative to the amount he could have had if he had bought the Value Line Index.

The experience of the bondholder in the late 1960's is similar to what would have happened to the prewar stockholder in a bear market. In a sense, there was still a chance to lose 50% —at least on a relative basis. Investment risks were still great despite the changed framework for investment.

Current Conditions

Let me now attempt to apply this background, admittedly sketchy and oversimplified, to the present situation.

The government in our managed economy has two main weapons to dampen inflation and to slow the economy— namely, fiscal policy and monetary policy. Most economists agree that one or the other of these, or some combination of them can be effective. A good deal of controversy arises over which one is the most important. At one extreme, some say that monetary policy is not very important, and, indeed, monetary policy was generally de-emphasized for many years until just recently. At the other extreme, some say that fiscal policy in itself is not too important. In between these two views, there are all shades of opinion.

What is significant now is that, whatever the theory, both tools have turned restrictive. The problem facing the investment people is not one of deciding which economists are right or wrong, but of choosing the right investment strategy in view of the evidence that both approaches are restrictive.

Fiscal and Monetary Policies

Let us take a quick look at this federal budget influence, as shown in *Exhibit III*. This is a concept which has influenced the Council of Economic Advisors. The zero line in the middle represents the point at which the budget would have a neutral influence at full employment. Deviations in the upward direction from the zero line represent a potential budget surplus and the downward deviations represent a potential budget deficit, each at full employment. The full employment surplus would be restrictive to the economy because the government would be mopping up purchasing power. The full employment deficit would be stimulative just for the opposite reason.

Over much of the 1960's, the budget became more and more stimulative. When the Vietnam war escalated, we entered a period of large deficit spending—which contributed to the inflation and the super boom of the late 1960's. More recently, the imposition of the tax surcharge along with other factors caused the budget to become restrictive. In general, there is agreement that there has been a major turn and that this is a significant factor; however, the argument is about the degree of its significance.

Exhibit IV shows two measures which are related to money supply. The upper one, representing the monetary base, is perceived by the monetary theorists to indicate outlook for the money supply. It does not necessarily move directly with the money supply at all times, but it does show the broad tendency. In the exhibit, it rises rapidly in 1967 and 1968, and then flattens out in 1969.

Federal Reserve Credit influences the monetary base and it also has turned down.

Effects of Government Policies

The impact of the government's dampening of the economy is reflected in *Exhibit V*. This is the gross national product in current dollars, which takes into account the impact of inflation.

Exhibit III. Federal Budget Influence* on Investment Strategy

Stimulus or Restraint

Billions of Dollars

Quarterly Totals at Annual Rates
Seasonally Adjusted

Billions of Dollars

9.4

STIMULUS
RESTRAINT

1961 1962 1963 1964 1965 1966 1967 1968 1969

* The High-Employment Budget, first published by the Council of Economic
Advisers.   Latest data plotted: 2nd quarter preliminary.

Source: Federal Reserve Bank of St. Louis

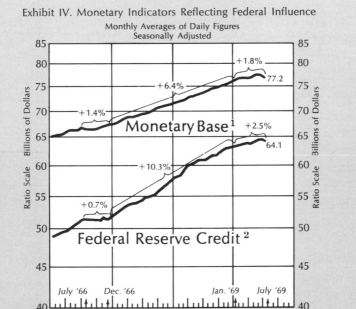

Exhibit IV. Monetary Indicators Reflecting Federal Influence

Monthly Averages of Daily Figures
Seasonally Adjusted

Billions of Dollars

Ratio Scale

+1.8%

+6.4%

77.2

+1.4%

Monetary Base[1]

+2.5%

64.1

+10.3%

+0.7%

Federal Reserve Credit [2]

Ratio Scale

Billions of Dollars

July '66   Dec. '66   Jan. '69   July '69

1966   1967   1968   1969

The lower curve suggests the real rate of activity, rather than the rate of activity distorted by a rise in prices. While this graph does not show clearly what happened, the lower line curls over a bit, which suggests a slowing down. Actually, in percentage terms, growth of economy in real terms has slowed substantially since 1968. In the second quarter of 1968, real GNP was rising at a rate of about 6% or a little more, but in the second half real growth was down to about 2%, which is a rather substantial change.

The Federal Reserve Board's Index of Industrial Production also turned down. The decline thus far has been too small to be significant, but there was a decline and this is something which traditionally would have been bad news; however, under 1969 circumstances, it was good news. The components of the FRB indicated various areas where this was happening, such as a flattening in production of appliances. One of the most dramatic areas in which the monetary policy was obviously hitting very hard was housing, both in the interest rate on mortgages and in the availability of mortgage money.

On the other hand, the restrictive influences have not thus far (mid-1970) slowed the uptrend in prices and wages. The continued rise in prices is certainly a disappointment and the rise in wages has continued at even a much faster rate. In another era, the buoyancy in prices generally might have been interpreted as good news for stocks, but now it must be thought of as bad news.

At this point, I might touch on the role of the Vietnam war as it relates to the stock market. At one stage, about a year ago, the slightest peace rumor sent the stock market up for a day or so. There was widespread assumption that the end of the war would be very bullish. I think there was validity to the idea that the end of the war would help us with some of our fundamental problems and contribute to a stronger stock market.

As time has gone on, however, investors have taken a more sober look at prospects for the end of the war and probably have come to two conclusions. One is that the end of the war will not

Exhibit V. Effect of Federal Policy to Dampen Inflation

GNP in Current Dollars

GNP in 1958 Dollars

	1965	1966	1967	1968	1969
1000					
950					
900					
850					
800					
750					
700					
650					
600					

mean such a dramatic cutback in military expenditures as they had hoped for earlier. The other is that there has been a good deal of discouragement with the idea that the war can end dramatically—full settlement coming all at once. As a consequence, anticipation of the end of the Vietnam war appears to be less a market factor today than it was a year or so ago. It appears though, that any important progress toward peace in Vietnam would still be significant in two ways.

One, since people associate a period of super boom and inflation with war, the phasing out of the war might exert a psychological impact which would help to hold down inflation and to bring some of the beneficial results that the government is trying to attain.

Two, the phasing out of the war might give the government an opportunity to squeeze a little harder on the economy. The reason is that, under such happier circumstances, people might be willing to take a bit more unemployment and dislocation, feeling that the adverse situation is only temporary and offset by the prospect of bringing our boys home.

What does all this mean for the stock market? The answer seems to depend in large part on whether we get enough bad news soon enough to bring inflation and high interest rates under control before they cause more mischief. I conclude that the bottom for stock prices has either been reached or is close at hand provided current efforts by government to restrict economic activity and control inflation progress on schedule. On the other hand, a flattening in general business activity—which traditionally was bad news in the pre-World War II days because it could spiral into a depression—should be limited in our managed economy by use of appropriate fiscal and monetary tools. With moderating inflation and some softening of interest rates, a slump should not result in a catastrophe. If accompanied by clear evidence of slowing inflation, it could be regarded as good news.

It is very difficult, nevertheless, to see interest rates coming down a great deal. The demand for funds is heavy from so many areas of our economy—housing, state and local governments, and the federal government itself with new programs in the welfare and urban areas. Not only all this, but capital formation has been rising relative to gross national product on a worldwide basis. I would like to suggest, though, that there is room for some kind of an improvement if we can begin to get inflation under control.

Floor Discussion

Question: What companies were in your *Quality Growth* group?

Good: There were about 20 companies in that group over this period. I can't recite the list to you offhand, but I can tell you very quickly what some of the criteria were, which would give you an idea. The companies had to increase their earnings at an average annual rate of 12% over the last decade, 15% over the last five years, and there had to be a very high degree of consistency. We made a few exceptions in those instances where we felt that the company was strong enough and had a well-defined growth trend. But the kinds of companies we're talking about are Xerox, Polaroid, and so on.

Question: What if capital expenditures continue to go up? What if the Federal Reserve Index doesn't turn down and we have the inflationary boom continuing? What happens with the balance of payments problem then?

Good: Let me point out something that I think may help as much as anything right now. Most of the major trading countries of the world are inflating. Germany, which had been most successful in holding down inflation, is now finding that it has an upcreep in inflation and that if it doesn't revalue the Deutsche mark, then it's importing inflation on its own country due to a boom in German exports.

What seems to be going on in the world right now is general inflation and this tends to keep our exports competitive in price. I'm quite sure that people who are closest to this balance of payments problem are not concerned that it can't be handled, at least during the period that we're talking about, through various forms of international cooperation.

Question: Will the Administration continue its policies until it is clear that they have either had success or failure, or will it "chicken out" too early?

Good: This, of course, is something that's debated a good deal. As far as looking in the period right ahead, I think it is clear that the Administration doesn't have much in the way of an alternative except to keep pushing its fiscal and monetary policies further. This is what seems to be happening when you look at the implications of what the Administration is doing.

Question: If we had continuing inflation, then bonds would not be a good alternative and, for most investors, the only alternative is stocks. Is there any place else where one could go to, including something like a pension fund?

Good: One of the most obvious alternatives, of course, is real estate. If you're talking about a large fund, whether a life insurance company or pension fund, there are ways of participating directly. There are also ways of doing this in the stock market but only to a limited extent.

Question: Turning this question around and looking at it from the point of view of the financial manager of a corporation faced with the problem of raising money next year, what strategy would you advise that he follow? Where does he go for money if he needs to get money in the 1970's?

Good: It would seem to me that if the financial manager has the kind of credit rating and so on that permits him to issue bonds, he might use that market for raising money. I think that any future easing of interest rates might be rather moderate— rather than a sharp drop. In other words, I don't think you're going to make the mistake of having committed yourself to long term debt, and then finding that you could have done it at much lower rates shortly thereafter.

Chapter 6

PUBLIC EQUITY FINANCING FOR EXPANSION

Peter A. Hager

How can we explain the phenomenon of a surging market for new security issues in the face of a fluctuating interest in existing equities? How do we reconcile the fact that the Dow Jones stocks have traded in a narrow range for over five years, while the public appetite for new equity security issues has grown nearly 400%?

I would like to suggest that the answers to these questions can be found by examining recent changes in investor attitudes. Who are the buyers of equities today? What motivates them to

Mr. Hager is a Partner of Goldman Sachs & Co. He is in charge of the firm's corporate client development activities in the northeastern United States, and handles all aspects of client companies' financial needs.

buy? Are the motivations which currently apply to the purchase of securities apt to change? Have we been witnessing a temporary growth in buyers' preferences for equity issues, or is this a long-range trend in the making?

Professionals Prefer Equities

The most striking fact that emerges from an examination of the demand side of the securities markets is the growing popularity of equities among professional investors. The institutional investor now accounts for nearly 50% of the volume of activity on the New York Stock Exchange. For some years now, individuals, on balance, have been sellers of listed stocks. In other words, they have sold more than they have bought. Their liquidation has been offset by net purchases on the part of bank trust departments, pension funds, mutual funds, insurance companies, closed-end investment trusts of various types, and by corporations themselves. It has been estimated that institutions now own more than 30% of all listed equities. And the proportionate value of their holdings climbs inexorably year after year.

Cult of Performance

During the last few years, we have seen changes in the attitudes of institutional investors. Traditionally, the manager of a mutual fund or pension fund acquired only the equities of America's most prestigious industrial corporations. Their portfolios resembled a cross section of the *Fortune* 500 list. And the degree of professionalism in investment management was limited to favoring the securities of different industry groups at different times.

For example, in the 1950's a well-run fund was one which held a greater percentage of oil stocks, and a smaller percentage of utility stocks in certain markets. The proportions would then be reversed when the economic outlook favored the utilities over the oils. But the individual equities which constituted the portfolios were always the same: Texaco, Gulf, Standard of

California and, for the daring, Superior Oil among the oils; Commonwealth Edison, American Electric Power, Southern California Edison and, for the daring, Tennessee Gas Transmission, among the utilities.

These investment policies were buttressed by a strict interpretation of the prudent man rule, which suggested that money managers invest in equities at their peril and that the principal justification for the selection of any particular stock was its appearance in other similar portfolios.

The cult of performance has changed all that. Institutional investors have come to regard the test of professionalism to be the ability of the portfolio manager to outperform the averages. Now it seems axiomatic that you cannot outperform the averages if you invest in stocks which make up the average. The point may be arguable because, after all, the timing of purchases and sales makes it possible to realize different results from investing in the same group of individual securities in different amounts at different times. Even so, this axiom is accepted as an article of faith by the new breed of institutional money managers, whose quest for better than average results has led them to look at a broader spectrum of equity alternatives.

New Growth Situations

The spectacular success of a few who have ventured far afield from the *Fortune* 500 and who have realized substantial investment gains from accumulating stocks of relatively small companies engaged in computer leasing, the operation and construction of nursing homes, and the franchising of convenience food distributors has prompted many imitators to seek new emerging growth situations.

Inevitably, this quest by the professional money managers has not gone unnoticed on Wall Street. Investment bankers are, after all, first and foremost merchants of securities. In a very real sense, they are responsible for creating the merchandise which the security buyers desire. Not that they manufacture companies out of thin air, but they do seek out the owners of privately owned enterprises which have particular investor appeal, and attempt to "sell" them on the advantages of public participation.

Another fact that has not gone unnoticed by professional money managers and investment bankers alike is the disparity which can exist between relative growth and absolute growth. The introduction of a successful new household product by, say, a major soap manufacturer with sales of $2 billion may result in a 2% growth in that company's sales and a 3% growth in its earnings; however, the corresponding effect on the market value of its stock is likely to be nominal or even nonexistent. After all, a major soap manufacturer is *supposed* to introduce successful new products from time to time.

But the same product, introduced with the same success by a company whose present sales and earnings are, say, $200 million and $10 million, respectively, may result in a 100% appreciation in that company's stock. The rewards which accrue to the finders of such a situation tend to stimulate the search.

The simple fact of the matter is that earnings growth, measured in percentage terms, is today the primary evaluative factor in the securities marketplace. If success is to be measured in terms of a compound rate of percentage growth, the mathematics of business favor the small and the medium-sized company. Shrewd professional investors are aware of this fact and have accordingly looked for small and medium-sized companies which have substantial percentage growth potential.

Is this trend a temporary phenomenon? Can we foresee a return to a time when investors' preferences will be focused on the giants of American industry? I do not think so. As Walter Lippman put it, the most significant economic development of our age is that we have learned "to invent invention." New developments are occurring with ever increasing rapidity. New industries are springing up overnight. New companies are being formed and reaching maturity in decades, rather than in centuries. It is no longer ludicrous for the manager of a company with sales of, say, $25 million to aspire to a ten-fold growth in a single decade. There are many examples of companies which have accomplished just such results.

In such a dynamic environment, the advantages of size and established market position can only be temporary. Success accrues to those enterprises that through technological skill, marketing prowess, or manufacturing economies adjust more rapidly to changes in consumer desires. The rewards for fulfilling those desires are enormous and immediate, and are quickly translated into financial terms.

Equity Financing Expense Overstated

Up to this point, I have been analyzing the current and probable future demand for new equity issues, because I believe that corporate managers, charged with the responsibility for financing the growth of their companies, should be aware of the demand trends in the marketplace.

When we turn to the other side of the supply and demand equation—the supply side—the outstanding conclusion which we can draw is that equity financing has until recently been decidedly unfashionable. In theory, at least, the astute corporate manager was one who obtained the required amount of external capital without expanding his equity base. He raised money through borrowings, both short and long term. And there was a reason for this. After all, the argument ran, equity financing is terribly expensive, both in terms of financing costs and more importantly in terms of its impact on the market value of the already outstanding shares.

Now that we are in a new era, characterized by diminishing opportunities for further credit expansion, perhaps the time has come to re-examine the theory that the sale of additional equity is the last resort of a smart financial manager. Does the issuance of additional common stock, or securities convertible into common stock, invariably depress the market for that stock? Does the marketplace automatically adjust for equity dilution? The answer to each question is an emphatic, "No."

For every instance in which the announcement of a new equity issue resulted in a market price decline, there is at least another instance in which a similar announcement had the opposite effect. Although this face may seem to defy logical explanation, in reality the reason is a simple one. Frequently, the potential demand for a particular security far outstrips the available supply in the secondary marketplace. Fund managers who must make commitments of substantial size find that they simply cannot accumulate such positions in certain stocks without driving up the price. They conclude that the market is too thin, that it has insufficient liquidity, and therefore that they are not interested in the security.

Since a new equity issue will serve to broaden the market, as well as to make it possible for an institution to accumulate a sizeable position at a single price, the professional money manager may be attracted to a situation simply *because* there is an equity issue in the offering. Moreover, because the price of equities reflects the demand for them and not some theoretical intrinsic value, the effect of dilution may or may not be felt in the marketplace.

The correct judgment as to whether a particular offering for a particular company at a particular time can be absorbed without any adverse affect on the market price of the stock is, of course, the real test of the investment banker. Suffice it to say that such a result can be, has been, and will in the future be accomplished.

Pertinent Questions

I hope by now to have established two points to your satisfaction: *first,* that public equity financing is growing in popularity as a source of expansion capital because professional investors prefer equity to debt; *second,* that the costs of this type of financing to companies which require expansion capital are frequently overstated. For the balance of this chapter, I should like both to anticipate and to answer your questions regarding the role of the investment banker and the financing process itself.

Choosing an Investment Banker

Perhaps the most frequent question asked is: How should I go about choosing an investment banker to manage my financing?

Since this question may really mask some confusion about the precise duties and responsibilities of a managing underwriter, perhaps the best answer is one that covers what a managing underwriter *does* as well as what he *does not* do. Taking the latter part first, there are two very important things that the managing underwriter does not do: (1) he does not sell your issue, and (2) he does not fix the price at which it sells.

The issue is sold, to a large extent, by the underwriting syndicate of which the manager is but one member; and, to a lesser extent, by a selling group of nonunderwriting brokers. Both groups are assembled by the manager, who generally distributes no more than 20% to 25% of the issue through his own organization.

Since the managing underwriter does not sell the entire issue, he obviously has incomplete control over its pricing; in fact, he consults with his fellow underwriters and makes a judgment as to the degree of enthusiasm of the selling group before recommending the price at which he thinks the issue can be successfully sold.

Moreover, since pricing cannot be accomplished until the distributing group is formed and the selling effort is completed, any estimate of the probable price some months before that work occurs is nothing more than an educated guess. Selecting a managing underwriter either on the basis of who promises to deliver the best deal, or who has the most salesmen on the payroll, is a most naive and irrational method of choosing an investment banker.

What does the managing underwriter do? He helps to tailor the particular security to meet both the needs of his corporate client and the demands of the marketplace. He assists in the preparation of the prospectus and the registration statement, bringing his particular skill to bear on the problem of presenting the company's distinctive qualifications in the most favorable light. He recommends the timing of filing the registration statement, which tends to establish the probable time of offering. He forms the underwriting syndicate and selling group, and controls the amount of the issue which each such participant will actually have available for sale.

Since these are the actual tasks he will perform for you, the best way to select a managing underwriter is to discuss with him the various steps in the process as they relate to your particular situation. In the final analysis, your decision as to which firm is likely to do the best job for you is going to be based on your confidence in its representative with whom you are dealing, its reputation for performance, and its enthusiasm for your particular project. By reviewing the details of the job which your investment banker will perform for you, however, you will at least have the comfort of knowing that you have made a subjective decision on rational, not uninformed, grounds.

Choosing the Right Type of Financing

A second, and frequently asked, question is: We have to expand our equity base, but isn't it more advisable for us to sell convertible debentures, or debentures with warrants, than to sell common stock?

The convertible debenture has two appealing features: (1) since the conversion price is usually set at some premium above the market, it is tantamount to selling common stock at a higher price than could otherwise be obtained; and (2), if the issue meets certain criteria, the dilution entailed in issuing the additional shares will not have to be accounted for until conversion actually occurs, which may be some years away.

The same advantages may hold true for debentures with warrants, which have an additional benefit in that convertibility is partial rather than total. Because of these features, some managements have decided that convertible debentures, or debentures with warrants attached, are the only sensible way to raise equity capital.

However, there is another side to the coin that is perhaps worth looking at. Convertible debentures are debt securities and must ultimately be repaid if not converted; the proceeds of a common stock offering never have to be repaid. Then, too, the right of the debenture holder to convert at a fixed price is a protected right. In most instances, the future issuance of additional common stock—below the conversion price—results in a downward adjustment of the conversion price, which may in fact eliminate the very attractive premium over market that existed at the time the issue was sold. The price at which common stock is sold is never subject to subsequent downward adjustment. Finally, there is the two-edged matter of equity dilution: the dilution factor involved in a common stock offering is significant if a company's stock sells at 10 to 15 times earnings; it is insignificant for a company whose stock sells at 20 times earnings, and nonexistent for a company whose stock sells at over 30 times earnings—as compared with the dilution in earning power which would result from a convertible debenture offering. This is simply because the after-tax impact of the additional interest charge is equal to, or greater than, the dilution attributable to the sale of that much additional common stock in the case of companies whose stocks enjoy high price/earnings multiples.

When all is said and done, convertible debentures are appropriate in many financing situations, as are debentures with warrants attached. Nevertheless, the cash sale of common stock is still the form of financing appropriate to most requirements that call for an expansion of the equity base.

On the other hand, rights offerings of common stock are difficult to justify under any circumstances, since they entail selling stock substantially below the market; in fact, they really offer the greatest benefit to those shareholders who do not wish to purchase additional stock. It is not surprising that rights offerings have declined considerably in popularity in recent years.

Pricing Equity Offerings

The next question I should like to address myself to relates to the pricing of an equity issue. It goes something like this: How do I know whether I am getting a fair price on my offering?

There is no aspect of the underwriting process that engenders more suspicion than the establishment of the price for the issue. This generally occurs the day before the offering is made, and usually it involves only the investment banker managing the issue and the management of the issuing corporation. During the preceding weeks, the company officers may have been besieged by friends who wanted to buy the new stock issue but claimed that they were unable to get the amount they desired through their normal brokerage connections. Brokers who did not receive adequate selling group allotments may have complained directly to the corporation, stating that the syndicate manager failed to recognize their distributing capability.

Experiences like this have led a company's management to believe that the demand for their issue is unlimited, or at least enormous. And now that the critical moment of truth has arrived, the managing investment banker may be talking in much more sober, or even somber, terms.

If the investment banker has not prepared his corporate client, or if he is not forthright and factual in his presentation of the marketing situation, the price negotiation can turn into a disaster. This is why the responsible investment banker prefers to discuss the underwriting process, up to and including the pricing of an issue at the very outset of the assignment.

The corporate client would do well to listen. If he does, he will understand that a premium over the offering price is essential for an offering to be a success. He will know that the quotations at that point are reflecting a demand for a tiny portion of the offering.

The real message I want to convey, however, relates to the delicacy of the pricing job. The line between success and failure, between underpricing and overpricing an issue, is frequently extraordinarily thin, and can turn on a half a point or even on a quarter of a point. On one side of the line lies success, characterized by an offering which gains momentum as buyers realize that the initial public offering price was, in fact, a bargain. On the other side lies disaster, as lower quotations accelerate the rush of sellers who want to cut their losses.

While investment bankers are all too aware of the importance—and the difficulty—of pricing an issue properly, corporate managements are sometimes totally uninformed or uninterested in the subtle judgments which are required to reach a pricing decision, and regard the whole business as nothing more than an elaborate horse trade. A negotiation between a fully informed party and a completely uninformed one is no negotiation at all.

Concluding Note

Underlying much of what I have been discussing in this chapter is a theme that I would like to develop in closing. In these times of rapid change and in a period marked by dramatic shifts in investor attitudes, it seems to me that it behooves corporate management to develop more meaningful ties with investment bankers.

There are strong trends suggesting that security issues, and particularly equity and equity-related security issues, will be a much more significant source of expansion capital for American business in the decade ahead than has been true in the quarter century prior to 1970. During the past two decades, most companies looked to commercial bankers as their key financial advisors, and those bankers provided the resources which fueled not only working capital expansion, but also more permanent asset needs as well.

There is considerable evidence that the role of the commercial banker is changing and diminishing in relative importance, while the role of the investment banker is expanding. Until recently, it was felt that well-managed companies should seek funds in the capital markets only infrequently. Except for utilities and finance companies, most corporate financial officers expected to use the services of an investment banking firm sparingly throughout their careers, and they treated investment bankers accordingly. As a result, a considerable mystique has built up around the investment banker, what he does and how he does it.

In my judgment, the time for many corporate managers to dispel the mystique, to start a dialogue with an investment banker is well before the time when a company must issue securities. For you, the best time may be now.

Floor Discussion

Question: Isn't there a conflict in going to an investment banker who will have to make a determination as to what is best for you—and then also—a determination as to whether he wants you for a customer?

Hager: I don't think so, any more than the conflict that a lawyer has as to whether he is interested in dispensing good advice, or whether he is primarily interested in collecting a fee from somebody who walks through the door. It's basically a question of the integrity of the individual. A good investment banker will be willing to give you sound advice even if he feels that he is not equipped to handle your problem.

Question: Does it make any sense to hire a completely independent investment banker to sit at your right hand during a price negotiation?

Hager: That really isn't a very practical solution. No investment banker who's worth his salt is going to be willing to take that position, unless he fully understands the facts that the firm you're negotiating with at that point has in its command. As a practical matter, I think you're talking about something that is not a problem, provided you're dealing with people of integrity. On the other hand, if you're not dealing with people of integrity, everything's a problem.

Question: If I understand correctly, the market is becoming more and more one that is dominated by the professional investor, and the professional investor is really limited to making investments in situations where the volume of trading is sufficient so that he can both get into and out of the stock when he deems it appropriate to do either. If that is the trend, doesn't this militate against the desirability of new equity issues for small companies?

Hager: Yes, I think it does. This is one of the inevitable trends. I think that the desirability of underwriting issues for new companies is increasingly going to be based on whether there is a sufficient amount of stock available, as a result of the offering, to attract the professional investor.

Question: Would you comment on the difference between the regional investment banker and the national investment banking firm?

Hager: Yes, I'll comment on it. I think there is now, and will continue in the future to be, a place for the regional investment banker who, in effect, specializes in underwriting smaller companies and makes a market in those companies in the locale where it is natural for such a market to exist.

Let me point out to you, lest there be any confusion on the point, that there are probably some 12,000 companies which today enjoy some sort of a market for their stock. Of these 12,000, less than 2,500 are listed on the two major national stock exchanges; the balance are traded over the counter, and in many instances on a purely regional basis.

As those companies with essentially regional markets for their stock grow and prosper, they may very well—and with every right—eventually get to the national markets.

Question: What's the significance of the after market in connection with the financing?

Hager: Let me say that, in terms of the qualifications of an investment banker or managing underwriter, I regard as very high his willingness and ability to continue to provide a trading market for the stock once the issue is in the hands of the public. I think that obtaining a good after market is an essential part of a new security issue. You're not simply selling the stock to raise money; you're also interested in what the value of that security is going to be long after you've sold it.

Moreover, you should be interested in how that after market is going to be made, and in who's going to make it. And these are the kinds of questions, I think, that you should bring up in the dialogue you have with an investment banker about your specific offering.

Question: Is it true that the role of the commercial banker as the key financial advisor to a company is changing and diminishing in relative importance, while the role of the investment banker is an expanding one?

Hager: I think it's entirely based on the realities of where companies are going to get their money in the future. In the last 25 years, for many companies, the primary source of capital has been the commercial banks. Since most of the alternative ways of raising capital today seem to involve the services of an investment banker, I would suspect that the investment banker is going to be relatively more important than the commercial banker in the future.

Question: What are the risks inherent in a company making the determination to have a private placement, rather than an underwritten offering?

Hager: Most underwritten offerings are firm contract deals. In other words, the underwriter purchases the securities, whether or not he can sell them.

On the other hand, a private placement, handled by an intermediary or by a company officer himself, is a best efforts arrangement. If you're uncertain about whether the private placement is going to be successful, and if that uncertainty actually comes to pass and the placement isn't made, the investment banker has no responsibility to find you that money.

Question: In pricing a common stock, is there a tendency to underprice an offering that involves only selling shareholders, as against much more realistic pricing on an offering that involves raising money for the company?

Hager: Emphatically not. An issue's price does not depend on who is doing the selling, but rather on who is doing the buying.

There have been examples of offerings where the company was more anxious than the underwriter to make sure that the offering appeared to be underpriced; it would therefore be well received and go to a substantial premium.

There are occasionally examples where for legal reasons an offering has obviously been underpriced. Frequently, unless you know the background of these situations, you can't draw conclusions as to why certain things occurred. And in the packaging of any particular offering, there may be countless considerations that the public is never aware of.

Question: I am curious regarding the fact that most companies which seek a public market are interested in maintaining clear-cut voting control of their companies. Is this a problem in connection with an offering? Is this a legitimate reason for not making one? Are there things that can be done in the structuring of the offering to ensure that result?

Hager: The New York Stock Exchange has what I consider to be an excellent rule. It is, in essence, that no stock can be listed where some artificial means exists to perpetuate the control of people who have sold most of their stock to the public.

I'm in favor of this rule. I don't think you should sell a man a participating interest in your company, and then not give him the right to have some voice in the company's affairs. Nevertheless, many companies have persuaded underwriters to create some artificial means to prevent voting control from ever leaving the hands of the management.

On the other hand, "going public" rarely involves selling a majority of a company's common stock. We, for example, will not undertake an offering for a company that involves more than a third of the existing stock. We figure anything higher than that looks like a bail-out—that is, it looks like the people behind the company are less interested in it than they hope the public will be.

Chapter 7

COMBINATIONS OF DEBT AND EQUITY

Charles D. Ellis

How should the financial strategist of a large corporation with publicly held debt/equity securities go about getting the best capital structure for its shareholders?

There are two ways to change the capital structure of a large corporation: first, by changing the total size of the capitalization, how many dollars the management has to work with; and second, by changing the source of those funds, the mix of debt and equity. In this chapter, I shall discuss both approaches

---

Mr. Ellis is a Vice President of Donaldson, Lufkin & Jenrette, Inc. He is an Associate Editor of the *Financial Analysts Journal,* has authored many articles in other financial and business periodicals, and has two books forthcoming on common stock repurchase and institutional investing.

and how they can be used jointly to optimize the capital structure over the long term.

Focus on Misunderstanding

The major stumbling block in trying to approach a question like this is that most of us have a pretty substantial misunderstanding of what debt really represents to the corporation.

First, we expect it to be paid off. This is unrealistic; most well-managed corporations that borrow will be steady, regular borrowers. Management may pay off a particular bond, but it certainly does not plan to be completely out of debt in the normal sense. A typical example of this is the American Telephone & Telegraph Company, which has no intention of being out of debt and yet has every intention of regularly paying off what it is obligated to pay.

Second, we do not understand how to measure debt. For example, we use balance sheet ratios, debt to equity, debt to total assets, and so forth. These are easy to calculate, and that is a saving grace; but these are not very useful measures.

Consider the left-hand side of the balance sheet. Here we accept historic cost bases for our fixed assets, and then depreciate them heavily for tax purposes. If we have heavily depreciated our factories, we have also sharply reduced our recorded stockholders' equity, which is treated as a residual figure on the right-hand side of the balance sheet.

Much more importantly, however, we do not put anything on the left-hand side of the balance sheet to show an asset account for the brilliance of management, important patents that are controlled by the company, good will in its marketing relationships with customers, research developments that might lead to sensational products in the future, or for the simple achievement of having developed a tremendously successful business.

In short, it is difficult to justify any long-term decision on corporate capital without including the most important assets of the corporation; yet, we go about making vital decisions in just this way. Thus my contention is that we should eliminate the use of balance sheet ratios of debt to equity. At least, then, we would not be deluding ourselves by using very precise decimal measurements of a meaningless ratio. However, if we reject balance sheet ratios, it is probably useful to insert a substitute, and this is one of the things I wish to suggest here.

Limits of Debt Policy

It seems to me that there are really three ways in which to view a corporation's debt policy, because there are three different interested parties involved: the *lenders*, the *corporation* itself, and the *shareholders*. Each of the parties has not only a different view of optimum debt policy, but a right to be represented in the final decision, and the reasons for this shall be clear in a moment.

Because the *lender*, quite obviously, wants to get his money back, he will put a limit on the amount of debt that he thinks a corporation should borrow or be loaned.

The *corporation* itself has a limited capacity to support debt or the debt service obligations of interest and principal repayment.

Gordon Donaldson offers a complete analysis of how to go about the process of working out and forecasting the amount of debt a particular company could handle.[1] He does it under a period of adversity in the business. In other words, if the going gets tough, how much debt could you then handle? Donaldson says that this analysis of funds flow under adversity will give you the capacity of the corporation to borrow.

Obviously, involved in this are the interests of employees, customers, the local community, and others who would rather you did not go bankrupt. Basically, then, the corporation's objective is protection from bankruptcy, whereas the lender is interested in protection from insolvency and nonrepayment.

---

1. See his book *Corporate Debt Capacity* (Harvard Business School, Division of Research, Boston, 1961).

As the third party, the *shareholder*'s interest is simply to have the highest per-share market price that is possible on a sound basis. Since the management can influence the price of shares by its debt policy, it has to be responsive to the interests of the shareholder.

Simulation of Probable Effects

Capitalization that uses debt up to but not in excess of the amount preferred by the equity investors will produce the highest market value for the common stock. Thus, in order to determine the explicit level of debt that would produce the desired maximum value of the stock, we have to analyze the probable effects on share prices caused by changing the various combinations of debt and equity.

The method of determining the appropriate blend appears to be quite complicated at first, but it is not at all difficult to grasp. Actually, it is a straightforward arithmetical analysis which assumes that funds obtained by incremental increases in debt are used to repurchase increasing amounts of outstanding common stock.

In this section of the chapter, I shall explain how this method, as shown in *Exhibit I*, page 91, can be used to analyze different debt/equity mix options on which to base decisions.

In this exhibit, let us first assume that the size of the capital structure is going to remain constant, but that the mix of debt and equity is going to change. I shall also assume that this corporation earns $30 million and presently has no debt. (The analysis could theoretically start at the other extreme and assume no equity.) Thus, on reported earnings of $30 million, with 10 million shares, the corporation earns $3 per share. Note that the operating income is constant under all options and that between options debt is rising by increments of $50 million. As the corporation borrows more and more, gradually the lenders' point of view comes to bear and interest rates rise. I calculated these combinations of debt and equity at an optimistic time in the debt market, and thus the interest rates may be actually higher or lower than those shown in this matrix, but the formula is valid in any case.

In Column D, we multiply interest rate with total amount of debt, and come up with interest cost after tax, to put it on the same basis as Column A at the far left.

Deducting the net interest cost from the operating income, we come up with hypothetical reported earnings for the corporation.

The corporation, we assume, has taken the money that it received with each added debt issue of $50 million, and it has spent that $50 million in repurchasing its own common stock. In other words, as we can see in Column F, the number of shares declines by 1 million per increment of debt. The reason for this is that at the starting point of zero debt, the shares are worth $50 apiece. (The reader may quarrel with this convenient assumption, but using it greatly simplifies the analysis.)

In Column G, we can see that there is a pretty substantial increase in per-share earnings each time debt is increased and equity reduced. But this does not solve the problem in terms of the per-share market price that will result from changing the debt policy. That is what the shareholder is interested in.

But if we borrow heavily, do we not add risk from the viewpoint of the company? Indeed, we do. Thus we might assume that after a Donaldson-type analysis of funds flows, management has decided that $300 million of debt in Column B represents the capacity of this corporation to handle debt service. Thus we eliminate from consideration the possibility of borrowing $350 million, $400 million, or $450 million.

Determining Stockholders' Debt Preference

Now we turn to the question: How can we maximize the share value within this constraint? In other words, how much debt do the owners want for this company?

The first step is to show how increasing debt-retiring equity will hypothetically increase the level of per-share earnings. We can get the earnings as high as $4.50. In addition, we increase the rate of growth in those earnings because the corporation is borrowing greater amounts each year to reinvest along with the retained earnings.

Further, because we are increasing the fixed cost of interest, as operating income varies, reported earnings will vary even more. Thus we are reducing the stability of that earnings growth while at the same time increasing the growth rate. These two factors will affect the price/earnings ratios as shown in Column H of *Exhibit I.* In this exhibit, we make the assumption that when no debt exists on the corporate balance sheet, the shares are priced at $50, or about 16½ times earnings.

I contend that as we make the first increase in the amount of debt we are willing to use, we increase not only the per-share earnings level, but also the growth rate, and without significantly reducing the stability of that growth rate. Thus we ought to have a higher price/earnings ratio because we are growing faster, and P/E ratios usually rise as corporate earnings growth rises.

By the time we get to $100 million borrowing, the P/E ratio might be up to 18. We are paying a reasonable interest rate, but we are not sure that our shareholders will be excited by our continuing to borrow more money. For example, they will be concerned about the increased variability in year-to-year earnings, which becomes increasingly significant as we assume greater and greater debt. On the other hand, the extra growth rate is not as large for that increment from $150 million to $200 million as it was from no debt to $50 million. Thus the shareholders may become a little uncomfortable about this borrowing practice, and reflect this in a reduced price/earnings ratio. The per-share earnings are still going up, but the price/earnings ratio is declining.

On this basis, we take the P/E ratios back down at the same rate they went up. As we go down Column I, which shows what the per-share price would be, we see that it is $50 with no debt; $54.20 with $50 million; and so on up to $75.10 with $300 million.

Exhibit I. Simulation Matrix of Possible Corporate Combinations of Debt and Equity

Operating Income (After Tax) (A)	Debt (B)	Interest Rate (C)	Interest (After Tax) (D)	Reported Earnings (E)	Common Shares (F)	EPS (G)	P/E (H)	Share Value (I)	Equity at Market (J)	Equity plus Debt (K)
$30MM	0	—	—	$30MM	10,000M	$3.00	16.7x	$50.00	$500,000M	$500,000M
30	$ 50MM	5%	$ 1.25MM	28.75	9,000	3.19	17.0x	54.20	487,800	537,800
30	100	5%	2.5	27.50	8,000	3.44	17.3x	59.50	476,000	576,000
30	150	6%	4.5	25.50	7,000	3.64	17.6x	64.10	448,700	598,700
30	200	6%	6.0	24	6,000	4.00	18.0x	72.00	432,000	632,000
30	250	7%	8.75	21.25	5,000	4.25	17.5x	74.30	371,500	621,500
30	300	8%	12.0	18	4,000	4.50	16.7x	75.10	300,400	600,400
30	350	9%	15.75	14.25	3,000	4.75	15.8x	75.00	225,000	575,000
30	400	10%	20.0	10	2,000	5.00	14.0x	70.00	140,000	540,000
30	450	12%	27.0	3	1,000					

Explanation of Exhibit One

Column A shows the tax adjusted operating income for the company. Incremental levels of debt are stipulated in Column B. As debt is increased, interest costs rise both because more money has been borrowed (Column B) and because lenders charge higher rates of interest (Column C). (The financial manager should have a quite accurate knowledge of these debt cost schedules from his prior investigation and analysis of the lenders' constraint on borrowing.) The expected after-tax interest cost associated with each possible debt increment is stated explicitly (Column D) and subtracted from after-tax operating income (Column A) to determine (Column E) the reported earnings available to common stockholders. Each possible increase in debt and simultaneous reduction in equity is treated independently (e.g., $100 million debt is an increase from no debt rather than an increase from $50 million) and the necessary number of shares is repurchased in all cases at the "no debt" market price of $50. (This price assumption is used to simplify the present analysis, although in practice a higher price may be required to buy in a large number of shares.) Dividing the remaining number of outstanding shares (Column F) into "reported earnings" (Column E) produces the resulting EPS (Column G) for each debt level.

Price/earnings ratios (Column H) are determined independently as explained earlier in the text. Multiplying EPS by P/E (Column G × Column H) gives the expected market price (Column I) for each level of debt. Total equity (Column J) plus debt (Column B) gives total capital value (Column K).

Then it goes down because the P/E ratio is going down even faster than the per-share earnings are going up.

From the shareholder's point of view, he wants this corporation to have $300 million worth of debt because that gives him the highest per-share market price for his stock. He knows he is going to have less net income. He knows he is going to have greater variability in the earnings report, but he will have a faster growing stream of per-share earnings and therefore he has a higher price. That is what I think the corporate financial manager should be aiming at.

You may not agree with the numbers in the price/earnings column of *Exhibit I.* You may think they should be higher and increase faster, or you may think they should not rise quite as rapidly. This is something that will depend, first, on the growth rate of the company under question, which we have purposely avoided mentioning because we do not know whether this is a company that grows at the rate of 10% or 50% a year.

Second, it will depend on the variability of operating earnings for this company. If it is a service company with a steady income stream, it may be able to handle a great amount of debt in comparison with that of a highly cyclical business. Since you understand your own company well, you should make these judgments as to probable P/E at each debt level. This is a way in which you can formally put down on paper that understanding and see what the results are.

In this particular case, we have a shareholders maximum value per share at $300 million of borrowing. The corporation happens to be able to handle that amount of borrowing. We are good on two scores.

The hard part is when we go to the lenders. Typically, they dislike to lend much. The trick is probably going to be, once you have convinced yourself of the correctness of a large amount of borrowing, to convince the lenders. I would suggest that after doing the same kind of analysis we have just discussed, plus the analysis presented in Donaldson's book on the corporation's real debt capacity, it should be relatively easy to persuade lenders that you understand what you are talking about, and therefore you may be able to change their initial views of the limit on debt in your company.

Changing the Size of Capitalization

The second way of changing capital structure is to change not necessarily the absolute size, but the size relative to need. There are two obvious ways of doing this: either to increase the demand for capital within the corporation, or to reduce the capital supply stored up in the company.

Companies that are thinking of increasing their capital demands rather vigorously—building new plants, entering new markets, acquiring other companies, and so forth—should thoroughly understand how such demands for capital will impact on the corporation. They can then decide whether they have enough capital, too little, or too much.

When I say "capital," I mean after adjusting the mix. Thus, if yours is an all-equity company and careful analysis shows that you should be a substantial borrower, then you have potential capital which is quite large relative to your present capital because you might borrow heavily without retiring equity. In that event, you should be thinking in terms of the potential capital level, and not the actual balance sheet amount that is currently shown.

Referring again to the same corporation discussed earlier, this company has in effect $300 million excess capital because it could borrow that much and be doing the right thing. If its demand for capital is not going to rise soon, it should reduce its present capital by reducing its equity base by repurchasing stock.

I think it might be helpful to put this proposition in the context of cost of capital thinking, as shown in *Exhibit II*, page 95, which consists of three graphs. The traditional point of view, shown at the left, basically holds that debt is relatively cheap. If you do not borrow too much, you will cut your average cost of capital; if you borrow too much, it will show up in your price/earnings ratio. The ideal situation is to borrow some judiciously, but not push too hard.

Exhibit II shows this proposition on a quantitative basis. Note that in the left half of this graph the equity cost does not go up because the price/earnings ratio holds. In addition, the debt cost is a lot lower. Thus the average cost of capital, as we increase the amount of debt, goes down. Then, we swing into a period where we have "borrowed too much," and the cost of equity goes up—that is, the price/earnings ratio goes down. At the same time, perhaps, our debt cost is going up. But the average cost of capital is really taking off, and nobody knows how far to the right that bend goes.

A second way of looking at capital structure is in line with the so-called "operating income theory," which holds that the cost of capital is a constant figure, without regard to the form in which you raise capital. This is called the operating income theory because it does not go all the way down to net income after interest costs in measuring earnings, but rather it goes right to the operating income in the market value of debt and equity securities.

The assumption is that lenders and stockholders are intelligent. They see that the corporation is taking greater risks. So at some debt level, they cut the price/earnings ratio to reflect that risk. The net of it all is that beyond some debt level, there is no advantage whatsoever to the corporation or stockholders in borrowing or not borrowing.

The third chart in *Exhibit II* displays the results of the concepts I have just been discussing. Debt cost is constant across a moderate range of borrowing, and then it gradually goes up as the amount of debt increases relative to equity. The price/earnings ratio goes up because the growth rate is accelerating as the corporation begins to borrow, and the cost of capital goes down. (Looked at the other way around, management does not have to earn as many dollars to get as many dollars from the market.) When we put more debt together with a higher P/E, the average cost of capital goes down as we start

Exhibit II. Three Ways of Looking at Capital Structure

1. TRADITIONAL OR
NET INCOME THEORY

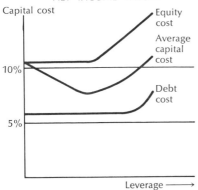

2. OPERATING INCOME THEORY

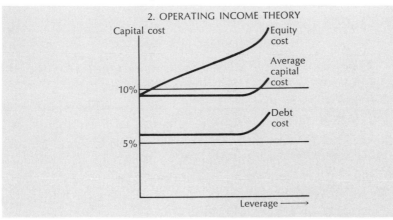

3. AUTHOR'S PROPOSED THEORY

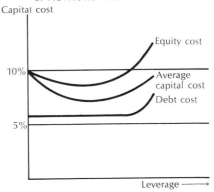

borrowing. Later, as heavier borrowing (going beyond $300 million) increases the interest charges and reduces the P/E on equity, the average cost of capital rises.

Exhibit II puts the three ways of looking at capital structure quite clearly. On the left-hand side is the traditional or net income theory that people have been operating on in Wall Street for a generation or two. In the center is the operating income theory, which is what the MBA's coming out of graduate business schools are trying to explain to their superiors. On the right-hand side is the theory proposed here. This is a new description of the results of blending different combinations of debt and equity in the capital structure. It is the only conceptual argument that is built up from independent and realistic components, rather than being imposed from an abstract hypothesis.

Floor Discussion

Question: What effect on the price/earnings ratio does the reduction of common shares outstanding have?

Ellis: Nobody knows. A study has been done of corporations that tender for substantial amounts of their shares. Another study has been done of corporations like General Motors, General Electric, Standard Oil of New Jersey. Large companies like these are substantial buyers of their own shares in order to fund the pension for their employees. These three companies, as a matter of fact, have bought 10% of the shares traded on the New York Stock Exchange year in and year out at a minimum. Thus we see tender offers and also steady repurchasing.

There is no statistical evidence that anything happens as a result of reducing the number of outstanding shares. But there are some assumptions that perhaps something does happen. With smaller companies, it appears to be true that there are transaction problems which, in the short run, may tend to raise the price, but it is a specious increase. With a large enough company, I think the answer is it won't make any difference.

Question: Does the quality of debt have some bearing?

Ellis: The lenders will tell you that that first $1 million is high class debt; that the last $1 million, or the last $50 million, is pretty suspicious. They do it in several ways: first, they don't lend it unless you really work for it; second, they will charge a higher interest rate; and third, they will probably ask for a kicker. Thus they are saying, "Gradually, you are getting the money you have borrowed from us to be more like equity because it is taking a risk, and we don't like that."

It is entirely possible that the problem is with lenders' attitudes rather than with the truth of the economics of the loans. It may be that the lenders are more suspicious of risk than they ought to be.

Question: I think that your theory by definition is academic because I have not seen any debt financing recently where you can use proceeds for the repurchase of your own equity. Am I correct?

Ellis: The reason you think it is academic is there aren't any examples of corporations borrowing money and simultaneously announcing their intention to use the money to buy stock. Unfortunately, that is not correct. I shall give you examples. Through 1968, American Standard had purchased about 20% of its common shares, and the company had borrowed a lot of money. I maintain that the two are tied together. Allied Chemical has been a substantial buyer of its shares—and a substantial borrower. Many of the oil companies have bought their own stock, and most of them had been borrowers.

A corporation that plans to take over another company with debt securities is really borrowing money to buy stock. I have seen several corporate mergers in which the company that was going to survive was not willing to bring those two balance sheets together and add them up. Instead, the parent corporations offered debt for virtually all of the other companies, eliminating the equity that was on the acquired companies' balance sheets on consolidation and substantially increasing the debt/equity mix.

Question: As debt goes up, won't the lenders impose some restrictions both on your financial operations and on what you can do as a corporation from a strategic point of view—that is, put limitations on mergers and things of this nature?

Ellis: I think this is clearly one of the costs of debt and that it should be added into interest. However, it should be specifically quantified. Most people say, "Gentlemen, they really hamstring you when you borrow money." Then they let their lawyers do the negotiating and they get hamstrung. I think they deserve it. Usually, there are some things that you do not want to do and some others that the lenders don't want you to do. You use those as trade-offs in the negotiation.

Ultimately, you may get stuck. There may perhaps be some things you simply cannot do because the lenders have said, "All right, if you want to go from $250 million to $300 million, you can do it. But we are going to insist on a big quid pro quo." Then you have to decide whether that *quid* is worth the *pro*.

I think it is too common to make broad statements like: "Gee, debt is risky," or "They hamstring you," or something like this, without carefully analyzing what difference it makes to you in the way you are running the business. If you can jump up two steps and only slide back one, like the frog on the muddy bank of the river, you may be gaining enough. It may be a struggle that is more difficult than the easy work, but, after all, you are well paid for being a brilliant financial manager.

Question: Does the theory extend equally to low-priced earnings multiples as well as high-priced ones?

Ellis: By and large, this theory is of much greater power the lower the P/E multiple, and also of greater power the higher the growth rate. But really it is mostly that the lower the multiple the more shares you can buy back for each increment of borrowing.

There is an obvious danger. Most companies that are badly run have low multiples, and many borrow money to buy earnings they cannot generate from within. I am not talking about that kind of situation; rather, about the man who borrows money because he has a really great way of using it.

Question: If you are going to show growth from $3.00 to $3.19, would that be a one-year operation?

Ellis: No, sir; both numbers are from the same year. You earn $3.00 with no debt, and you can get $3.19 by reducing the numbers of shares outstanding. The operating earnings are the same, only the debt/equity mix is changed.

Question: It looks as if you can do this just once and get the benefit. What does changing the debt/equity mix do to change the characteristics of the company so people will re-evaluate it at a higher price/earnings ratio?

Ellis: The really important thing is a change in the growth rate of the company, the stream of per-share earnings over time. For example, if I have retained earnings each year of $10 million, and I have a policy that I will only invest retained earnings because I am an all-equity company and pay as I go, I am going to be limited to investments of $10 million a year. However, on the other hand, if I am willing to borrow $10 million to add to every $10 million that I earn and retain, I can invest $20 million, and thus my company can grow faster, and per-share earnings will increase faster.

Question: Doesn't this impose super-acceleration?

Ellis: Yes, sir. We are trying to take advantage of the corporation's tremendous earning power for a better split between shareholders and others. We have no reluctance, I hope, about working for the stockholders.

The corporate treasurer is going to work harder. He is not going to have as large cash balances. He is not going to be sure he will have money for anything, come what may. Unfortunately, he is also the fellow who has to say, "I think what we ought to do is repurchase some of our shares and reduce our total equity capital and borrow more from the banks. I am prepared to go out on the road and talk to different banks and work out a really good loan agreement. I am willing to work harder." He may not be willing to work harder, however, and this would stymie the play.

Question: How did you establish that $300 million was

the debt capacity of this company in your chart?

Ellis: Rather than going through all the steps involved in the Donaldson analysis of the corporation's capacity to carry debt during adverse business periods, I have simply made a judgment as to what amount of debt seems high to me.

Of course, that is an oversimplified way of doing the analysis. You have to understand the nature of each individual company's business and really study it carefully. It is a sophisticated, time-consuming job. But once you understand it, you really have a corporate asset.

Question: You mentioned that companies don't expect to pay off debt. In this last case, are you now saying that with $300 million debt you will be paying off a certain amount? If, say, at the end of 20 years, you have only paid off 30% or 40% of the debt, what is the attitude of the public when you go out for a refinancing in order to pay off the original loan?

Ellis: It is difficult to explain this sort of thing orally. When I say that we would borrow $300 million, I mean as of today. Next year, we would have earned some money and retained some earnings. Thus we would borrow more.

Now the way you write a bond agreement or a loan agreement is that you pay off some every year or every quarter. You will continuously be borrowing enough to meet the repayment obligations of the existing debt and to increase the total debt, which is what AT&T does.

Question: Will you give us your definition of the cost of common equity capital?

Ellis: In an all-equity company, you take the market value of the shares and divide it by the earnings. The only hard part is to figure out which earnings. Certainly, not the current year, because people are paying for future growth. So it must relate to future earnings stated in present value terms.

When you get debt and equity combined, it is a lot harder. For simple convenience, in my own mind, three to five years from now is the farthest that the Wall Street analysts can reach out in their most careful and elaborate projections. In the investment business, five years is a pretty good projection for infinity. Therefore, I take the present price and divide the earnings by three or four years out to determine roughly what the cost of equity is.

Question: Would a company repurchase its stock on the market if it were selling at a high price/earnings ratio?

Ellis: The problem is: Is it a high price/earnings ratio relative to what it ought to be? Is the P/E ratio higher than is proven sound? By that I mean, if the price/earnings ratio should be 80 times earnings and it is now 120 times earnings, it is a high P/E ratio. If it should be 6 times earnings, and it is 8 times earnings, it is a high P/E ratio.

However, if its earnings are growing very rapidly, a company should probably be buying back its stock because the market almost never pays a fair price for a really great company. For example, the best investment IBM could have made 10 years ago would have been to buy back its own stock; the P/E was high, but not as high as it should have been.

Question: Do you know of any legal restrictions, SEC or otherwise, regarding the repurchase of your own stock and the use of treasury stock thereafter?

Ellis: There are several kinds of limitations. The New York Stock Exchange insists that a corporation report on a regular basis the shares it repurchases. Lawyers are increasingly coming to the conviction that it is wise to disclose to your shareholders if you are buying back your stock in significant amounts in order to avoid anything that could be considered manipulative practice. The SEC has promulgated some restrictions on certain companies that appear to have been abusing the repurchase technique which limits their repurchase to something like 15% or 20% of the shares in a given day, and prohibits their bidding the stock up at the close of trading and engaging in other prohibited practices. Most corporations follow guidelines to prevent unintended abuse.

Question: Going back to the debt/equity ratio, is there an obvious answer as to what you should do?

Ellis: You should not use balance sheet ratios. Really, it is so easy to use them, and they seem to make so much sense. For example, a group of financial executives talking about balance sheet ratios will tell you the right ratios for different industries. But all they are really telling you is what people are doing and what history proves. It is interesting conversation, but it is not very helpful in creating a really progressive, intentional financial strategy.

Let me be very clear: I am arguing the case for borrowing a lot of money. It may be you should not borrow any. But at least you should analyze what amount to borrow to your own satisfaction. There are no obvious answers. But this discussion does offer a clear format for analyzing a complex problem.

Question: How do you evaluate the cyclical aspects of the economy as a whole and inflation in regard to this subject?

Ellis: I think that the magnitude of fluctuation in our society in the long run is going to be less than it has been in the past for four integrated reasons: (1) because we are a larger, richer, and deeper kind of society; (2) because we have made some substantial changes in our institutional structure to reduce cyclicality; (3) because we have developed substantially more sophisticated theory and understanding in the way our economy operates, and thus have a better understanding of what to do about specific problems; and (4) because people have better forecasting capabilities than they used to have, and thus are avoiding some of the obvious mistakes that used to multiply and compound themselves.

Tremendous changes have taken place in this country as to what we want to do, how much we want to understand how to do it, and the means for accomplishing it—all of which tend to reduce cyclicality. And this means—all other things being equal—that more debt can be carried over the long term by prudent managers.

Chapter 8

ALTERNATIVE SOURCES OF GROWTH CAPITAL

John M. May

Decisions relating to financing have to be looked at from several viewpoints by the owner-manager of a business. Each of his varying interests, as listed below, may lead to different objectives to be coordinated in a long-range program for the company. Consider:

- His interest as stockholder.
- His interest and responsibility as trustee for family, investors, and so on.

Mr. May is Executive Vice President of William E. Hill and Company, a leading international management consultant firm.

- His interest as manager of a business to satisfy business needs.
- His interest as employer to keep and motivate managers and employees.
- His interest and responsibility to customers, suppliers, real estate investors, franchisees, and others.

Raising Capital

In considering alternative sources of growth capital, the goals to be accomplished should be analyzed and measured. Different objectives can be accomplished in different ways. I shall categorize these aims as *personal risk, financial liquidity, immediate value, capital growth,* and *long-term considerations.* After taking a closer look at each of these in the first section of this chapter, I shall then discuss the alternative methods of financing and the sources of capital to look for. Following that, I shall examine the sequential steps needed to carry out the various possible alternatives.

Different Objectives

The initial decision to raise outside capital is not an end in itself, but a first step toward a continuing program. The first step, however, sets the direction and course of action, which in many cases is irreversible. Thus the end objectives, as well as the immediate aims to be accomplished by the first step, must be considered.

Personal Risk. The first and most important reason for raising money is to minimize the personal risk that the owner-managers take in consort with the other stockholders they represent. Stated very simply, it is a desire on their part to share the risk by using outside sources of money.

In effect, the owner-manager of a business may very well be the greatest risk taker of any individual in our society. His salary, his income, his capital, his career—everything—is tied up in that business. And all of it is at the mercy of a strike, a price increase, a competitive situation, a lawsuit, a fire, or other factors. These risks can be particularly worrisome in times of tight money, in industries where competitive pressures are increasing, and in products and markets where technology, market changes, and other influences bring rapid change.

Eventually, there comes a time when an individual says, "I'd like to play with somebody else's money."

Financial Liquidity. This second objective in raising money, again for the individual stockholder, also relates to risk. However, even apart from risk considerations, it is questionable whether owner-managers are prudent to have 100% or even 80% of their personal capital tied up in a single business or industry. Obviously, it would be sensible to have a certain portion of one's capital outside the business. The owner-manager's problem could be stated: "Can't I take cash out of the business in salaries; or in dividends or income or expenses, and put it into oil wells or cattle or other forms of capital diversification?"

The answer is that the opportunities to take capital out of a privately held business (particularly, a growth business) are very limited and difficult. The way to build capital value is to convert the company's tangible assets into marketable stock and take *that* money out and put it someplace else—whether in investment-grade stocks or in speculative ventures, in income securities, or whatever.

Immediate Value. How can one get the most value out of the company immediately? Briefly, a company's value is entirely different, depending on whether it is raising money with debt, raising equity capital privately, selling out, merging into another company, going public, or some combination of these alternatives. For example, a company's value in raising money through debt financing is based principally on its book value plus its ability to cover interest and debt payments.

In other words, a company with $1 million of book value and $100,000 of earnings might have a capital-raising limit in terms of debt financing of perhaps 25% of book value or $250,000. The exact amount would of course vary; it might be as high as $500,000 or as low as $100,000, depending on how well the company's cash flow could cover the payments on interest and principal.

A company with $100,000 in earnings might have a value of, let us say, 10, 15, or 20 times earnings, or $1 million to $2 million, if it were to go public. By comparison, it might have a value of 30 times earnings, or $3 million, if it were to sell out. Then, again, it might have a value of $1.5 million, or $1 million or less, if it were to raise money privately.

There are, of course, many variables, but often the greatest immediate value for the owner-manager of a company is in a merger whereby he would not only get 100% liquidity, rather than some smaller percentage, but often the highest multiple of book value and earnings.

The next highest value generally lies in a public offering whereby the owner would usually get a smaller multiple than if he were to sell the whole company. On a first offering, he might thus end up with 20% or 30% of his equity out in public ownership.

Usually, the lowest value in terms of raising absolute dollars immediately is in some form of debt financing.

Capital Growth. The converse of what I just discussed is true about growth. The least growth in capital would accrue by selling the entire business now, because if it were sold for cash the owner-manager would have no further equity participation in the future growth.

If a company were to sell out for stock, then the shareholders' growth in capital would depend on the increase in the value of stock of the buying company and not on its own stock. Again, if a company were to raise debt money and give up no equity, the owner would retain the full equity participation in future growth. Thus growth in the future capital value is almost the direct opposite of getting the most out now. Another factor having an influence on financing decisions is whether capital is desired for the company or the shareholders.

Usually, the private placement of capital is to raise money

for the company, and certainly debt financing is a source of capital for the company rather than the individual. A first, public offering is likely to be for company money, although the individual often gets his money in a second offering. Merger often has the individual taking his money out and the parent company providing additional capital immediately or later for the business.

Because of these various ramifications in raising money, the owner-manager has to determine the timing and sequence of capital for himself and the company.

Autonomous Control. Any time money is raised outside the company, some autonomy and control are given up. The investor who puts money into a business—whether it is in the form of a bank note, an insurance company loan, venture capital, or whatever—earns the right to have a say in the company.

The venture capital route probably gives the greatest autonomy in the sense that most venture capital firms are not interested in taking over the operation of a business; they eventually want to get out and turn the business back to the owner-manager.

The public, especially if represented by investment bankers, will exercise some control and the owner-manager will have to do things differently as a public company than he did as a private company. Certainly, if a company merges, it will give up a great deal of autonomy.

Business Vulnerability. Other motivations or objectives to consider in choosing sources of capital concern the extent of vulnerability of the business. If the profits or liquidity of the business are vulnerable, going public or merger may be the worst thing to do because public ownership and merger magnify unfavorable as well as favorable results. If a company were to merge and suffer a downturn, for example, the seller would feel badly about the merger partner getting stuck, and he would feel even worse about the effect of the downturn on the new public stockholders.

Long-Term Considerations. This brings us to the question of long-term considerations such as management succession. How is the raising of money going to affect management's ability and prerogatives in choosing a successor—whether he is a son, another relative, or an outsider? Obviously, if management were to merge the company, the chance of a son becoming president would probably be diminished. If there were a public offering, it would be greater. If there were a venture capital placement, it could be still greater.

Overlooked Point

If a company has never raised growth capital outside of its own resources, management should keep in mind that raising capital is not a final step; it is only the first step in a continuing process. I think this is the one thing that is probably overlooked more than anything else. They say: "I want to go public;" or "I want to get the bank in;" or "I want to merge;" or "We want to get our estate planning in order and therefore let's go public"—as if these were end-objectives.

Let us look more closely at that last item, for example. Going public often does not allow owner-managers to diversify their holdings and put their estates in order; it merely establishes the market value that the IRS can use for determining an estate, which may in fact increase the value of the estate.

When a company floats a public issue of its security, it sets a market value; the stock may go up, and then, at some future time the company sells, say, 20%. At some still further time in the future, it sells another 30%. Thus raising capital is a continuing process.

In the same way, venture capital is really an interim step to going public or merging. At some time in the future, the private investors will want to get out, because the venture is of no value to them unless in putting up, say, $100,000 now, they can hope to get $1 million back later. Thus they can get out only by merging or doing a public offering. In short, venture capital is not an end; it is only the beginning.

A friend who has a successful manufacturing business remarked not long ago, "When we started out, we had three people in a garage and we borrowed $150 in order to buy our first supply of parts. Now, I'm into the banks for $18 million . . ."

Growth feeds on itself and always needs capital. Once you start, you never stop. If you want to borrow $1 million to build a plant, next year it could be $2 million or $3 million. The only way to stop is to stop growing.

Methods of Financing

In this section, let us turn our attention to the alternative methods of financing and what the sources of capital look for when they invest money in a business. There are many ways to raise debt capital. Among them: factoring; mortgaging assets; borrowing money from customers, suppliers, banks, and insurance companies; and convertible securities. The sources of debt money are typically interested in two things:

1. Ability to pay back the debt. In other words, the security of repayment of the debt with interest. Therefore, how secure is your business?

2. Some nonfinancial benefit. For example, a customer may loan money because he needs to create a market.

Thus, in taking a broad, over-simplified look at it, the needs of the source of debt capital are either security in the sense that the loan is going to be paid back or some nonfinancial reward. A company has to measure whether borrowing money from a supplier or customer would tie the company on a long-term basis to the lender, and whether that is advisable or not.

Various Sources

Going public runs the greatest spectrum of any as to what the source of money wants. One source of public money is "faith, hope, and charity" money. This is the unsophisticated public that does not want anything but a chance to make $1 million. This has no relation to earnings or anything else, but just the speculation where an investor calls up his broker and the broker says, "I'll give you 50 shares, and believe me it's another Xerox."

Contrast that lack of sophistication with the opposite extreme of dealing with an investment banking firm that is the most sophisticated, represents the public, asks the toughest questions, and so forth.

Basically, what the public should want is growth in capital, security, and dividends. If a company is going public, it should be reasonably certain of growth in per-share earnings, and in some glamour and potential. Those factors add up to growth in market value.

What do the private placement or venture capital people want in terms of their money? Basically, they want (a) to get out quickly and make their investment liquid, and (b) to have a much greater growth in capital value than the public demands. Specifically, most sources of private capital want to get back five or ten times the money they put in within two, three, or four years. To loan $100,000, they have to see a means of getting back $500,000 to $1 million within three or four years at the outside.

If these figures seem high, examine the situation. The reason they want such a return is that they are locked in. That money is sterile; it cannot be used, and there is the risk that it might be sterile for a long time, whereas the public always has the option of getting out if things start to turn down.

By the way, in terms of private venture capital, there are, again, alternatives, such as investment banking companies, mutual funds, SBIC's, large industrial companies, union pension funds and company pension funds, in addition to wealthy individuals and families. Thus there are all kinds of venture groups, each of which tends to specialize in a particular type of security.

Another source of money comes through merger with

some other company. What does that other company want? It wants to be sure it will not dilute its per-share earnings in buying a company. It wants to be sure that the original company will be well managed. It wants to increase its per-share earnings and it may want synergy.

Yet another source of raising money is to acquire companies that have certain assets, such as a public listing, cash flow, diversification, integration, and so on. Although opportunities exist for private companies to build their earnings through acquisition, it is relatively difficult these days; this is a route that is much easier for the public company to take.

Sequential Steps

Let me touch on the moves that should be made in dealing with any of the alternative sources of capital just discussed. There are five definite steps that are necessary but are seldom taken formally. The company that wants to steal a march could well consider following these steps and being way ahead of everybody else.

First, make up your mind that you are willing to change certain practices of your company if they need to be changed to raise capital.

By this, I mean that many businessmen who are now private and who are dealing with their own money (1) do not disclose much financial information; (2) do not keep their books on the basis of how much profit they can show; and (3) do not have an objective outside auditor or lawyer. Let us examine these three points more closely.

Private companies are often run for tax and individual income purposes, rather than for maximization of profit. In order to raise capital, it is important to shift the company's objectives to making money, rather than to saving on taxes.

The second point is perhaps the most difficult one of all. If the owner-manager is an entrepreneur who controls his own destiny, he has to mentally attune himself to the fact that he may have to answer to someone else. If he really does not want to do that, he possibly should not start the whole process of raising capital in the first place.

I have seen many cases in which men who owned and operated businesses could not bring themselves to the position of having to ask or report to or disclose to someone else.

The third point is to start thinking in terms of getting formal audits and legal counsel, talking to the bank, and doing everything more formally than has been done as a private company.

The second step is to put a dollar value on the company.

Either the company management should do this for itself, or hire somebody to do it for them; but, in any case, management should determine in advance whether the company is worth $10, $15, or $20 million, or worth only $500,000, $1 million, or $2 million. Appraise the company realistically, in terms of book value, earnings, what comparable companies sell for, and so forth, and raise money on that basis.

For example, let us say that management figures out—before they ever start the going public process—objectively that the company is worth $1.5 million. This means that if they sell 20% of the company to the public, the company will get $300,000. Will they settle for that, or are they thinking about raising money only if somebody will do it on the basis of the company being worth $5 million?

Establish objectives, as I discussed earlier. What is management trying to accomplish? Is it sharing risk, liquidity, or money for the company? How much autonomy do they want? Get the priority of these objectives firmly in mind. Then try to decide which alternative is right; because, depending on the objectives and the value that is set, one alternative is going to be better than the others for each particular situation.

The third step is to write a selling memorandum.

I do not use the word "prospectus" because it has certain legal implications. But write out a clear memorandum which can contain projections and all kinds of qualitative statements that a prospectus does not have. Write down the history of the company. Include the management members and their ages and abilities, competition, record, and prospects, and all the other kinds of data one normally would find in a prospectus. Thus when trying to raise money, it is important to project as a professional and give the source of money a basis for making a decision. That makes all the difference in the world.

The fourth, and a most difficult step, is to select the best candidate.

This requires a knowledge of the financial community, its investors, and the companies that might be merger candidates. Do as much advance preparation as possible; of course, if you cannot do it alone, get help—whether from an investment banker, a consultant, an accountant, a lawyer, a commercial bank, or a businessman who has been through it.

Here is an oversimplified rule of thumb: in planning to go public, keep in mind that there are some major investment banking firms which will not take a company public unless it has $1 million in net earnings. Thus, if your net earnings are considerably less than that figure, there is another fine group of investment banking firms which will take a company public at $500,000, another group at $100,000, and so forth. Go to the right one.

The same thing is true if one is considering a merger or raising venture capital. Certain venture capital firms have set minimums on earnings. Moreover, certain firms have industries that they like to be in and industries that they shun.

Find the right place and try to go in at the top level where decisions are made. Get a hearing at the top so that it can be established whether the investment policy of the source of money is favorable to the particular situation.

The fifth and last step is, of course, to negotiate.

My personal feeling is that the negotiation in raising money is usually the most haphazard, disorganized, amateurish exercise of all. Typically, and mistakenly, people go in and say: "Here's my company. I can tell you all about our earnings and all these unstated assets and so forth. What do you think we're worth?"

The correct way to negotiate, I think, is to set a dollar value, set the objectives, and go into the source of capital and say: "This is what I want. Here's my documentation to support it. Here's what we have to offer. Here's why we think it's reasonable. Let's talk on these terms."

In recapping, go through these five steps, reserving the option at any time to decide not to raise money at all.

The twin objectives of growth and control of the company are almost mutually exclusive—that is, it is difficult to have maximum growth and still have maximum control without giving up equity. The trick is either to compromise between the two and get the most growth and the most control, or to select the objective which is more important.

Concluding Note

The decision to merge, acquire, go public, or raise money is not an end in itself, but a first step toward a continuing program. The first step, however, sets the direction, and a course of action which, in many cases, is irreversible. Consider the end objectives as well as the intermediate objective accomplished by the first step.

The change from owner-management to other capital structure which uses outside money implies a significant change in philosophy of operation. This includes emphasis on earnings versus tax and other considerations, changes in disclosure and reporting practices, increased responsibility to outside stockholders or lenders, more formalized procedures and decisions regarding capital and policy planning, some limitations on autonomy, and particular problems created for the entrepreneur.

There is an inverse relationship between growth and control: growth requires infusions of capital, and capital demands some control. It is necessary to decide on the relative importance of growth and control, and to reach a compromise between highest growth potential and absolute control.

Floor Discussion

Question: Let's say you financed everything through retained earnings and put your eggs in one basket and then you died suddenly. Wouldn't it be too late then for the company to go public? Should you have done it beforehand?

May: I think, in all fairness to your question, it depends to a great extent on how valuable you are to the business. If the business is worth more with you there, you're certainly better off doing it ahead of time, from the business standpoint. However, from the estate standpoint, which is the problem a lot of people are conscious of, your company may not be any better off.

You may compound the problem by going public before you die, because you may raise the estate value of the business. To do it beforehand, set the value, have the stock continue to rise, and then—over a period of time and several offerings—liquefy your estate.

Question: Will it be a distressed sale after you're dead?

May: Again, I think it depends on, as far as the business is concerned, how much less the business is worth without your management. If you have capable management, the business may be worth just as much, unless the estate is forced to sell it.

Question: Under what circumstances would a company be better off selling for stock, rather than for cash?

May: There are two advantages: (1) the deal is normally not taxable until you sell the stock, and (2) the management, if it's going to continue, has greater motivation.

What would override that is a situation in which the ownership and the management of the business are separate. In other words, a case in which there's an absentee owner, who may prefer not to have his future based on either his old company or the new one. He may just want to get out. Therefore, the buyer can purchase for cash and can give the stock options and so forth, not to the owners, but to the management.

Question: But suppose you have an owner-management?

May: If the owner-manager is going to continue, it's difficult to see where he's better off selling for cash because, in his capacity as a manager, he now becomes an employee. Many buyers look on that situation with great distaste because they're inviting him to take his cash and go away.

Question: How long does it take to liquefy an estate starting out with a public offering?

May: I have to say that depends on the company and a lot of other things. But I think, as a rule of thumb, approximately five to ten years would be true. It is difficult to envision a situation where an estate could be cleared up in less than that time.

Question: In your reading of the marketplace, as far as price/earnings multiples are concerned, what are most buyers looking for today?

May: In most cases of publicly held companies, there are four main considerations:

1. *The buyer does not want to dilute his per-share earnings.* In other words, say he made $1.00 a share this year, he's going to make $1.20 next year, and he's selling it at 10 times this year's earnings or $10. He won't buy anything that will result in his next year's earnings being $1.18 instead of $1.20.

2. *The buyer wants to acquire something that will increase his per-share earnings over, say, a five-year period.* If it's not going to contribute to his company growth and per-share earnings over five years, it would be of little interest to him.

3. *The buyer does not want to pay out more in dividends than a certain percentage (say, 50%) of what he is getting in earnings.* Thus the relation of earnings

to dividends is important and also, as a part of that, he does not want to dilute his book value by writing off good will.

4. *The buyer wants to see your company and his worth more together than either one is worth alone.* In short, he wants synergism so that the total effect is greater than the sum of the two effects taken independently.

Chapter 9

FINANCIAL ANALYSIS AND LONG-TERM CAPITAL STRUCTURE

Wesley W. Marple, Jr.

For the purposes of this discussion, I shall make the standard assumption that the role of the corporate financial manager is to make decisions that are in the best interest of the common shareholders. As a result, his goal is to maximize their wealth as represented by the market value of their common stock.

There has been a change in the teaching of corporate financial management over the years away from an orientation that was principally concerned with the periodic affairs in the life of the corporation, such as the establishment of the corporation,

Dr. Marple is Chairman of the Department of Finance and Insurance, and Professor of Finance, Northeastern University.

the raising of capital, its liquidation, and so forth. The change has been to consider the day to day corporate financial affairs, such as the management of working capital, the decision to pay a dividend or not, and other recurring financial management decisions. This newer orientation is frequently characterized as the management of the flow of funds actually and potentially available to the corporation. When we consider the long-term capital structure of a business within this orientation, the financial manager of the corporation is primarily concerned with allocating earnings before interest and taxes (EBIT) in such a way as to meet the needs and objectives of his common equity shareholders. I like to think of this as the merchandising of the EBIT for the maximum price.

We can modify the risk associated with the business depending on how we merchandise the EBIT. For instance, for a given percentage change in EBIT, there will be a higher percentage change in our profit after tax if we use a lot of debt than there will be if we use a little amount of debt. This is what financial experts mean by leverage or gearing from the use of debt. These wider swings in profit after tax with leverage increase the risk to the common shareholder which may be justified in good times by the higher per-share earnings the financial leverage produces.

One of the problems in financial management is that it is difficult to prescribe ways to make trade-offs between higher risk and higher return for common shareholders. Given two alternatives that offer the same risk, we would prefer the one with the higher return; given two alternatives with the same return, we would opt for the one with the lower risk; but when we have different risk and return combinations, it is difficult to know which alternative is the better one to take.

It all depends on the individual who is making the decisions. The problem of determining appropriate risk and return combinations is encountered in many areas of financial decision making, and practical decision-making tools are lacking for many of these areas.

Against this general background of goals of financial management and difficulties of prescribing risk and return trade-offs, let us look at some tools used by financial managers in the day-to-day practice of their craft. The first tool is financial ratios derived from income statements and balance sheets.

Common Financial Ratios

Utilizing the figures shown in *Exhibit I* for the income statement and the balance sheet of the ABC company, let us examine some of the common ratios used in financial analysis.

Balance Sheet

Because of our emphasis on long-term capital structure, I shall first describe some ratios frequently used to characterize the long-term capital structure of a company, and then I shall discuss some other ratios often used in financial analysis.

The most relevant measures of a company's capital structure are ratios characterizing the proportionate contribution each source makes to the total long-term capitalization.

One such ratio is long-term debt to total long-term capital. In *Exhibit I*, it is the long-term debt of $1 million divided by the sum of the long-term debt plus the long-term equity capital which total $5 million, yielding the ratio of 1 to 50 or 20%. This ratio gives us a measure of how much of the total long-term capital is coming from debt sources and how much is coming from nondebt sources, such as preferred and common stock. Frequently, the same figures are combined to produce a debt to equity ratio; in this case, it is 1 to 4 or 25%.

Another measure of the total use of debt is the ratio of total debt to total assets. For the ABC company, this is the sum of current liabilities of $1.5 million plus long-term debt of $1 million compared with total assets of $6.5 million or a ratio of 39%. In this case, debt includes current liabilities, such as accounts payable and the like.

Another balance sheet ratio, although not of the long-term

Exhibit I. Ratio of Long-Term Debt to Capital

Balance Sheet
ABC Company
December 31, 1970

Cash	$ 500,000		Accounts payable	$1,000,000	
Accounts receivable	1,000,000		Loans payable	500,000	
Inventory	1,000,000				
Total current assets		$2,500,000	Total current liabilities		$1,500,000
Net plant and equipment		4,000,000	Long-term debt		1,000,000
			Equity		4,000,000
Total assets		$6,500,000	Total liabilities		$6,500,000

capital sector, but essential as background for financial analysis, is that of current assets to current liabilities. For our ABC company, it is $2.5 million to $1.5 million or 1.7 to 1.

Income Statement

Another source of ratios is the income statement. Frequently, all components of the statement are converted to percentages of net sales. One of the most important ratios is net profit to sales which in *Exhibit II* (see page 125) is 10%.

A more significant ratio, net profit divided by net worth, tells us how well a company is utilizing the book value of the stockholders investment. For the ABC company, that ratio is $580,000 divided by $4 million or 15%. Often this ratio is derived by multiplying the ratio of profit to sales by the ratio of sales to net worth, reminding us that return to shareholders may be enhanced either by increasing the profitability of sales or increasing the level of sales with a given net worth.

Finally, there is a ratio which indicates the relationship of the operating profit of the business (EBIT) to the total long-term capitalization, which in our example is $1.25 million divided by $5 million or 25%.

How does one know whether a particular ratio is satisfactory? Ultimately, there are only two sources of standards for determining the satisfactoriness of a ratio. One is to examine companies in the same business and the ratios that those similar companies have; the other is to look at the same company at different periods in its existence to determine the trend in the affairs of the company.

Looking at the sources of standards quickly calls attention to the fact that ratio analysis really does not give the definitive answers that we would like to have as financial managers. Ratio analysis does not reveal whether we have achieved, say, the optimum use of long-term debt or total debt in our capital structure.

One of the features of financial management in recent years has been an attempt to find ways of thinking analytically that go beyond the ratios which are essentially descriptive, and to answer questions such as: how much of earnings should be paid out as dividends? How much use should we be making of long- and short-term debt? These analytical approaches are useful in asking questions, but at their present stage of development they are not going to provide certain answers. An approach to thinking about debt capacity which goes beyond the descriptive ratios is discussed in the next part of this chapter.

Burden Coverage

I indicated earlier my dissatisfaction with looking solely at balance-sheet ratios to determine whether or not a company is making appropriate use of debt. Here, I would like to describe another approach, called "a burden coverage ratio."

The burden associated with long-term debt is the sum of the interest that has to be paid on this debt, plus the funds that have to be provided to amortize the debt. Because interest expense is tax deductible, the effect of having $100,000 of interest—again as shown in *Exhibit I*—and a tax rate of 50% is a reduction in after-tax profits of only $50,000. The interest component of the burden of debt is then $50,000 after taxes.

If the $4 million principal of debt in our example were to be repaid at the rate of $200,000 per year, the burden for repayment would be $200,000 after tax, thus raising the total after-tax burden to $250,000. Having determined the burden of the debt, we must determine the funds available to meet that burden. The most readily available source of funds is the operating profit of the company—$1.25 million in our example. At a 50% tax rate, this translates into $625,000 after tax, thus providing a coverage of $625,000 divided by $250,000 or 2.5 times.

This means that the profit at the present operating level will produce funds equal to 2.5 times the requirement of our long-term debt. Whether this indicates that the company can use more debt depends on how thin the borrower and lender are willing to let the ratio become.

Accordingly, the financial manager might want to develop some pro forma income data for comparison with the burden associated with the debt. This would enable him to determine the corporation's ability to use debt by looking at the funds generated from future operations, rather than by taking a snapshot of the balance sheet with or without new components of debt.

Source and Use Statement

One final analytical device that I find extremely useful is called the "sources and use of funds statement." This statement helps a financial manager to see where he has obtained and used funds in his business. Increasingly, corporations include in their annual reports the sources and use of funds statements to supplement their income statements and balance sheets.

In its simplest form, a source and use of funds statement may be constructed from any two balance sheets for a particular company. Sources of funds are decreases in asset accounts or increases in liability accounts. Uses of funds are increases in asset accounts or decreases in liability accounts. *Exhibit II* provides an additional balance sheet for the ABC company and an elementary source and uses of funds calculation derived from the 1969 and 1970 balance sheets.

If one of the balance sheets is a projected or pro forma balance sheet, the source and use statement will be a projected statement.

Cost of Capital

In obtaining funds for a corporation, we realize that a return is anticipated by the providers of long-term capital. In this section, I shall discuss the various ways of determining cost of capital for the three principal sources of long-term capital: *debt, preferred stock*, and *common stock*.

The cost of long-term *debt* is not difficult to assess, for we have a contractual arrangement under which debt is provided to the corporation. Let us say, for example, that we have a contract with the lender which obligates us to pay in a tight money market 10% interest. This is, of course, a tax deductible expense. Accordingly, if our tax rate is 50%, the cost of our debt capital at 10% on an after-tax basis is only 5%. Thus there is no particular trick in determining the cost of debt capital. The repayment of debt does not enter into our cost calculation because the discharge of the obligation is not an expense.

The cost of the second source of long-term capital, *preferred stock*, likewise may usually be readily determined because of the established return to the investor. A preferred stock issued at $40 a share and paying a $4 dividend has an after-tax cost of $4 divided by $40 or 10%. No adjustment is made for taxes because the preferred dividend is paid from after-tax earnings.

When we turn to the third major component, *common stock*, we run into a thicket because the return to a common shareholder is not contractual as it is with debt and preferred stock. Assume that we have a common stock selling at $7.38 a share which historically has paid a dividend of $.10 a share out of recent earnings of $.51 a share. Over the past five years earn-

Exhibit II. Use of Funds Statement Constructed From
Two Balance Sheets

A. Income Statement
ABC Company
Year ending December 31, 1970

Net Sales	$6,000,000	100%
Cost of goods sold	4,000,000	67
Gross profit	$2,000,000	33%
Selling, general administration Expenses	750,000	12%
Earnings before interest, taxes, (EBIT)	$1,250,000	21%
Interest	100,000	2%
Profit before tax	$1,150,000	19%
Taxes	570,000	9
Profit after tax	$ 580,000	10%

B. Balance Sheet
ABC Company
December 31, 1969

Cash	$600,000	Accounts payable	$900,000
Accounts receivable	900,000	Loans payable	500,000
Inventory	900,000		
Total current assets	$2,400,000	Total current liabilities	$1,400,000
Net plant and		Long-term debt	900,000
equipment	3,500,000	Equity	3,600,000
Total assets	$5,900,000	Total liabilities	$5,900,000

C. Source and Uses of Funds Statement
ABC Company
December 31, 1969 to December 31, 1970

Sources of Funds		Uses of Funds	
Cash	$100,000	Accounts receivable	$100,000
Accounts payable	100,000	Inventory	100,000
Long-term debt	100,000	Plant and equipment	500,000
Equity	400,000		
Total sources	$700,000	Total uses	$700,000

ings have increased at an annual compound rate of 11%. What is the cost of this common equity?

One approach has been to divide per-share earnings by market price, or $.51 divided by $7.38 or 7%.

Implicit in this approach is the expectation that the providers of new common stock should make an earnings' contribution at least equal to the rate of earnings provided by the old common stockholders; therefore, the prevention of dilution in per-share earnings.

However, when we compare the cost of equity of 7% to the cost of preferred of 10%, something begins to look a little bit strange; we find that the cost of common equity is somewhat below the cost of preferred stock, yet the risks associated with investing in the common equity are much greater than those of the preferred stock.

As a result of thinking along these lines, an alternative formulation for determining the cost of common equity has been developed. It is based on the common stock's dividend yield plus the rate of growth in per-share earnings—that is, how much the earnings have been growing over the past four or five years on an annual compound basis.

Using that formula with the example seen earlier, we have $.10 over $7.38, or about a 2% dividend yield added to the 11% annual increase in per-share earnings, thus producing a cost of capital calculated on this basis of approximately 13%. This seems more reasonable.

Neither of the approaches to determine the cost of equity is wholly satisfactory and, because of the problems in determining common equity costs, some people have been skeptical about the utility of cost of capital concepts. However, even though it is easier to conceive of a cost of capital than to calculate one, I find the concept useful in analyzing financial problems.

To some extent, this skepticism is more likely to apply to a large corporation than to a medium size or small business in which the principal shareholders may be able to avoid using either of these common equity formulas. The principals in a small company may be able to determine their costs directly by asking themselves what minimum outside rate of return they would require on the equity capital tied up in the business to prompt them to withdraw it and invest elsewhere.

In such companies, the solution might be to think about the cost of the common equity in terms of an opportunity rate—the rate that could be expected on another investment of presumably similar risk—and to avoid formulations like those we have been discussing. If there is no public market for the common stock, this is the only alternative.

Weighted Average Cost of Capital

How does one take the costs of various capital components and put them into a figure which may be helpful in making management decisions?

This is frequently done by determining a weighted average cost of capital. This approach argues that we should weigh each of the components in the capital structure by the proportion which they bear in the market value of the company.

For instance, if it turns out that a corporation has a million shares of a common equity outstanding, which sell at $7 a share, the market value of that common equity holding is $7 million. In addition, if preferred stock is outstanding and has a total market value of $2 million that should also be reflected. Moreover, if the debt that is outstanding has a market of $1 million, the company has a total market value of $10 million. In terms of percentages, the debt is thus 10% of the total long-term capital structure; preferred stock, 20%; and common equity, 70%.

We are now in a position to weigh the cost of these various components by their proportion in the total market value of the company:

- If we assume that the common equity has a cost of 13%, for purposes of this illustration, we would have a common equity component weighted by 70% of 13% to yield a contribution of 9.1% to the weighted average cost of capital.
- If the cost of preferred stock is 10% and 20% of the long-term capital structure, it would yield 2% to the weighed average.
- If the cost of debt is 5%, which is 10% of the capital structure, it would yield roughly .05%.
- And if we add all these together, we come up with a weighted average cost of capital of 11.6%, reflecting the fact that we have combined with some relatively expensive equity, some less expensive preferred stock and some much less expensive debt.

At this point, the reader may be wondering "What is the use of weighted average cost?" I think the answer to such a question is that it is an indication of what one should be making on investments. In the previous example, investments should return no less than the 11.6% weighted average cost of capital. Keep in mind that the ability to issue debt is dependent on the company already having some common stock outstanding. Thus, to the extent that the company issues additional debt, it is at some future time going to have to provide added equity either through an additional issue of common or through retained earnings.

The general prescription is that one should be using as his standard for return on investment the return expected by the providers of the capital which makes the investment possible, even though it is difficult to specify the expected return for the common shareholder.

Debt's Increased Popularity

By far, the most interesting development in the practice of corporate finance has been the increasing use of long-term debt in corporate capital structures. I take no stand on whether or not it is wise; only the future can determine that, but many practitioners of finance appear to believe that it is.

There are several reasons for this greater use of debt. One is that the people who recall the recession of the 1930's are increasingly leaving executive suites. Some of their successors believe that we are entering a new type of economy with less severe swings which favor the greater use of debt. Another is that there have been developed new analytical approaches, which some people believe are helpful to them in deciding whether or not to use debt. Still another development has been the design of issues of convertible debt.

The new analytical approaches free financial managers from balance-sheet considerations and look instead at burden-coverage ratios, as previously discussed, and the funds freed from contracting operations during recessionary periods. To the dismay of some conservative financiers, these approaches frequently appear to justify more debt than the older approaches would justify.

Use of Convertibles and Warrants

There are a number of reasons why convertible issues have had a measure of appeal, and may have again if the stock market improves its performance. One of these is the fact that a somewhat greater borrowing margin is available on convertible securities than on common equity investments. Investors themselves find the convertibles offer more leverage.

Another is that sometimes it is possible to issue a subordinated convertible debenture, which will provide the basis for additional debt where it might not be possible to issue the debenture if it did not have the conversion feature.

Finally, the use of convertibles has generally allowed a somewhat lower interest rate to be paid on the debenture than would otherwise be paid if it were not convertible. The interest saving is on the order of a .05% a year with a conversion premium generally being about 10% above current market price.

Another new device is the use of warrants, sometimes in conjunction with equity securities as well as with debentures. The warrants have an advantage of frequently being separable from the debt instrument. When the investor buys a convertible debenture, he cannot separate the conversion feature from the debenture. But if he buys a debenture with warrants, he can hold the debenture and later on sell the warrants. This is frequently an attraction.

The two have some characteristics which are quite similar, as well as different tax and financial implications for the company. One of the most important, it seems to me, is that there is a mechanism for forcing conversion by calling the convertible debenture, but there normally is no similar mechanism for forcing the exercise of the warrants.

Having briefly reviewed some analytical approaches and concepts which I find useful in resolving financial problems, let me try to answer your questions.

Floor Discussion

Question: Would you comment on new techniques being developed to determine the cost of a warrant or a convertible issue?

Marple: The question of the cost of a warrant or the cost of a convertible issue is, I think, a very serious one because presumably these sources of funds would only be used if they were cheaper than alternatives. To determine the cost, one theoretically should have an idea of the market price of the common at the time the debenture is converted or the warrant is exercised. It is therefore difficult to think of them in terms of cost.

My concern about the use of convertible debentures and debentures with warrants is that in many cases you would be better off with a straight debenture refinanced by a common stock offering than you would be with a convertible. This is particularly true if you expected the market price for equity to go quickly beyond the point where conversion would be desirable.

Question: On the basis of an assumption that you can have an equity issue, which is more attractive, a convertible debenture or debt refinanced with equity later?

Marple: If you were reasonably certain that the market price of the equity would soon increase beyond the conversion price, I'd prefer the latter alternative.

Question: In reaching some decision as to how much debt ought to be in your long-term capital structure, you're taking into consideration the market value of stock, are you not?

Marple: Yes indeed, I am.

Question: Would you discuss the market value versus the book value in this consideration?

Marple: Some people have argued that the weights to determine long-term weighted average cost of capital should be on book value, but the book value weights reflect the net proceeds that were realized on prior issuance of stock, plus accumulated earnings.

The resultant figure is the value that can be realized from the sale of common equity today, and the rate of return that is expected by the purchasers of that common equity, on their investment in the company today. Market value weights are argued for, rather than book value weights because the cost is based on market prices, not on book values.

Question: The equity cost is an after-tax equity cost, correct?

Marple: Correct.

Question: In your EBIT formula is depreciation not considered as an operating expense?

Marple: Yes, it is an operating expense and the EBIT is after depreciation. You are correct in raising the question as to whether depreciation couldn't as well be considered an operating source of funds for the burden coverage calculation. It frequently is added to the after-tax amount of the EBIT to determine the coverage.

Question: With what do you contrast the average cost of capital?

Marple: One of the uses of the average cost of capital is to determine the rate of return that you need from new investments to justify the employment of corporate funds in a new endeavor. In other words, it is a basic standard for determining whether or not to make a capital expenditure.

Question: And then there were earnings in terms of net worth that you were comparing it with. You arrived at an 11.6% figure there, and you were comparing that with which other ratio?

Marple: I cited no other ratio. I was comparing it with a return from a hypothetical investment which you, as a manager of business, would consider making. For instance, you might decide to expand a product line and put some corporate funds into that expansion. The notion is that you should at least get an 11.6% return in order to justify that investment.

Question: Would this be true if you have a company which you know is under leveraged?

Marple: If you have a company which is under leveraged, you should determine your cost of capital, not in terms of present capital structure, but in terms of the appropriate capital structure, which presumably involves additional leverage.

Question: If you do that, do you have a dynamic situation and do you change your cost of capital?

Marple: Indeed, you will change it.

Question: Could the internal rate of return then be used for capital budgeting decisions?

Marple: I have avoided use of the phrase "internal rate of return," but it could be one way of calculating the return from a new investment and it would also be the figure to compare with the 11.6%.

For instance, you might say that an investment in a new product line, using the discounted cash flow technique, has an internal rate of return of 12% which exceeds cost of capital; therefore, we should make it. Actually, you might go on to say that in the capital structure which we envisage, the cost of capital will be reduced to 10%, because of the use of greater amounts of debt. This means that the margin is even greater and the project is relatively more attractive.

Question: What other uses are there of the rate of average cost of capital?

Marple: There are two other uses of the rate of average cost of capital that come immediately to mind. It is (1) a standard for thinking about the design of your capital structure. It causes you to ask whether you have the appropriate amount of debt or preferred stock in your capital structure, both of which are customarily less expensive sources of funds than common stock.

It causes you to ask yourself whether you can reduce your cost of capital by the use of these additional sources of funds, therefore bringing into a zone of consideration some of the investments that might not previously have been considered attractive.

However, remember that you cannot have a capital structure that's 100% debt. If the percentage of debt in the capital structure becomes too great, the advantage of the lower cost debt will soon be offset by the accelerating cost of the equity capital.

The cost of capital is also used (2) in performance appraisal schemes where the compensation of executives is related to the excess of the return on investment above the cost of funds employed by the corporation.

Chapter 10

INTERMEDIATE AND LONG-TERM FINANCING FOR CORPORATIONS

W. Giles Mellon

My discussion in this chapter will focus on the general subject of intermediate and long-term financing for corporations. More specifically I should like to cover three main points: (1) to review briefly the major sources of intermediate and long-term financing; (2) to pinpoint some of the recent trends in the most important of these sources of funds, and (3) to raise some questions about the long-term cost and availability of such financing.

Mr. Mellon is Professor of Money and Banking, Graduate School of Business Administration, Rutgers University.

Sources of Funds

The main sources of intermediate and long-term financing—that is, from a year or two on out—available to U.S. corporations include: ordinary term loans, revolving credits from commercial banks, sale of regular and convertible bonds in the open market, direct placement loans from life insurance companies, mortgage financing, miscellaneous loans from the federal government and nonbank financial institutions, sale of common and preferred stock, and long-term leasing as an alternative to direct purchase.

Of all these sources, I shall restrict myself to a discussion of bank term loans, and the sale of debt and equity in the open and direct placement market. Let me mention something about these briefly one by one, starting with the intermediate term loans from banks.

Term Loans

These are bank credits of one year or longer in one of two forms: *business loans*, with an original maturity of more than one year, payable in lump sums, in even periodic installments, or in installments that balloon on the end; and *short-term loans*, under formal revolving credit arrangements in which the borrower has a definite commitment.

Banks also provide over one-year credit in two ways: by routinely renewing short-term loans, without having a formal revolving credit arrangement, and also by lending against real property.

However, in view of the fact that the available statistics are set up to reflect the first two, I shall confine myself to them.

The growth of term lending in recent years reflects the fact that such credit offers four distinct advantages to corporate customers:

> **First,** they are a source of medium-term credit to small businesses which cannot pass the security mar-

ket, at least at less than the high rates that some investment bankers have charged.

Second, for large businesses, term loans provide greater flexibility, often at a lower cost than the sale of securities in the market.

Third, term loans provide interim credit for financing initial stages of new construction with the final long-term credit needs provided usually by bond sales or long-term mortgages.

Fourth, revolving credit cannot only provide convenient coverage during short-term periods of uncertainty about needs for funds, but it can also be converted into term loans, if the longer term need for funds becomes much clearer.

Nonfinancial U.S. corporations had about $307 billion of credit market instruments outstanding at the end of 1969. About $85 billion of this was in the form of business loans by commercial banks. Unfortunately, we do not really have any comprehensive figures for term loans of all commercial banks; but, we can estimate that something in the order of 40% or more, say, $35 billion is in term loans.

Growth in term-loan lending, which had been very rapid over time, has slowed down and this reflects to some extent the general hesitancy of commercial bankers to commit themselves over the long term, what with the unsettled environment we have had in the last few years.

Debt and Equity Financing

Let me now comment briefly on the sale of regular and convertible bonds in direct placement—that is, long-term debt financing. At the end of 1969, total outstanding corporate bonds of U.S. nonfinancial corporations amounted to about $148 billion. Again, we do not have exact figures, but let us say that 50% of this represents insurance company direct placements and the other 50% direct sales to the public in the open market.

Normally, direct placements exceed open market sales by a sizable margin, but the remarkable acceleration in corporate bond financing in recent years to a level approximately triple that which prevailed in the period from 1960 to 1965 swamped the ability of the steadily rising insurance company reserves as a source. The demand, of course, spilled over into the open market and resulted in very high interest rates.

Sales of common stocks have constituted a relatively minor source of corporate funds in recent years. During the last five years, for example, U.S. nonfinancial corporations raised about $144 billion in the credit markets. In contrast, sales of common stock raised only about $7 billion in the entire five-year period. Thus, in this time period, debt financing as a source of corporate funds has outweighed equity financing by a factor of something like 20 to 1. For corporations, and for that matter for the whole U.S. economy, the expansion of the later 1960's was based on straight debt financing.

However, 1969 and early 1970, a period characterized by unparalleled high interest rates and uncertainty in the credit markets, saw major shifts in this pattern. The key elements of corporate finance in that period are easily apparent from a brief examination of the data. One, corporate financing demands moved to record levels. Two, long-term debt financing stayed at record levels during 1969, but was accompanied by a sharp increase in sales of equity and short-term financing via the commercial paper market.

To induce investors to absorb these huge additions to the stock of debts, interest rates obviously had to move up to postwar record levels. In addition, investors were induced to part with the necessary funds only by a sharp shift into equity-type participation in corporate activities during 1969.

Future Trend Outlook

I want to turn now to the main issue—namely, (a) the future outlook for cost and availability of the major sources of corporate external intermediate and long-term financing, and (b) the resulting trend in the composition of such financing and therefore the corporate financial structure.

To begin this discussion, we need a series of future assumptions about the economy in the 1970's, the relative position of corporations within it, and also projections in current dollars in those sectors which show both the product and income side of the GNP accounts. We need to know not only what each sector of the economy spends, but also what its total receipts are, since the difference between the two will represent either what the sectors save, and thus have available for investment, or the deficit they must finance in the credit market.

Most GNP projections lack this detail, and, therefore, are really quite useless for the person who is looking at the future of the financial markets. Recent projections, however, by the National Planning Association have been done well on this basis. Thus the National Planning Association model calls for a 7% growth in GNP during the decade of the 1970's, consisting of 2.5% inflation, and 4.5% real. Now let us project everything relative to this NPA growth figure. In other words, if the demand for funds or the supply of funds grows less rapidly than 7% in the economy as a whole, or if it does not represent a pressure on the financial market, or if it represents a net pressure, we will be able to isolate points of relative pressure without getting involved in the exact numbers, which would turn out wrong in any case.

The Government Sector

Rising receipts allow a general balance of government expenditures by the year 1980, even with providing for a reasonably rapid expansion in government services, additional tax cuts, or the retirement of securities. No matter how you slice it, the government, which caused much of the recent trouble in the credit markets, is not likely to be a significant net demander on balance in the market under normal circumstances.

A near balance is also projected for the state and local

government sectors. This, however, is of a very particular nature, and reflects the fact that state and local pension fund receipts will rise sharply during this period. In turn, this will tend to balance off the increased necessity to sell more and more state and local debt (i.e., municipal bonds) which means that the sector is likely to be only a moderate net demander of funds from the credit market.

The total government sector has a number of really unsettled issues. For example, one is the extent of housing programs for the poor. If we are to actually provide and finance these, somebody has to come up with the money. To do so, the federal government will either have to raise taxes, which would hurt the financial market by decreasing the supply of savings, or sell securities in the financial markets. Failure to provide the housing funding at the national level would mean that the state and local governments, or some combination of the two, would have to do it. Naturally, as more of this program is financed by government—and it is strictly a political situation—the more pressure there will be on the financial markets.

Moreover, massive programs to improve our environment, such as eliminating air and water pollution, will all have to be government financed.

Another unsettled issue revolves around what the final extent and form of the federal revenue sharing program will be. Federal government receipts rise slightly more rapidly than income, which tends to create an automatic surplus over time. By contrast, state and local receipts, which are heavily dependent on property taxes, sales taxes, and so forth, rise slightly less than income. Thus the financing gap between state and local governments grows even as the surplus of the federal government tends to increase.

As a result, we need some massive system for sharing this revenue. The exact nature of a new system, one in which all the securities are sold by the federal government, or one in which state and local securities would be sold with or without the tax exempt feature, or some other pass-through system, would heavily affect the impact of the government sectors on the capital markets.

The projections I am dealing with here assume that these sectors do not get out of proportion, and that the growth of the federal government sector will parallel that of the economy as a whole. Costs of state and local expenditures will in general rise much more rapidly than costs in the economy as a whole because of heavy personnel disbursements. This will cause the state and local expenditures as a percentage of the GNP to move up during the 1970's.

Consumer spending and consumer credit will obviously rise rapidly. Housing outlays will also be up sharply because of the demographic mix, but much of this will be due to the very young age of people coming on the housing market who can be expected to seek apartments, rather than single-family homes.

The Business Sector

Here, we can see a clear pattern in almost any of the projections made of capital expenditures.

Plant and equipment spending should rise rapidly because of the amount of plant and equipment necessary to produce so many units of new output, plus replacement and modernization. In addition, the shift into multi-family housing, as we just noted, should require heavier business financing in place of individual savings and loan type financing. Thus total capital spending by business will rise very sharply, more rapidly than the economy as a whole, and thus outstrip the internal corporate sources of funds.

Obviously, this means that we will have a continuation of the rapidly rising trend toward long-term financing, since there is a gap between sources and uses of funds which reflects heavy long-term investment, which is usually financed by long-term borrowing.

The cost at which this demand will be satisfied in the credit market in this decade depends on the conditions of supply and demand—particularly, in those markets which absorb corporate debt and equity.

The Individual Sector

At this point, therefore, I should like to comment briefly on what may happen in those particular markets on which businesses must depend to absorb this large volume of long-term borrowing, plus whatever equity is thought desirable, beginning with the individual market. Here, two facts are immediately apparent.

One, individuals normally are not very good markets for private securities on a direct basis. They hold only about $20 billion of the $175 billion dollars of corporate and foreign bonds outstanding, and while they hold hundreds of billions of dollars in common stock, they have been heavy sellers of noninvestment company common stock to institutions in recent years.

Individuals, of course, are on balance very large savers. They added, for example, some $50 billion to their holdings of financial assets in 1969. However, they tend in normal times to save through financial institutions; for example, in 1968, $57 billion of the year's total acquisition of $59 billion of financial assets represented savings accounts, pension funds, insurance reserves, and the like. The remainder represented their direct acquisition of securities.

To get them to buy this really quite extraordinary projected increase in their holdings of corporate bonds, it will be necessary to pay exceedingly high rates to induce the purchases. In fact, one rule-of-thumb system of forecasting interest rates which is widely used in the financial community says: add up all the demand for funds and all the sources of funds, and if the source of funds is made up to a large extent of selling to the individual consumer or to the foreign sector, then interest rates will be high, since this sector demands high rates to absorb securities directly. At high rates, the individual sector will take debt directly. In 1969, with high rates, individuals increased their direct purchases to nearly $19 billion as compared with $9.5 billion the year before.

Two, while consumer savings will rise as incomes grow, savings as a percentage of income will remain quite low. This reflects the easiest thing to project—that is, what happens to existing people as they get older. In the period of the 1970's, the number of young people in this country will increase rapidly, the number of old people will rise very slowly, and the numerical size of the middle-aged group will remain constant. In fact, by 1980, there will be fewer people in the age 40 to 55 bracket than there are today.

But young people are poor savers. People in the age group 25 to 34, for example, save only 2% of their income in comparison with the overall average of 6% or 7%. It is the middle-aged group which saves and that will be in short supply during this decade. The importance of this simple fact cannot be overestimated. It is the net surplus of financial savings over borrowings by the individual sector, which finance the perpetual deficits of U.S. corporations and the frequent deficits of the government sector. Individual savings, either directly or through financial intermediaries, are the source of funds in the capital markets, and if these savings are low relative to income, money will tend to be scarce and expensive.

The Institutional Sector

Insurance companies, both directly and through their operation of insured pension funds, have been for many years the single major source of long-term debt financing of corporations. However, if we look at the industry we can see certain trends which will affect this relationship.

First, individual and group life—that is, the ordinary life insurance aspect of the business—has been growing with the economy. Premiums for this kind of insurance, for example, have been running at a comfortable 3.25% of disposable income for a decade; thus this reflects very steady growth.

At first glance, the decade of the 1970's would seem to offer some very good opportunities to the industry because, in fact, the group that will be increasing in size is precisely the young people who are the ideal insurance company prospects. Of course, whether or not the industry will be able to capitalize on this is another question. There are other problems involved, and I really would expect only a moderate improvement in the relative rate of life insurance sales and growth of life insurance reserves.

In any case, moreover, the life companies will be pushing equity products, which compete with their ordinary sales, and they will also be trying to put more equity into their own portfolios. We have witnessed revisions which have increased the proportion that the life companies can put into equity form, and this trend will continue.

After many years of being rapidly outdistanced by noninsured funds, the insured pension funds have actually been growing in recent years just about as fast as the noninsureds. However, this will again be, as a market for bonds, affected in two ways: (1) by the general slowdown in pension fund growth, which I will get to in a moment, and (2) by the fact that this recent improvement has been accomplished through segregated accounts in which more funds go into equities, enabling them to be more competitive against the noninsured funds.

Pension funds, which were once good bond customers, have been shifting steadily into stock purchases in recent years. For example, in 1969, they bought something like $5.5 billion in common stocks in comparison with only $500 million in corporate bonds.

One of the major financial phenomena of the 1970's will be the maturing of U.S. pension funds, both the insured and noninsured, as the increase in numbers of additional plans slows down and as large numbers of workers reach retirement age and start to draw benefits.

Projections made by the National Bureau of Economic Research clearly show that pension funds as a group will tend to level off in the rate of growth of assets within a few years. This means that their relative importance in the financial market will start to decline steadily and pension managers will also probably continue to shift more funds into equity.

Partially offsetting this relative decline in private pension funds will be the growth of state and local pension funds. The absolute rate of growth of private plans will level off at a fixed rate of about $7.5 billion annually in, say, three or four years. Meanwhile, state and local funds, which currently provide a surplus of about $4 billion a year for investment in financial instruments, will rise to, say, something like $8 billion or $9 billion by the end of the decade.

These plans, which already are a major factor in the corporate bond market, by 1980 will be *the* major stable factor in the capital market, and particularly in the bond market. Here again, however, we see the maturing of investment philosophy. State and local pension funds, which once bought mainly federal— and some state and local—securities are now buying corporate bonds of generally higher quality. In addition, they have been steadily shifting into equity as their operating restrictions allow.

The Banking Sector

By this time, I hope the general pattern that I have been developing is relatively clear. Corporations will have a heavy demand for borrowing, especially for the long term. Individual savings will be relatively low and tend to go through financial intermediaries, which have been shifting away from bonds. If this were all we had left, we would be stuck with a situation in which the individual sector would have to pick up directly a huge volume of corporate bonds plus all the federal, state, and local securities.

The only remaining sector is banking, which I come to at the end. It is certainly possible that the banks will be able to fill much of this long-term corporate financing gap, although in the process, of course, they will not be able to buy much in the way of municipal bonds.

Businesses are preferred customers of banks. By year-end 1970, the banks knowing that interest rates had already passed their peak, were more willing to lend long term. Major money market banks have shown some great ingenuity in devising deposit instruments to attract funds and to compete with the rates available in the open market. Thus they are in a position to finance a great deal of this long-term debt.

The question mark here, obviously, is monetary policy. The Nixon Administration, which is with us until 1973 at least, has shown an inclination to use monetary rather than fiscal policy or direct controls. Now, with an economy growing very rapidly and with strong pressures on prices, continuous reliance on monetary policy as the major stabilizing force means that most adjustments in terms of fighting inflation will have to come through the money and capital markets in the form of tight money. Thus while the banks when money is easy can pick up this long-term financing and may be quite willing to do it, they may simply be unable to do it. The adverse factor, of course, would be periods of tight money when the only available source of funds to the banking system—the Federal Reserve—would dry up.

In Summary

It seems clear that during the decade of the 1970's there will be strong demands on the capital markets by the private sector, in combination with a relatively reduced flow of savings and a reduced flow of funds into financial institutions on balance. Dollar totals will rise, but the big question is whether or not they will rise as rapidly as the economy as a whole. While this will result in a shift to debt financing through banks, there will still have to be a considerable amount of direct sales of corporate securities, both debt and equity, to individuals—which is a switch over the pattern of many years.

Thus to balance the sources and uses of money it will be necessary to throw some of the debt into the private sector. The question is at what level will this equilibrium be reached.

I suggest that all these considerations mean that the level of interest rates necessary to balance demand and supply of funds in the economy will be very high on the average, with occasional credit squeezes of even higher rates where monetary policy will be used to stabilize the economy. Moreover, it will be necessary to include more convertibles and equity-type financing in the corporate structure as the years wear on, and particularly in tight money periods. High bond yields will of course increase demands for them, and increased supplies of equities will somewhat—when combined with the high bond yields—diminish the appetite for equity, leading to equilibrium in the two markets.

This pattern of generally quite expensive money, with reasonably brief periods of credit tightness, will likely persist moreover, even if we do succeed in getting the rate of inflation down from its current level to the (perhaps optimistic) 2.5% or so envisioned in the National Planning Association projections.

A widespread current concept in financial circles holds that investors tend to demand a fairly constant rate of interest, say, 3%, plus an amount equal to the expected rate of inflation. Thus, if the rate of inflation were to dip by 2% or 3% from its current level, the interest rates would automatically go down by that amount.

For the corporate borrower, however, I think that this concept just does not hold water. Statistics indicate a poor relationship over the long run between inflation and interest rates. There can be periods of rapid growth with low rates and vice versa.

It is quite true that expected inflation may accelerate borrowing and force up rates, so that an easing of inflation will produce some temporary drop in rates. Of course, as the economy eases in coming months, credit demands, interest rates, and economic activity would all be correlated with one another. Thus credit demands would dip, causing market rates to come down as well, and this would be associated presumably with a lower rate of inflation.

But over time, long-term interest rates—that is, the price of the use of money for extended periods—will depend on the balance between the demand and supply of such funds. I believe that this balance will result in very expensive money in the years to come.

Chapter 11

THE CASH FLOW FORECAST: A NEW APPROACH

Salomon J. Flink

A cash flow analysis is generally accepted as a useful tool in short-term financial planning. The planning horizon, encompassed in the cash flow forecast, may vary from one season to one fiscal year of the company; or, in some cases, it may extend over several fiscal years. Financial institutions, especially commercial banks, quite frequently request the submission of such cash flow forecasts as one of the factors influencing the final determination by the lender as to the amount of the line of credit to be extended to the company.

Dr. Flink is Professor of Finance, Graduate School of Business Administration, Rutgers University. He is a widely respected advisor and consultant to business and government, and coauthor of *Managerial Finance* (New York, John Wiley & Sons, Inc. 1969).

A cash flow forecast is invariably requested by financial analysts and term lenders, as well as by investment houses in conjunction with a proposed public offering of securities. A typical cash flow forecast would be along these lines:

Estimated cash inflow—
        collections on credit sales
        cash sales
        sale of temporary investments
        sale of plant assets
        rentals from tenants
Total estimated cash inflow

Estimated cash outflow—
        payments to suppliers of materials
        payments of operating expenses and interest
        payments on long-term notes
        down payments on plant assets acquired
        payments of dividends
        purchase of temporary investments
Total estimated cash outflow

Net cash position from current operations

excess of inflow over outflow

or

excess of outflow over inflow

Shortcomings of Traditional Schedule

A cash flow forecast along the traditional lines is unrealistic, irrelevant, and obsolete. It is unrealistic for the reason that the projected figures have but a single "dimension." In other words, the figure in each "cell" implies a definitive forecast of a particular income or expense item. As a matter of fact, no company or

member of the company can realistically claim to be in posses-
sion of a crystal ball that will enable him to make a definitive
projection. Such an assumption ignores completely the element
of uncertainty that surrounds every forecast, with the exception
of some expenditure items which are fixed in advance for a
definite period of time (e.g., rent payments, interest on capital
debt, and the like).

The element of uncertainty in economic and financial predictions requires therefore the use of the probability tool.

It is precisely the element of uncertainty as to the exact
course of future events in the market which makes the traditional cash flow forecast an expression of wishful thinking rather
than a reflection of hard-boiled evaluation of future probabilities.

The deficiencies of the single-cell projection can be easily
overcome by the substitution of a minimum-maximum range of
probability. Let us take a simple situation:

Suppose the sales manager of Company X predicts
monthly sales for the next season to be $320,000, $415,000, and
$700,000, respectively. Let us next assume that in making this
prediction the sales manager has attempted to be "conservative." This still leaves the question open as to the probable
volume of sales if the market should prove to be more favorable
than the conservative estimate implies; and, conversely, what
the sales volume is likely to be if the market should be even less
receptive than had been assumed by the sales manager.

To determine the range above and below the sales manager's sales estimate calls for a final determination by top management on the minimum volume of sales which it expects in
each of the three months if the market should turn downward;
and, conversely, what the probable maximum is likely to be if
a reasonable degree of optimism is applied to the forecast. Thus
the range of projected sales is limited at one extreme (minimum) by a fair degree of pessimism. The maximum of the range
is in turn fixed by what top management regards as a reasonable
degree of optimism.

Clearly, many of the projected inflows of funds as well as outflows of cash will be affected by the assumption of pessimism or optimism, respectively. For instance, credit sales will in all likelihood constitute a high proportion of total sales if the sales projection reflects pessimism. This compares with a higher proportion of cash sales if optimism (maximum of range) is applied.

The effects of the points just discussed on the cash flow forecast will be demonstrated a little further along in this chapter.

Irrelevance & Obsolescence

The customary cash flow forecast "lumps" all inflows and outflows, regardless of whether they (a) arise from the day-to-day operations of the company, (b) are tied to the sale and purchase of capital assets with a relatively short lifetime (3 to 10 years), or (c) involve changes in the long-term asset structure of the company. Such conglomeration of sources of inflow and outflow fails to take into account three factors:

> **First,** the financial management of inflows and outflows involving capital assets with a relatively short lifetime usually gives management greater flexibility in scheduling either inflow or outflow during a particular month or other period of the year.
>
> **Second,** the conglomeration of sources deprives management of a useful tool in decision making, especially in the area of expenditures.
>
> **Third,** the conglomeration of sources makes it difficult, if not impossible, for top management—as well as the external supplier of funds—to determine quickly and effectively the specific source of weakness in any one month or other period of the year.

The commercial banker, in analyzing the demand for a line of credit, is primarily concerned with the inflow-outflow of funds from the day-to-day operations of the company. A temporary inflow of substantial funds from the proceeds of a term loan will unquestionably relieve the pressure during that period of the fiscal year. The reverse will occur when the expenditures for which the term loan is intended are incurred.

By separating the inflow-outflow of funds by types of sources—operational, medium-term capital assets, and long-term assets—both management and external suppliers of funds (commercial banker, term lender, investment banker) can quickly evaluate the relative importance of each source in the cash flow forecast for the fiscal year.

I cannot too strongly emphasize that the cash flow budget is a *tool* of managerial *decision making*. A single-cell schedule leaves little, if any, room for actual decision making. It simply confronts management with a fixed set of financial facts.

On the other hand, the decision-making process involves a presentation to management of a set of alternatives from which it may subsequently select the one alternative that top management believes to best meet the dual test of desirability and feasibility.

In the case of the cash flow forecast, this calls for an identification in the appropriate schedule of those items which are postponable in terms of time. Furthermore, it should identify the time range over which they are postponable.

For instance, a contemplated major repair job may be postponable by one, two, or three months. Or the payment schedule as submitted by the bidder may lend itself to renegotiation. The terms of royalty agreements, rental contracts, and other programmed expenditures—in terms of their respective time schedules—can frequently be renegotiated by management in order to shift the incidence of such payments or receipts, respectively, with the financial needs of the organization.

Suggested Basic Changes

To make the cash flow forecast a realistic, and thus useful, tool of decision making, two basic changes are necessary. The *first* change is purely structural in that it involves a separation of inflows and outflows into three distinct categories: (1) operational, (2) medium-term assets, and (3) long-term fixed assets.

The first category would be confined only to those incomes and expenditures that arise out of the daily operations of the firm. These are usually embodied in the current assets and current liabilities as summarized in the balance sheet.

The second category involves incomes and expenditures that are generated by replacement of, or addition to, medium-term fixed assets (e.g., machinery, equipment, tools, fixtures, and so on).

The third category identifies incomes and expenditures which arise from additions to existing capital assets.

The preparation of separate inflow schedules is designed to serve a dual purpose. For one thing, it clearly indicates to top management whether, and to what extent, any of the three distinct categories has an excess or insufficiency of funds in any given month, and it also indicates the need for a reverse shift of funds in a subsequent period of time. For another thing, management is also informed as to whether a particular inflow or outflow, respectively, may be shifted forward or backward in time if such action is needed to reduce the cash deficit in any one month.

The *second*, and equally important, basic change involves a substitution of a minimum and maximum range for any given item, instead of the characteristic single figure of the traditional cash flow forecast.

The nature and application of these two basic changes are explained and illustrated in the following sections.

I. Operational Cash Flow

The starting point for every cash flow forecast is the projected level of sales for each month, say, of the fiscal year. As I pointed out earlier in this chapter, the projection of a single figure for each month is unrealistic.

Now let us assume that a hypothetical company wants to

prepare a cash flow forecast in October for the next calendar year. Then, let us further assume that knowledgeable and highly reputable economists in and out of government are divided in their opinions on the economic outlook for the next year.

Such being the case, it is not likely that the sales manager of our hypothetical firm will, or can, claim greater expertise in predicting the economic trend for the impending fiscal year. Thus, in making his own forecast, he will certainly be on safer ground if he allows for each of two possibilities:

1. A level of sales that reflects in some measure the prediction of a slowdown in general economic activity and a corresponding contraction in the market for his own company (assuming that his company's products follow pretty much the general trend).

2. A prediction of sales that accepts a more optimistic outlook for the new year. This procedure is illustrated in *Exhibit I* which covers the first three months of the year.

Based on the minimum and maximum sales prediction for, say, the month of January, it will usually be necessary to make some adjustments in the "normal" collection period. Experience indicates that the percentage of sales in which a customer will take advantage of the discount is smaller in a period of economic contraction than in a period of expansion.

This tendency is reflected in *Exhibit I* in the two items "Credit Sales" and "Cash Sales." In this instance, it is assumed that in a contracting market ($300,000 sales) only a sixth of the accounts will be paid within ten days, whereas in an expanding market more than a third of the sales will result in payment within the discount period.

In *Exhibit I*, let us assume that in this particular case there will be no savings in labor cost if the volume is $300,000 compared with $350,000. This assumption may prove to be incorrect in a given situation in which wages and salaries may actually be reduced by more than a seventh if sales are $300,000 compared with $350,000. This may very easily result by eliminating from the labor force marginal or submarginal employees who would otherwise be required if sales are $350,000. The same could well be the case with selling expenses.

Note also that in *Exhibit I* five items are followed by an asterisk. These indicate the feasibility of some shifting in time. For example, it may be feasible to rearrange the schedule of royalty payments (either inflows or outflows). It certainly is within the realm of feasibility to negotiate with the bank for a shift in the due date of notes to coincide more closely with a month in which the company will have excess funds.

One item that comes readily to mind is property taxes. While these are due each quarter, top management may decide to shift the actual payment by one or more months. True, this will involve a penalty in the form of interest payment. However, the interest charged by the local tax authority will usually be no more, and probably less, than the interest rate on borrowed funds.

A look at the last line of *Exhibit I* shows substantial differences in the financial position of the company at the end of each of the three months, depending entirely on whether actual sales will be at the lower limit or the upper limit of the prediction for that particular month. Top management will then have to decide whether or not it wants to, or can, make some time adjustments in each item indicated by an asterisk; and, if so, the effects of such adjustments on the company's financial position.

This, in turn, makes it possible for management to negotiate more effectively, as well as more realistically, for a line of credit which, in effect, represents a "range of credit." At the same time, the prospective lender will view such a cash flow projection as a realistic tool of financial planning.

II. Medium-Term Assets

The items in this category *(see Exhibit II)* are self-explanatory. Here, again, postponability becomes an important factor. More important, however, is the not readily visible connotation of this separate schedule. Sound financial policy requires that in an expanding company fixed assets be financed largely, if not entirely, with long-term capital funds.

Exhibit I. Operational Cash Flow Forecast

(in thousands of dollars)

	Jan Min.	Jan Max.	Feb Min.	Feb Max.	March Min.	March Max.
Projected Sales	$300	$350	$400	$430	$600	$750
Estimated Cash Inflow:						
Cash Carry-Over (1)	0					
Credit Sales (collections)			250	225	325	255
Cash Sales	50	125	75	175	100	300
Rent (from tenants)*	25	25	25	25	25	25
Royalties (from licenses)*	50	50	50	50	50	50
Interest on investments	20	—	—	20	—	—
Estimated Inflow	145	200	300	495	500	630
Estimated Cash Outflow:						
Accounts Payable			95	120	125	150
Notes to banks*	100	100	—	—	100	100
Purchases (Cash)	50	60	65	75	100	210
Wages & Salaries	60	60	70	70	100	135
Selling expenses	30	30	35	35	50	50
Administrative expenses	15	15	15	15	15	15
Rent Payment*	5	5	5	5	5	5
Royalties Payment*	5	6	6.5	7	10	12.5
Taxes, Insurance, etc.	2	2	2	2	2	2
Estimated Outflow	267	288	293.5	329	507	679.5
Inflow (Outflow)	(122)	(88)	6.5	166	(7)	(49.5)
Cumulative			(115.5)	88	(122.5)	38.5

Assumptions: Sales are 1%-10, net 30 days EOM; Purchases are net 30 days EOM.

(1) For the sake of simplification it is assumed that the cash carry-over from the preceding month of December plus the corrections in January from credit sales in the previous month will be offset by the accounts payable in January for purchases made in the previous month. In a real life situation, the accountant will naturally have to enter these 3 items and their appropriate figures.

* Indicates feasibility of shifting the income (expense). The appropriate member of management would indicate the number of month(s) by which the item can be moved forward or backward, respectively.

Exhibit II. Medium-Term Asset Forecast

	Jan		Feb		March	
Estimated Cash Inflow:						
Sale of fixtures, equipment, etc.*	—	—	—	—	30	30
Proceeds from term loan*	100	100	75	75	150	150
Proceeds from lease-back*					75	75
Estimated Inflow	100	100	75	75	255	255
Estimated Cash Outflow:						
Replacement of fixtures, equipment, etc.*	75	75	125	125	125	125
Major repairs*	50	50	—	—	—	—
Maintenance	10	10	10	10	10	10
Estimated Outflow	135	135	135	135	135	135
Inflow (Outflow)	(35)	(35)	(60)	(60)	120	120
Cumulative			(95)	(95)	25	25

* Indicates feasibility of shifting the income (expense).

It is a basic truism that retained profits which are channeled into net working capital (current assets) are too frequently insufficient to maintain the same proportionate relationship to the increase in receivables and inventories. Too frequently companies find themselves in a financial squeeze as a result of ignoring this fact.

Studies by the Small Business Administration and my own research in this field[1] clearly demonstrate that such diversion of funds from current operations into investments in capital assets are one, if not the major, cause of financial illiquidity in applications for intermediate-term loans.

There is nothing improper in using an excess of funds generated temporarily by a fixed asset to meet a deficit in funds generated by current operations. On the other hand, it is important for management to be fully aware of the fact that it has "borrowed" from Category II to meet the needs of Category I. Being aware of such a "loan," it will use this device only as a

---

1. *Equity Financing of Small Manufacturing Companies in New Jersey,* New Jersey Department of Conservation & Economic Development, 1962; *The Role of Commercial Banks in the SBIC Industry,* American Bankers Association, 1965.

temporary expedient and take the necessary steps in advance to make sure that these funds will again be available for "repayment" to Category II.

III. Capital Asset Expansion

As in the previous case (roll-over assets), the items in *Exhibit III* are self-explanatory and the procedures pretty much the same.

In both cases—Category II and Category III—the feasibility of shifting the time schedule of either inflow or outflow, respectively, becomes important. Its significance is in relation to Category I.

In other words, if the operational outlook for, say, January shows a prospective deficit of funds, a shift in an expenditure in Category II or Category III to March may generate a surplus in the latter categories sufficient to cover most, or all, of the January deficit in Category I. The same result would be obtained if it proves feasible to shift an inflow of funds from either Category II or Category III or both in, say, January instead of March.

Summary Table

Note that at the end of *Exhibits I, II,* and *III* there is a summary of the last lines in each of the three categories. We now have a picture of the projected range of inflow and outflow resulting from the total monthly cash flow activity of the company *(see Exhibit IV)*.

The application of this new approach should present no difficulties insofar as the individual items in the several schedules are concerned.

The central problem is the determination of the lower and upper limits of projected sales. Once these are established, the necessary calculations for each of the items under the two assumptions—lower limit and upper limit—can proceed exactly as it customarily does if one single assumption is made about projected sales.

Exhibit III. Long-Term Fixed Assets Expansion Forecast

Estimated Cash Inflow:	January		February		March	
Sale of Securities	—	—	—	—	250	250
Sale of fixed assets*-11	100	100				
Estimated inflow:	100	100			250	250
Estimated Outflow:						
Payment Schedule on New Plant, Machinery*-12	—	—	100	100	150	150
Payment Schedule on major Leasehold improvements	75	75	—	—	—	—
Estimated Outflow	75	75	100	100	150	150
Inflow (Outflow)	25	25	(100)	(100)	100	100
Cumulative			(75)	(75)	25	25

Exhibit IV. Total Monthly Cash Flow Activity

	January		February		March	
I. Operational	(122)	(88)	(115.5)	88	(122.5)	38.5
II. Asset Roll Over	(35)	(35)	(95)	(95)	25	25
III. Long-Term Capital	25	25	(75)	(75)	25	25
Total Inflow (Outflow)	(133)	(98)	(285.5)	(82)	(72.5)	88.5

Chapter 12

SEGMENTAL FINANCING

Thomas E. Myers, Jr.

I should start by trying to define "segmental financing," because I suspect that you may not be familiar with the term. By my definition it is financing a corporation's operations, or part of a corporation's operations, by the sale of a minority interest in a division, or the sale of 100% of a division of a corporation. By division, I mean any operation which can be segregated from the rest of the company and make sense as an independent business entity.

The topic here emphasizes "financing," but we are dealing in an area where one cannot separate the raising of the money

Mr. Myers is a Principal of Harlan, Betke & Myers, Inc., specialists in negotiating investments that include programs to effect the purchase and sale of companies.

from some broad aspects of corporate strategy. Thus I shall be referring to factors that do not directly relate to financing, but are nevertheless quite important.

At the outset, we should distinguish between the two categories of activity that I have just described: (1) the sale of a corporate division in total, and (2) the sale of a minority interest in a corporate division. Generally, when the latter is done, less than 20% is sold so that the parent corporation can still consolidate the results of the subsidiary. The two actions have, I think, different objectives. They require a different type of analysis and the implementation is quite different.

Some General Considerations

One interesting influence on the subject of segmental financing is what the SEC is doing in requiring that corporations report results of various separable operations—and not just total corporate sales and earnings, as has been done historically. The SEC is in fact removing one of the big reasons why many corporations have not taken advantage of segmental financing. In the past, it has been very easy for large corporations to have an operation which was not profitable or which was not up to industry standards but to keep it hidden, because only total corporate results were reported. However, the SEC is now moving to stop that practice. No longer can the promise of a degree of secrecy keep a corporation from taking advantage of segmental financing.

Moreover, when a corporation reports its divisions separately—that is, when it tells what its divisional sales and earnings are—top management is exposed to questions from bankers, security analysts, and other interested parties, such as: "Why aren't you doing better?" "Why don't you take advantage of a potentially high price/earnings multiple on another division?"

There remains one big stumbling block that we have to recognize. U.S. business has one central and pervasive theme, and that is to grow. Not all companies subscribe to this theme as all important, but most do. And one of the problems when you sell an operation—whether it is any good or not—is that you are growing in reverse; nevertheless, there are many cases where the need to grow in reverse should be accepted.

Sale of a Minority Interest in a Division

Let us get down to the fundamental question: Why would a company management think of segmental financing? First, the objective is to raise money; therefore, management should have somewhere else to put the money to work. This is a fairly obvious point, but one which is easy to overlook. Second, the more normal sources of financing are likely to be tight. For example, in the depressed economy of recent months, it has been pretty difficult to float a stock offering or to secure debt financing.

A third reason why a management might be interested in segmental financing would be a situation in which the company has a stream of business earnings hidden away in a corporate division and which the stock market or another buyer would evaluate more highly than the company management does. I think one of the classic examples of this was the case of LTV Aerospace, a subsidiary of LTV. It had a book value of $6 million. LTV sold a minority interest in it, and immediately the market value of LTV's remaining ownership in LTV Aerospace was about $60 million. That valuation later went as high as $150 million.

Still another reason for segmental financing would be if the company had an asset, not necessarily an earning asset, that other people might evaluate more highly than the company management does. I think here of a major forest products company, Weyerhaeuser, which has owned thousands and thousands of acres of land since the 1800's. Much of this land is carried on its books at $2 or $3 an acre or less. Up until the recent past, bankers, and certainly the stock market, tended to value that asset at its carrying cost. Weyerhaeuser might well have decided to package some of that land and sell it—not as potential timber sources, but as development property, for example, in order to reflect its true value more adequately.

Financial Leverage

We have examined the sale of a minority interest in a corporate division. Why does one do it? First, to raise money. It is a way to bring dollars directly into the till, and yet maintain control of an operation. Let us say that you sell 20%. You still control the division, you can still consolidate it; but you have in cash whatever you receive of the 20% interest sold. Also you may have a market evaluation of assets, as I described in the LTV case before, that can permit an increase in borrowings. The reason why this may be possible is that traditionally bankers and insurance companies—that is, fixed interest investors—have looked more at assets than earning power in evaluating the credit worthiness of a company.

Let us go back to LTV Aerospace. LTV had a subsidiary carried at $6 million on its books. Even a daringly aggressive banker probably would not loan more than twice the value of those net assets or roughly $12 million in this example. At that he would be taking a risk by conventional banking standards. However, when LTV sells a minority equity interest in the operation, it has stock with a market value of $150 million (although it cannot be readily sold). In view of this, the banker might well be justified in lending more than $12 million. The reality of the situation has not really changed, but there is a different way of looking at that situation.

Then the other opportunity which might exist here is the opportunity for what I call a holding company type of leverage. *Exhibit I* gives an example of what I am thinking about. It is oversimplified but illustrates the point. The example is a company with two divisions equal in every respect except earnings. The company, for borrowing purposes, has an equity value of $100 million. We work down to the income statement and see that Division A is earning $8.75 million. If 20% of that division

Exhibit I. Examples of Possible Leverage Through Segmental Financing

Assume XY Company is made up as follows:
  (a) Net assets equal to $100 million represented by two divisions, each with $50 million net assets.
  (b) Total earnings before interest and taxes of $25 million. Division A earns $20 million; Division B earns $5 million.
  (c) Borrowings of $50 million at 10%.

XY Co. Income Statement
(millions)

	Div. A	Div. B	Total
Earnings before interest & taxes	$ 20.00	$ 5.00	$ 25.00
Interest	2.50	2.50	5.00
Earnings before taxes	17.50	2.50	20.00
Taxes	8.75	1.25	10.00
Earnings after taxes	$ 8.75	$ 1.25	$ 10.00

XY Co. Balance Sheet
(millions)

Total Assets	$100.00	$100.00	$200.00
Current liabilities	$ 25.00	$ 25.00	$ 50.00
Long-term debt	25.00	25.00	50.00
Equity	50.00	50.00	100.00
Liabilities and equity	$100.00	$100.00	$200.00

  (d) XY Co. sells publicly 20% of Division A for 20× earnings, or $35 million ($28 million after capital gains tax).

XY Co. Balance Sheet (nonconsolidated)
(millions)

	Securities Valued at Book Value	Securities Valued at Market Value
Other assets	$128.00	$128.00
Securities	40.00	140.00
Total assets	$168.00	$268.00
Current liabilities	$ 25.00	$ 25.00
Long-term debt	25.00*	25.00*
Equity	118.00	218.00
Liabilities and equity	$168.00	$268.00

* - Plus guarantee for $25 million in debt of Division A.

were to be sold at 20 times earnings, the company would have brought $35 million into its corporate bank account, and have $28 million remaining after capital gains taxes. The result is that it would have brought in cash equivalent to more than half of the original carrying value of this division, while only giving away a 20% ownership interest.

The new balance sheet might show the securities valued at market value, and suddenly we would see that the company had an equity value at market of $218 million—a very substantial change from the $100 million of before. The reality would be the same, but people might look at it differently. I am not accusing bankers of being stupid; remember that this is an oversimplified example. However, many bankers and insurance company loan officers are traditionally accustomed to lending some proportion of net asset value, because of their desire for protection in case a loan should go bad.

Whereas originally this hypothetical lender might have loaned this company $50 million, now if he looks at the market value of those securities, he might be able to justify lending more than twice that amount. That is specifically what has happened in some of the cases with LTV and other companies that have taken advantage of this segmental method of financing.

One might also have a lender who is more interested in the more valid measure of debt carrying capacity, interest coverage. This is what I mean by holding company type leverage, because the subsidiary borrows and pays its interest, and the parent company consolidates the earnings of the subsidiary. The parent company can then, in theory, justify a higher level of borrowing. The reality is the same, but it looks different.

This method of financing has value. Many companies do have more borrowing capacity than traditional methods suggest. I would not recommend it for every company in every situation. The depressed marketplace in recent months has raised some questions about its validity.

Sale of a Total Division

The other type of activity we are considering in this chapter is the sale of all of a division or an operation which can stand on its own. Our operating assumption is again that the seller has a need for money. Perhaps the bank is asking for 2 points over prime, plus a 20% compensating balance, and an effective 13% interest rate is not appealing. The underwriter is unwilling or unable to float a public stock offering. The company needs money.

Divestiture Implications

As in the case of most major financial steps, the sale of a corporate division should not be undertaken without a thorough consideration of what other implications it has. One cannot just look at a division as an asset which can be bought or sold, because one has to consider whether, in fact, the remaining operations are interconnected with the one being sold and whether its disposal will cause problems in other areas.

Another reason why one might decide to sell a division is because of a change in corporate strategy. At one time, for example, W.R. Grace was solely a shipping company. As the years passed, the corporate focus moved almost totally away from shipping. Thus it really made very little business sense for the corporation to remain in shipping. There was only a loose fit between the Grace lines, the chemical operations, and the other parts of the company. Accordingly, it made a great deal of sense to sell Grace Lines. In the case also of Grace National Bank, there was no direct business fit and the money realized from the sale could be used elsewhere.

One might also have a situation where (1) there is a major need for capital in the corporation, (2) there are parts of the business which do not tie in with the major thrust, and (3) the corporation wants to focus its assets in one area. For example, a growth company—that is, a company with a commitment toward rapid earnings growth—might have an operation that is very profitable, well run, and very successful, but which has reached a degree of earnings maturity where the earnings growth has moved more in line with the growth of the economy. It might make sense to sell that division, because its slower rate of earnings growth could slow down the total earnings growth of the corporation and exert a negative influence on its price/earnings ratio.

Or one might have a situation of the opposite extreme— that is, a conservatively managed company that comes across a product with rapid growth characteristics, but with high risk and heavy capital investment requirements that the company either cannot or will not undertake. Here again, it might make sense to package this and sell it outside to someone else who can exploit it, and to whom it will be more valuable.

Finally, the obvious divestment situation that comes up frequently is an FTC decision or other external pressure to get rid of an operation. Here, one does not have a great deal of choice other than a little time, because somebody else makes the decision.

All of these situations might lead a corporation to sell a total division. I reemphasize that it is an important decision. One of the themes of our business—we call it "negotiated investments"—is that this is an investment decision which is only made and implemented once. Once a corporation sells a division, it can bring it back only in very rare cases.

We have reviewed reasons why we might consider selling a corporate division and what some of the implications are. In a divestment program, as in most other business activities, planning is really vital. One must think through the implications. What does the sale mean to the remainder of the business, and what can one get out of the sale? Implementation takes time. There is no established marketplace for selling corporate divisions. Nor is there an immediate marketplace for a minority interest in a division. Public sale requires the registration of securities and a considerable time lag.

This means that one cannot rely on segmental financing to meet short-term needs for funds. Moreover, if one tries to push through a sale too rapidly, it takes on elements of a fire sale. Anything that is sold in desperation is unlikely to get a top price. Another problem with timing is that the market can go against the seller. For example, if a company was relying heavily on selling part of, say, an aerospace division in mid-1969, one might not have been able to get even an underwriting, let alone at a favorable price.

Implementing the Public Sale of a Minority Interest

How should one go about the sale of a minority interest? First, company management has to package what it has. Look at it from the point of view that what one probably should sell is the thing that is going to have the most value to the public. The public is fickle and inconsistent in its assessment of earnings growth; thus current market psychology might influence one's decision of what to sell. If possible, one would want to sell a combination of operations that showed a good historical growth pattern.

Because the seller wants the best price he can get, he will want to include operations which have some degree of current market appeal. In one year that might be an operation in the computer software business, and in another year it might be an operation related to real estate. One should look for areas that meet these criteria, and which also are not too interdependent with the rest of the business.

Once management makes up its mind to sell and what operations it is going to tie together in a package, the actual implementation—while not easy—is fairly straightforward. Management really has three alternatives: (1) it can distribute this ownership directly to its stockholders; (2) it can sell the shares representing the minority interest of this division to present stockholders—an interesting concept, selling somebody something that he already owns; or (3) it can have a public underwriting in which an investment banker sells the securities to his clients.

The choice depends in part on whether management wants its stockholders to have the opportunity to acquire what was being distributed, and how much cash it wants to raise from the actual sale. Once management decides what it wants to do and how to do it, the implementation can be handled by the underwriting community.

Implementing the Sale of All of a Division

It is a somewhat different matter to sell a total division. This is especially difficult, and we feel that practically everybody needs outside help in doing it. Generally, selling a corporate division tends to be reactive. The company management reacts to an offer to buy or to a need for financing, or to poor results in a given year by saying, "We're fed up with the business; we want out."

I am reminded of a fairly large chemical company that needed financing at a time when the market was tough for debenture issues. The money was needed quickly because of debt refunding problems, so management decided to give itself 45 days to sell a division. The division was not very profitable and not very saleable; altogether, it was an unexciting business. They prepared a short writeup on the operation and distributed it to a few venture capital firms to see if the money could be raised rapidly. The result was that it was impossible to sell such an operation in that short amount of time. All they got out of it was a myriad of problems. Some of their key people left in the interim. Moreover, they wound up with some slightly shopworn merchandise, which a lot of people knew the parent company had tried unsuccessfully to sell.

The Reactive Transaction

When there is a bidder for a division, typically, the selling process is in reaction to an offer. One may go a step further, and call in commercial bankers, attorneys, or even an investment banker. But this is not defining what one wants to achieve, and working to achieve it. Frequently (and this appalls me), a company that decides to divest itself of an operation will turn it over to the manager of the division to find a good home. There is an obvious problem of misguided incentives in this situation, because that management is not likely to have as its prime objective to get the best price and the best terms for the owners. Its objective is most likely to be to find the best home for itself.

The problem in all of these cases is that the potential buyer has the initiative. He sets the initial price, he sets the initial offering terms, and he knows what the operation is worth to him. Conversely, the seller does not; he is just reacting to an offer. In fact, the offer may be totally unrelated to the real value of the operation.

As an example, consider a privately held company we were working with that needed to be sold. The owners started thinking about selling out because of an offer from a large publicly held company. The original offer was 60,000 shares of this company, which, at the time, seemed interesting. After a positive program was developed to sell the company, the original interested public company offered a price of 140,000 shares—two and a third times the original offer, and that offer was not good enough.

Had the owners restricted their activities to reacting to one offer—the first one in this case—they might have ended up with 75,000 shares and would have sold out much too cheaply.

'Positive Selling Program'

The alternative to the reactive sale, and the one that we think makes the most sense, is what we call a "positive selling program."

Think about your own business. You have a product—whether it is physical or whether it is a service. You do not sell your product by sitting back, waiting for people to come through the door, and asking you if they can buy it. You develop a marketing program to get the message across to prospective buyers about what you have, what it is worth, and why they should buy it.

This is the kind of program that we advocate for selling a corporate division. It *is* a product that has value to somebody. Most companies need outside help. They need outside help because they are not in a particularly good position to document to a prospective buyer what their operation is worth; they are too close to it. Typically, they fail to do a good job of screening the range of possible buyers and focusing in on the ones that are real prospects.

In the case of a smaller company that has no active acquisition program, one usually finds a situation where the person to whom he is selling may have a lot more clout at the bargaining table. I can think of a number of managers whom I know well, even from large companies, that would be "eaten alive" sitting across the table from shrewd bargainers. Thus there is frequently the need to bring more ammunition on the smaller company's side.

In the event that outside help is utilized, it makes no sense at all to use the typical compensation structure in the "deals business." That structure, as you perhaps know, is a declining percentage of the value of the operation sold, payable contingent on the sale. If an outside party working with the seller gets 5%, for example, of the first one million dollars and 1% of the tenth million he does not have much incentive to bargain for the best price. He is more interested in doing a deal, and not necessarily doing it at the best price.

Evaluating the Operation. What does a positive selling program entail? First, it entails maximizing the value of what is being offered for sale. This can include tying together operations that make sense, fit together well, and are attractive to a prospective buyer. It can mean paring off redundant assets from a division, because if there are assets which are not used in the division, the chances of getting the maximum price for them in a sale are minimal. It requires a documentation of the earnings capabilities in the operation—not just "these are our plans," but "these are our plans and this is why they are a reasonable expectation." This is not an easy operation. It is one that requires a lot of imagination and work.

The question that will frequently be asked by a potential buyer is: "If this business is going to triple its earnings in the next three years, why are you selling it?" It is frequently hard for a seller to respond convincingly to this question. Here again, an action approach, which addresses the question before it is raised, is convincing.

Moreover, the value should be documented in terms of how this operation fits in with that of the particular acquirer. Why is it worth more to him? What kinds of opportunities exist for profit improvement, or for leverage? Are there opportunities for product line expansion through the investment of a little more capital or through further acquisitions by the acquirer?

Altogether, the seller should identify the value of what is being sold in the buyer's terms—that is, the maximum value as the buyer will see it. The seller will get a much better price if he can paint an objective picture, one that does not brush over all the negative aspects of the operation.

The seller should sit down, probably with outside help, and decide exactly what his own objectives are. What does he want in terms of price? Is he willing to give terms? Does his payment have to be all cash today? Could there be some deferred payment? What sense of responsibility does he feel toward the employees of the operation that he is selling? Should the managers of that division have long-term employment contracts with the new parent? Is he interested, primarily, in face saving? Does he want to be able to say, "I got 15% more than book value for that division," without mentioning that his price was paid with 20-year notes with a 1% interest rate.

These objectives should be spelled out beforehand, because one of the worst things that can possibly happen is to get down to the end of the line—in any sort of business transaction—and have second thoughts about some important item.

Indentifying the Right Buyer. I mention this because we are dealing in a very sensitive area. Management is selling a division where there are people. The operation has some value as cold assets, but mainly its value is as an ongoing business. If one starts shopping the operation around, there can be tremendous internal morale problems. For one thing, when the competition hears that the particular division is for sale, they will be on the phone calling up the good people in the operation. Thus the more that management can do in secrecy, the better off it is.

If management can approach the right buyer—one who can meet the terms and who needs this operation—and close a deal with him, the whole process may be done in virtual secrecy. The right buyer is one who has some reason, like a good business fit, or a probable favorable impact on his price/earnings multiple or brand name, to place a higher value on this operation than anybody else. Whatever his reasons are, they are all factors that can and should be identified beforehand. It *is* possible to focus on the right buyer; if one does his homework and knows what his operation is worth, there is really no need to shop it around and establish an auction for it.

Tailoring the Package. Once the seller has figured out what his operation is worth and identified a sequential list of preferred buyers, we feel that it is important to tailor a selling document to the needs of the particular buyer. This document serves a number of purposes, but mainly it presells the buyer and does his homework. Its use helps him to make a positive decision, and it emphasizes the things that are most important to his particular situation.

It is equally important to spell out the terms that the buyer will have to meet, and to have those terms such that the buyer can, in fact, meet them. The seller is not operating in a vacuum. Rather, he is saying, "I know that you can do this in this way, and that is the way you will have to do it to make the purchase."

Then the final factor, and I have referred to this earlier, is to approach potential buyers sequentially, because it reduces morale problems and also avoids overshopped merchandise which has less value.

To summarize, probably the most important part of the whole procedure, whether one is selling all or part of a division, is to plan and allow enough time to think through the alternatives and to develop a rational approach to the problem. Generally, professional help of an underwriter or other outside party is necessary to do a good job, and to take an action posture.

Case #1: Lender will lend 50% of Net Asset Value.

	Borrowing Capacity (millions)
Before sale of 20% of Div. A	$ 50.00
After sale of 20% of Div. A if securities valued at book	$ 59.00
After sale of 20% of Div. A if securities valued at market	$109.00

Case #2: Lender will lend up to a point where earnings before interest and taxes are 5× interest. Interest is at 10%.

	EBIT	Maximum Interest (millions)	Debt Capacity
Before sale of 20% of Div. A	$25.00	$5.00	$50.00
After sale of 20% of Div. A Division A	20.00	4.00	40.00
XY after consolidation of 80% of Div. A	17.80	3.56	35.60
Total Debt Capacity			$75.60

Chapter 13

SECURED FINANCING

Herbert E. Ruben

In the broad redundant sense, secured financing is the lending of money against security. More specifically, it refers to the lending services typically provided by commercial finance companies: short- and medium-term lending against accounts receivable and inventories, loans against machinery, equipment and other chattels, and real estate construction and second mortgage financing.

While everyone knows what commercial and investment bankers do, many businessmen are not familiar with the services provided by commercial finance companies.

Mr. Ruben is Vice President of Walter E. Heller & Company. He is a senior credit officer of this leading commercial finance company and has designed many imaginative commercial loans.

Commercial Finance Services and Techniques

Ten years ago, you might have been told that a commercial finance company is where you went to borrow money out of desperation in order to buy time; where some very tough, hard people would charge you an exorbitantly high rate of interest, take a lien on all your assets, dry up your lines of credit, and finally drive you into the bankruptcy courts.

Today, I would hope that you might be told that a commercial finance company is where you go when you cannot meet your requirements from internal growth or bank borrowings, and the time is not right to give up equity; it is where you go with an under-capitalized seasonal business, or if you have an opportunity for a favorable acquisition, or to buy out a partner, or to get medium-term financing for a new venture or rapid expansion, or to tide you over during a temporary reversal. And you would understand that our interest rate on a daily money-in-use basis, about 6% over prime, is fair, not so much more than you would pay your bank after compensating balances and drawing down unneeded funds, and certainly much cheaper over the long run than giving up equity.

Ten years ago, our clients were usually small private businesses, often referred to us by commercial banks. Today, they are typically medium-sized public companies, often brought in by investment bankers.

I would like to discuss briefly the services and techniques provided by commercial finance companies.

Old Line Factoring

This service is the buying of accounts receivable with assumption of the credit risk by the factor. This encompasses three categories of services:

> I. A loan service in that the factor at his client's request advances the face amount of assigned invoices on the day of assignment and prior to the maturity date of the invoice.

2. A credit insurance service in that the factor sets the credit lines for his client's customers and assumes the credit risk of non-payment of the account because of the buyer's financial inability to pay. Many factoring clients utilize only this service in what is called "maturity" factoring since the client is not paid for the invoices sold until their maturity date on shortest selling terms plus a collection period.

3. A bookkeeping and collection service in that the factor takes over the ledgering, billing and collecting functions. In recent years small and medium sized manufacturers selling directly to retailers in relatively small dollar amounts per invoice have been inundated by the paper work. Moreover, for the most part they lack both the overall sales volume and expertise to computerize these operations. Since the factors who are computerized can perform these functions much more efficiently and economically, retail factoring is assuming greater and greater importance.

For the foregoing services, the factor charges a commission of from ¾% to 2% of the net invoice amounts factored, the commission determined by the number of invoices that have to be processed, the average amount of the invoice, the total volume of business projected, and the projected loss experience and credit risk assumed. The factor also charges interest on money drawn down in advance of the average maturity date of the invoices purchased, currently about 3½% over the prime rate.

Accounts Receivable Financing

This is the lending of money against the security of a floating lien under the Uniform Commercial Code against the client's accounts receivables and inventories. Unlike factoring, the lender does not assume the credit risk and the accounts are not placed on direct collection. In fact, other than the Code filings, the account debtors are not aware that their accounts have been assigned.

Typically, accounts receivable financing involves setting a rate of advance after allowing for disputed items, past due accounts, contras, and the like, of about 80% of the face amount of the accounts receivable pledged. The client's availability is adjusted each month based on the last available monthly aging of accounts. During the month, daily schedules of new accounts are sent in to the lender, along with collections on previously assigned accounts, and a running balance on the outstanding loan and availability is kept until the next monthly aging.

Our clients can draw funds on a daily basis, as required. Typically, we enter into a one-year contract, thereafter renewable from year to year or terminable on 90 days notice by either party.

A Case Illustration. Let me give you an example of an accounts receivable financing we recently booked:

Company A is a large, listed manufacturing conglomerate with annual sales of $100 million. It caught the acquisition virus and during a three-year period it acquired over 20 unrelated companies which it could not assimilate and many of which were losers. The company sustained a large loss in its last fiscal year, much of it nonrecurring, and its banks asked to be paid out.

On investigation, we satisfied ourselves that the company had hit bottom and was on its way back. Management had closed down and was selling off the unprofitable divisions, cutting costs, and revitalizing the profitable divisions. The company had receivables on a conservative basis to support the $9 million line it requested from us.

We obtained two banks as participants, which cut our concentration and brought down the client's money cost. The loan agreement contains typical bank loan restrictions and working capital requirements. The mechanics of closing and handling were complex because, for legal reasons, we made individual loans to each of the twenty-plus operating subsidiaries and parent, all of which loans were fully cross-collateralized.

This meant Code filings all over the United States, and in order to save clearance, the opening of Heller bank accounts in all of the locations where these subsidiaries are located, for the deposit of collections on the assigned receivables.

The biggest problem here was the liberal return policy traditionally permitted in the parent company's industry, which means that in the event of serious trouble we could expect to get back a lot of relatively worthless inventory instead of dollars. We resolved this problem by agreeing to only a 70% rate of advance against receivables, plus a special reserve for unallocated credits and returns, plus a special contingency reserve. We expect this company to be bankable in a year or two if it meets its projections.

Inventory Financing

Inventory loans are rarely made alone; instead, they are made in conjunction with accounts receivable financing or factoring. Typically, these loans are made to accommodate a seasonal buildup or in connection with opening letters of credit to finance the importation of merchandise.

Currently, for example, we extend inventory loan accommodations to a swimming pool manufacturer, a greeting card manufacturer, a food importer, and a shoe importer. The first two have a long buildup period and a short selling season. The second two require letter-of-credit accommodation, which means financing for the period it takes for the goods to be shipped from overseas, cleared through customs, repackaged, and reshipped. In the case of the shoe manufacturer, he is also required to carry a large inventory of varying types and sizes to accommodate his customers.

On occasion, we will utilize warehouse receipts as a security device, usually a field warehouse. But, for the most part, we will rely on a Code filing and periodic reporting by our borrower.

Term Loans Against Fixed Assets

These take a variety of forms with respect to terms and collateral. Maturities can run from six months to seven years. The loans may be standing, or repayable in level payments, or carry a small monthly amortization with a balloon at the end. The collateral is as varied as machine tools, airplanes, real estate, computer equipment, and dining cars. Consider:

Company B was a supplemental airline which wanted financing to purchase a Boeing 707 jet liner. We were unwilling to provide this financing without a stronger credit standing between us and disaster; accordingly, we brought in a creditworthy plane dealer and operator in whom we have confidence and who was to be compensated with the residual plane values for assuming the risk.

The loan was structured in this manner: we lent the plane dealer $3.5 million, and he bought the plane for $4 million. The difference in the price was made up by the supplemental airline in the form of an advance deposit and advance rental payments. The plane was then leased to the airline and the lease and lease payments assigned to us as collateral additional to our chattel mortgage on the plane.

Unfortunately, the airline went bankrupt and the plane dealer has repossessed the plane. The plane dealer is meeting his payments on our note and expects to eventually realize enough money out of the rental or sale of the airplane to meet his obligations to us and still make a profit.

Industrial Time Sales Financing

This is the business of providing finance plans for manufacturers or dealers who sell income producing equipment or consumer products which are usually paid for in installments over a period of time. This paper is bought with or without full or limited recourse, depending on the quality of the paper.

This used to be very big business indeed until the banks took most of it over and historically we have run the gamut of financing automobiles, construction equipment, juke boxes, coin operated laundries, and bowling pin spotters. We still do some of this business but nothing like in past years.

We engage in refinancing small loan company paper but today, with the small loan companies caught in a squeeze between the fixed rates they are permitted to charge their customers under state small loan statutes and the greatly increased cost of money, we are not adding to our existing portfolio.

We also engage in real estate construction loan financing and second mortgage real estate financing on a selective basis.

Changes in the Industry

We have now reviewed the categories of finance business that the commercial finance companies have historically engaged in and continue to engage in. In the last few years, however, there have been three developments which have significantly affected the nature of our business:

1. *The banks have gone extensively into secured lending.*

There have been many reasons for this, including having excess funds in the early 1960's which the banks were anxious to employ in new ways; favorable changes in the law, primarily the adoption of the Uniform Commercial Code which simplified the problems of obtaining and administering a floating lien on accounts receivable and inventories; younger and more aggressive management assuming control of many major banks; and finally a tight money market in which the banks have sought to employ their funds in higher yielding business.

The banks not only started taking collateral to secure their weaker loans but also set up separate divisions to do secured financing and, in several instances, acquired existing factoring companies. As a result of this competition, commercial finance companies have been required to become somewhat more resourceful and innovative in keeping their funds employed.

2. *The rise (and fall) of the conglomerate movement.*

While it seems a long time ago, we all remember vividly the booming conglomerate movement and the fantastic growth of many new industrial and commercial giants, some of which have fallen on very hard times.

There were many reasons for this boom: the ready availability of investment funds, a rising stock market and an insatiable demand for new issues, the apparent loopholes in the antitrust laws which appeared to favor conglomeration, the use of convertible debentures in acquisitions, and favorable accounting treatment resulting in hyped-up price/earnings ratios.

Leverage became the magic word and this resulted in new opportunities for financing acquisitions. During this period, there was considerable demand for "bridge" or interim financing and the larger commercial finance companies were often in a position to move quickly and be of service in these situations. Let me cite one example:

An investment banker came to see us with this problem. He had a client who had negotiated the cash purchase of a business for $30 million, and the purchase was to be financed with $20 million in the form of a two-year unsecured senior revolving credit from a group of banks, and $10 million in subordinated short-term bank debt which was to be repaid within six months by a public underwriting.

The subordinated lenders were to be secured by something called a "hell or high water put." What the borrower had arranged was to issue six-month subordinated convertible notes for the $10 million, which would have a conversion price for common stock at a very low price most unfavorable to the company's existing stockholders. The borrower then went to some investment groups and in exchange for some warrants bought a "put" for these subordinated convertible notes. If that put were ever exercised, it would represent a substantial dilution of equity.

Some 24 hours before the closing, $5 million of subordinated debt became unavailable, and the underwriter and buyer came to see us that afternoon. They told us that there was another bidder for the company they had contracted to buy, and they did not want to ask for an extension.

We worked all night and put up the necessary $5 million the next day. We took the loan essentially as it had been structured with two modifications: (1) we went in on a parity with the senior bank debt, and (2) we required that the stock of the acquired company stand as collateral for the entire $30 million borrowing which was financing the purchase.

We were paid out six weeks later with bank borrowings.

3. *Tight and expensive money.*

In the 1968–70 period, the prime rate went up; bank funds were unavailable for acquisitions, capital improvements, and new customers; the stock market declined drastically and many underwritings aborted; and the acquisition boom ground to a screeching halt.

It happens that the large commercial finance companies were in funds, and at a time when the banks by and large were not. Accordingly, we have been upgrading our portfolios and markedly increasing our outstanding loans. Since long-range economic forecasts indicate that capital will be in short supply for the foreseeable future, it would appear that the skills of the commercial finance industry in allocating capital intelligently will be much in demand and the future of the industry is bright.

Obtaining a Secured Loan

It is probably self-evident that a prospective borrower approaches a commercial finance company in essentially the same way as he would approach a commercial bank or an investment banker. He can, of course, find us in the yellow pages or answer one of our ads, but it is only fair to say that an introduction helps —from your banker, investment banker, lawyer, accountant, or some brokers. Such an introduction is a prescreening factor, and we are interested in accommodating these people who are in a position to refer business to us.

If we indicate initial interest, these considerations are of importance:

- We want to see reliable historic financial statements, with the underlying schedules and detail, audited statements, a respected auditing firm on the account, and, hopefully, an unqualified certification.
- We expect full disclosure and we will check the borrower's trade report, bank references, and available registration statements and proxy material filed with the SEC.
- We want to see budgets and projections, and to be convinced that they are sensible and achievable.
- We want to be satisfied that the collateral to be assigned is adequate in realistic terms. However, we are very profit and loss conscious, and most concerned as to how our loan is going to be repaid. We are not interested in presiding over liquidations, no matter how well collateralized we may be.
- It is perhaps trite but true that we want to be con-

vinced of the intelligence and capability of the borrower's management.

• Finally, we want to be paid our going rate of interest and to get a reasonable term for the employment of our funds.

We are not seeking equity participation from our borrowers. We do not knowingly assume legal risks as opposed to credit risks. Accordingly, we will not (a) finance a buyout where nonconsenting minority shareholders are involved, (b) finance an insolvent company, and (c) knowingly make funds available for an improper purpose. While we will support our clients to the extent possible, by and large, we do not make unsecured loans nor throw good money after bad in trying to stave off a loss.

Concluding Note

Anyone seeking funds for any legitimate business purpose should not overlook the financing provided by commercial finance companies, particularly in a tight money market. Many of us are large, well capitalized, and receptive and willing to consider new approaches, new situations, and new lending techniques.

Chapter 14

SELLING
COMMERCIAL
PAPER

Philipp H. Lohman

The volume of commercial paper is for the most part made up of short-term unsecured promissory notes, sold by corporations either to a dealer or directly to an institutional investor. The paper is placed with only about 20 of the largest sales finance companies.

The tour of these instruments varies from a few days up to nine months, but no longer, because under the Securities Act of 1933 the proceeds are required to be "for current transactions." Any prospective issuer who questions whether his issue is ex-

Dr. Lohman is an adjunct full professor at the Graduate School of Business Administration at Pace College. He has been interested in commercial paper for over 30 years and has written numerous articles and books on finance.

empt from the registration requirement because he is unsure what "current transactions" means need only write an explanatory letter to the SEC in Washington. Assuming all is in order, the Commission will simply issue a so-called "no action" letter indicating that no legal problem is encountered with the note issue.

Treasury bills are to government what commercial paper is to private corporations. Both instruments are sold at a discount, and the two mature at par. In contrast to the large secondary market for treasury bills, there is no comparable market for commercial paper. However, recently changes have been introduced.

For example, a large dealer will make secondary markets in the paper the firm sells. Of course, as the volume of dealer-placed paper has multiplied, the resulting increase in liquidity or marketability has increased its attraction to investors. Therefore, if you have not thought of it before, by investing your temporarily idle funds in commercial paper, you can ride the yield curve by selling paper before maturity at a lower interest rate and thus at a higher price. Then, if you have funds left, you can reinvest the proceeds in longer maturities at higher yields.

The use of such sophisticated techniques in riding the yield curve gives, in turn, a greater marketability for commercial paper, and your secondary market therefore becomes more active. This, of course, is also helpful in developing either the acceptance of your own paper or of the commercial paper market in general. A corporation such as a sales finance company, which places its paper directly with investors, may be willing to redeem that paper when asked to do so before maturity. But, why should you buy finance company paper if you can do better through dealer-placed paper?

Issuing Your Own Paper

Let us say that your company wants to issue commercial paper. How does it go about doing so? The answer is quite simple; your board of directors simply authorizes the issuance of unsecured short-term promissory notes by means of a corporate resolution. This resolution should give specific company officers—the financial vice president, treasurer, comptroller, and others—authorization to sign and issue the notes. Then, their names and specimen signatures should be filed with the commercial paper dealer through whom you intend to offer the notes. The notes should show the amount, issue and due dates, and where payable.

Any corporation dealing with, say, a New York City securities house (and there are now seven national dealers in the commercial paper market, as well as seven or eight smaller ones who are regional dealers) should appoint a New York City bank as the paying and issuing agent. As is customary with bonds, the issuing bank countersigns the notes. The agent bank, then, should be supplied with numbered notes, signed by the duly authorized company fiscal officers. Subsequently, the issuing bank, upon your instructions, can at any time fill in the due dates and amounts, the payee and the bank where the notes are payable. Your agency bank should also be authorized to pay the notes when presented on maturity. And as you probably know, all transactions in commercial paper are made through drafts drawn on any Federal Reserve Bank.

Commercial paper can be viewed in two ways: (1) as a liquid asset for the investment of temporarily idle funds at a yield higher than that available through other investments such as treasury bills, or (2) as a source of funds, as we noted earlier.

Topping the Money Market

As an indication of the tremendous figures involved, consider that the Federal Reserve Bank of New York reported the volume of commercial paper outstanding at year's end 1969 had reached almost $34 billion, which is an impressive increase from the $6.7 billion outstanding as recently as six or seven years ago. Of the $34 billion total, nearly $13 billion had been placed through dealers, and $21 billion through finance and bank holding companies with corporate investors. On the principal issuance of dealer paper on nonfinancial corporations, about 100 of the smaller sales finance companies also used the dealer market.

That more and more corporations are placing their paper through dealers can be seen by the figures from 1965 to 1969 in which the amount of paper sold through dealers rose from $1.9 billion to over $11 billion. In comparison, the commercial paper sold directly by large finance companies went from $7.2 billion to $20 billion.

A dealer's commission of ⅛ of 1% per annum is charged on prime paper. In case you are curious as to why there is such a low yield on the finance company paper, there is a very simple illustration. Investors—for example, the trust department of a large bank—buy a master note in commercial paper in maturities that they want. It is a one-day note, indefinitely renewable, which is then allocated to accounts.

The investors of directly placed papers are willing to accept the lower yield to gain a source of steady supply and usually tailor-made maturities. Surprisingly, the way the dealer paper market is developing, if you want a specific maturity, you can have your cake and eat it, too. You can work with a dealer; he can give you the maturity you want, and you can still get the higher yields—particularly now that utilities are in the commercial paper market.

No company will sell commercial paper for direct placement without first obtaining a rating from Dun & Bradstreet's national credit office and/or from Standard and Poor's. The rating determines the cost and possibility of raising money. Of course, as larger companies, particularly the utilities, enter the commercial paper market, getting a rating on the paper receives less emphasis as time goes by. But as far as your own company is concerned—unless yours is a large one—the rating is likely to be essential.

Types of Paper

About 70% of the paper currently outstanding is rated *prime*, most of the rest of it is rated *desirable*, and there is also a category rated *satisfactory*. Comparable with bond ratings, your own commercial paper rating is determined by your net worth, performance, financial position, previous record, prospects for growth and future earnings, and quality of management.

To receive a *prime* rating, a corporation must have a net worth in excess of $25 million, assuming that all the other standards just referred to have been met satisfactorily. Usually, it must maintain a bank line of credit equal to its commercial paper notes outstanding.

A company with a net worth of at least $5 million, which meets all the other standards, is eligible for the rating of *desirable*. This kind of commercial paper is almost exclusively traded regionally.

A company with a net worth of at least $1.2 million and on up to $5 million, which can meet all the standards, qualifies for the rating of *satisfactory*.

The Future Outlook

The growth of commercial paper will be determined by two factors: (1) on the demand side as investors are corporate fiscal officers who are becoming more and more sophisticated in buying this paper; and (2), on the supply side are the corporate fiscal officers who are sufficiently sophisticated to avail themselves of tapping the money market for funds.

As an alternative, have you ever thought of investing in high grade preferred stocks? On preferred stock dividends, a corporate investor has an 85% tax exemption. Of $1,000 interest on commercial paper, about half goes to the tax department in Washington, fully taxed as corporate income. On the other hand, with a $1,000 dividend on high-grade preferred stock, you pay not 50% tax but, roughly speaking, 7½% tax.

But what will happen if the price of the high-grade pre-ferred stock goes down? You may be worse off than if you had stuck to commercial paper or treasury bills. This can happen if you invest at the wrong time in the interest cycle. In view of this, from here on, if you have any opportunity to catch a couple of dividend days, you might remember that I mentioned there is an 85% tax exemption on dividends paid to you as a corporate investor, on common or preferred stocks. I am sometimes sur-prised, as I discuss commercial paper, that this fact is not par-ticularly well known.

Pressure From Borrowers

Why has the commercial paper market grown so successfully in the past? Why will it continue to grow in the future? For one thing, the credit crunch of 1966 brought many companies into the commercial paper market because they felt the pressure of developing an alternative source of funds. The banks may ration credit, but no one asks any questions in the money market. With an appropriate rating and a willingness to pay the going interest rate, any company may borrow. The growth of sales finance companies, and the expansion of consumer credit, has let both the large and small finance companies tap the money market for funds. The decline of internally generated funds, in the face of larger corporate expenditures and decreasing corporate liquid-ity, has attracted still other companies. Further, the large yield spread favors commercial paper over bank loans.

Attesting to its growing popularity, the Federal Reserve Banks of Chicago, San Francisco, Richmond, and St. Louis have all come out with fairly recent articles on commercial paper. Moreover, several prominent investment houses have under-taken a more active solicitation of business, as shown by the interest volume of business done by dealers.

The recent history of the commercial paper market once again demonstrates the flexibility of our American financial system and its almost instantaneous response to a new challenge or to pressure. Not only has there been a shift of borrowers from bank loans to commercial paper, an even more striking development has been the emergence of new borrowers. Seasonal borrowers—such as food processors, canners, grain dealers, textile companies, tobacco companies, and wholesalers—have been sellers of commercial paper for a long time. Steel, chemical, oil companies, and the railroads use the commercial paper market. Most recently, the utilities—gas, electric, and telephone companies—as well as aerospace and electronics companies have gone into it. And the airlines and conglomerates have shown definite interest.

Bank holding companies have also recently issued commercial paper. As you may know, they had been squeezed by the rates, and so the bank sells the loans to the holding company which sells the commercial paper, and the money is turned over to the banks.

Lower Cost Advantages

What are the advantages of tapping the money market by selling commercial paper on a national or regional basis? Interest costs are decidedly less on commercial paper than on bank loans. This is the case particularly during times when banks demand 20% or more of a loan as a compensatory balance. For example, an 8½ % prime rate plus the cost of maintaining 20% of the loan as a deposit raises the effective cost of a bank loan to 10 5/8%.

It is interesting to note, particularly in view of our economic climate, that this difference in cost between bank loans and commercial paper will widen during times of reduced credit demand. The prime rate of the bankers is very sticky. The money market rate for commercial paper reacts instantaneously to changes in the demand for the supply of funds. At any given moment, the market rate on commercial paper is the result of several factors:

1. Changes in the supply of, and the demand for, commercial paper. If your company wishes to tap the money market and offer its paper, and the demand for it does not increase corre-

spondingly, the interest rate will move up. Like any merchandiser, the dealer will have to shave his price to market the paper, and that means of course a higher discount rate.

2. Commercial paper competes with such other money market instruments as treasury bills, bankers' acceptances, CD's, and of course the bankers' prime rate. When these instruments offer higher yields, commercial paper must become more attractive, too. When the yields come down, the dealer of commercial paper can raise his prices—that is, lower the discount rate on the paper.

3. The Federal Reserve authorities, our national money managers, change their monetary policies at times so that money may become easier or tighter. When less money is available, yields will rise. Investors will thus be more anxious to exchange nonearning cash for income yielding money market instruments.

As I mentioned earlier, the cost of selling commercial paper through a dealer is small. It is a standardized ⅛ of 1% per annum for prime names; on smaller names, you might pay ¼ of 1%; and, if you really are small and have a regional dealer, it may go to 3/8 of 1%.

Increased Bargaining Power

The ability to sell notes through dealers, of course, gives your company a certain amount of bargaining power in dealing with the banks. Furthermore—and do not underrate this—open market borrowers are able to obtain valuable financial advice from their dealers. Corporations that continuously maintain a credit position strong enough to enable them to borrow through dealers acquire financial prestige and obtain favorable publicity in all sections of the country in which their notes are purchased.

For example, if you were to come to us, or go to any other investment banking outfit, and say, "We want to sell our securities to you, but we want you to resell them in this, that, and the other area"—you are the boss; we would have to listen. This is the relationship between the corporate issuer and the investment banker—whether short or long term. Investors are probably much more likely to buy your securities if they know about your company through the commercial paper market.

As a company becomes better known through the sale of its paper, public distribution of a straight or convertible debt issue or, for that matter, an equity issue will be easier for it to make. To be well and favorably known in the commercial paper market will substantially ease the way to all types of long-term financing at a lower cost with a large, responsible, and prestigious underwriter.

This is particularly important for a company that contemplates going public, since a responsible underwriter will make a good after-market for the new securities. There will always be a bid and an offer in the market, and for more than just 100 shares or 5 bonds, as the case may be. The alleged disadvantages of open market borrowing are either nonexistent or of little consequence.

Should the country again experience in the near future a prolonged bull market, such as the one we saw between 1962 and 1965 when the Dow Jones Industrial Market went up 75%, many business firms will probably replace short-term loans with long-term debt or common stock issues. This, however, would not necessarily spell a decline in the volume of commercial paper coming to the market. From 1962 to 1965, when the industrial averages rose by 75%, the commercial paper outstanding rose by 50%.

The future growth of the paper market will probably depend to a large extent on the continued willingness of bankers to maintain for their paper issuers the open lines of credit which have in the past assured the paper buyers that repayment schedules would be met on time. On prime companies with more or less continuous borrowing, such as the utilities, the stress formally placed on the bank credit line tends to be reduced. One great advantage of commercial paper to investors rests primarily on a higher yield. Another advantage is the excellent safety record of commercial paper. And of course, there is no renewal in the market; it is an impersonal relationship between issuer and buyer investor which must be paid on maturity.

Dealer paper consists of notes in denominations of at least $5,000 and ranging up to $100,000. The trend has increasingly been toward larger minimum denominations. Minimum investment requirements tend to be at least $100,000, if you are looking on the demand side as an investor. However, sometimes you can get below that. I know of one investor who recently was able to buy $35,000 in commercial paper.

Changing Corporate Needs

In closing, I believe it is safe to assume that the commercial paper market will continue to expand. This is particularly so since future recessions are much more likely to take the form of a slowing down in our economic growth rate rather than of an actual decline in national income.

Commercial banks may well hold the key to the commercial paper market's expansion. The paper market certainly could not have operated as it did in the past without the services of the banks and their supporting lines of credit. Today, there are bankers who feel (and not surprisingly) that they have encouraged their competition too much. Commercial paper must compete with bank loans—and the finance companies that sell their paper must compete with banks in the consumer loan area, in arranging dealer inventory financing, in the leasing of industrial equipment, and in accounts receivable financing. Moreover, the banks sell negotiable certificates of deposits.

Another variable affecting the volume of commercial paper is, of course, the relationship of the long-term and short-term interest rate to the cost of long-term funds that decline substantially. Many companies that now borrow on the short-term basis would certainly fund these debts and sell long-term credit instruments when their equity is selling with a high P/E ratio.

However, with a gross national product of $2 trillion in sight for at least the mid-1980's, we face a great expansion. I think nobody yet comprehends what this means in terms of impending change. Certainly, any thoughts of substantially lower long-term interest rates seem to me to be completely unrealistic for the decade of the 1970's.

Corporations will need more money to finance plant and equipment expenditures. We have already begun to see a change in corporate debt structure. Therefore, it seems realistic to say that huge demands for savings are on the horizon.

Concluding Note

Those of you who are responsible in this new arena for equity financing will have to work out some way to make more financial decisions from your income statement, rather than from your balance sheet. You will have to take a good, hard look, and see whether you can meet your interest charges and sinking fund charges, which as you know come after taxes when it gets rough. This is where your money market tapping ability may well come in handy.

You will also have to know how to present your case differently to the different agencies. I often hear the criticism from various financing agencies that the individual who makes the presentation for the financing is not aware of the particular financial expertise of each of these different agencies.

Then, of course, you should look at the motives on the other side. What kind of an individual am I dealing with? Am I dealing with somebody who is interested in my business? Or is he merely stepping on my back to make some money? What is the investor looking for?

The thread that runs through what I have been discussing is this: plan carefully. Know what you are doing. Keep in mind a tremendously shifting historical context. If you think ours is an affluent society, wait until the 1980's. We will continue to have problems, but it is going to be a new ball game. All records are going to be broken. Things are going to be done differently. Institutions will be different, and customers will think differently. And all of us will have to work out new concepts.

Chapter 15

EURODOLLAR FINANCING— IMPORTANT SOURCE OF CAPITAL

Harvey P. Dale

U.S. corporations have learned, since 1963 and particularly since 1968, that their needs for capital can often best be met by selling their securities *outside* of the United States. There are many reasons for this, some of which I shall discuss.

Part of the planning for any kind of Eurodollar offering is to avoid too much taxation. As we go along in this chapter, I shall also try to outline some of the structures that are commonly used to accomplish that objective.

A discussion of all aspects of financing abroad is beyond the scope of this paper; therefore, I shall start out with a few

Mr. Dale is a General Partner of Schaeffer, Kahn, Dale & Vogel, a New York based law firm.

definitions and then focus on the most common forms of financing abroad.

A "Eurodollar" is a bit of a misnomer; it is a dollar deposited anywhere outside of the United States. For example, a dollar deposited in Canada is a Eurodollar; likewise a dollar deposited in Mexico is a Eurodollar. For our purpose, I shall concentrate on the Eurodollar market, but on occasion make a reference or two to the use of currencies other than the dollar for foreign financing.

An "international bond," as I use the term, means any bond sold outside the country in which the borrower is incorporated to do business. A "foreign bond" is one kind of an international bond; it is different than a "Eurobond" in that it is usually sold by a local syndicate in one country in the currency of that country. For example, if a German company through a British underwriting syndicate floated a bond issue in the United Kingdom in sterling, each bond would be a foreign bond. By contrast, a Eurobond issue is generally sold internationally by an international syndicate and, therefore, of necessity in currency other than that of at least some of the countries in which it is sold.

Customary Pattern

I shall concentrate primarily on Eurobond dollar offerings, dividing my discussion into two parts: one, going to the Eurodollar market for the purpose of raising money to use *outside* the United States; the other, going to that market to raise money to use *within* the United States. The technical structures—that is, the forms used to borrow—vary substantially for reasons which we shall come to shortly, depending on the place where the proceeds are eventually to go.

As a matter of prudence, U.S. based corporations that are thinking of going into Eurobond financings, or into the Eurodollar market in general, should specifically use their U.S. investment banking house at the start. Its contacts will in turn lead to foreign investment banking houses.

I shall discuss only sales to the public, not institutional financing through banks or similar entities abroad. Moreover, I shall confine my discussion primarily to Eurodollar financings, not other Eurocurrencies, and to the use of debt issues by a subsidiary of the parent corporation, guaranteed by the parent, and (sometimes) convertible into stock of the parent. These are the most common methods of raising money abroad.

The customary pattern, to repeat, is to have the U.S. parent form a wholly-owned subsidiary corporation; the subsidiary borrows money from the public; the parent guaranties the debt of the subsidiary; and sometimes the debt is convertible into stock of the parent. We shall now explore that pattern, *first* from the standpoint of structuring a Eurodollar borrowing when one wants to use the proceeds inside the United States, and *second* when the proceeds may be used abroad to finance foreign ventures of the U.S. corporation.

Domestic Use of Proceeds

The subsidiary which borrows from the public will have to pay interest on that debt. In order to make the net cost reasonable, it is important that there not be a withholding tax imposed on the payment by that subsidiary of interest to the foreign borrowers.

The subsidiary will in turn take the money and reloan it, or reinvest it in some form, inside the United States. Here, again, it is important that there be no withholding on the payment of interest or dividends from the United States to that subsidiary.

It is also important that any net profit to the subsidiary not be subject to too much tax. The net profit, if any, would probably be created by any "spread" between the interest income the subsidiary receives from the loans or investments it makes inside the United States and its net cost of doing business, including interest paid by it to the foreign lenders.

For these reasons, almost invariably, when borrowing abroad for use of the proceeds inside the United States, the borrower is a foreign corporation that is also entitled to certain tax treaty benefits.

Netherlands Antilles Treaty. There are a number of jurisdictions which have been used for Eurodollar financing, but by far the most popular—and for good cause—has been the Netherlands Antilles. I think the best way to explain why is to trace what happens in the absence of a treaty. Then, I shall explain what having the treaty does for the corporation.

Let us assume, for example, that a foreign corporation, which was entitled to no treaty benefits with respect to the United States, loaned money to a U.S. borrower. The payment of interest by the U.S. borrower to the foreign corporation would be subject to a 30% tax, collected by withholding at the source.

(There are exceptions to this rule. One, involving a U.S. borrower that itself derives less than 20% of its gross income from U.S. sources, will be discussed shortly. The second excepts from the 30% withholding tax payments which, as to the foreign corporation, are "effectively connected with the conduct of a trade or business within the United States" by the foreign corporation. However, in the latter case the interest would be subject to U.S. taxation because the foreign corporation would be taxed on its "effectively connected" income just as a U.S. corporation is. In addition, the foreign corporation might itself then have to withhold 30% on its payments of interest to the foreign public lenders.)

Thus, if the foreign corporation needed to receive 10% on its loan to enable it, in turn, to pay the required interest to the public lenders, it would have to charge the U.S. borrower not 10% but approximately 14.3%, because it would actually receive only 70% of the stated interest (the other 30% being withheld and paid over to the IRS). It is clear that this would substantially increase the cost to the U.S. borrowers from the foreign corporation.

The Netherlands Antilles Treaty and several other treaties contain provisions that make the transaction workable: (1) interest is exempted from U.S. tax altogether when paid from the U.S. company (the borrower) to a Netherlands Antilles subsidiary company (the lender)—that is, no withholding is made on the interest payment from the U.S. parent to its foreign Netherlands Antilles subsidiary; and (2) payments by the Netherlands Antilles subsidiary to the foreign public lenders are also exempted from U.S. tax altogether. (This second exemption protects against the risk alluded to earlier that the foreign corporation might itself have to withhold 30% on its payments of interest to the foreign public lenders.)

Other jurisdictions have treaties that may work equally well. For example, both Luxembourg and the Netherlands have been used on occasion. These other jurisdictions should be explored in detail by U.S. corporate managers and their legal aides and investment bankers.

In order to ensure that the foreign subsidiary is treated as a separate entity, for foreign and U.S. tax purposes, it is generally capitalized so that the debt-to-equity ratio, net after the borrowing, will not exceed 5 to 1. If a U.S. manager borrows $20 million, he has to capitalize the foreign subsidiary at $4 million which is a high cost. Although this original capital may be indirectly of some use to the U.S. parent, any "recircling" transaction must be carefully checked and will almost certainly cost at least some interest.

For example, if the manager wanted to capitalize the foreign corporation with property (e.g., stock, securities) in lieu of cash, he would have to pay tax on the transfer unless he got a tax ruling under Section 367 of the Internal Revenue Code before contributing the property to the foreign corporation. Such rulings are difficult if not impossible to get. (The guidelines used in granting this type of ruling do not contain any indication that rulings would be obtainable under this set of circumstances.)

As a general rule, the foreign corporation is capitalized with cash—and that involves a substantial outlay. In capitalizing the foreign corporation at $4 million to borrow $20 million, as we noted in the example a moment ago, the U.S. manager is putting up, in effect, one sixth of the total assets that the foreign corporation will have.

In order to get the benefit of an exemption from withholding under the Netherlands Antilles Treaty, the foreign subsidiary has to certify that it is not a "holding company" in the Antilles (and thus is not entitled to the special tax reductions available to such companies there), and there are procedures set up for certification to that effect in the United States. The earnings of the Netherlands Antilles subsidiary, determined under U.S. tax concepts, will be treated as income to the parent corporation in the United States because of certain provisions dealing with "controlled foreign corporations" in subpart F of the Internal Revenue Code.

However, its earnings should be fairly low. The reason for this is that the U.S. manager will probably try to calculate his net cost in such a way that the interest income on the loan by the subsidiary to the U.S. parent will exceed by very little the amount of expense that the subsidiary incurs on its own interest payments.

Even though the Antilles subsidiary has little or no taxable income according to U.S. concepts, it will have some taxes to pay in the Antilles. Under the current system of taxation in the Antilles, the foreign subsidiary will probably have to pay tax as though at least 1% of the face amount of its foreign borrowings was net income. Thus, if the foreign subsidiary borrows $5 million, it will probably be treated in the Netherlands Antilles as though it has taxable income of at least $50,000, on which it will in turn pay a tax ranging from approximately 24% to 34%. It may be necessary to get a special ruling from the taxing authorities in the Antilles to assure this result. Absent such a ruling, interest paid by the subsidiary may not be deductible under some circumstances, which would perhaps result in quite heavy taxes to pay. There is no withholding tax imposed by the Antilles with respect to payments made by the foreign subsidiary to the foreign lenders.

Before talking about securities laws, one area that should be mentioned is the Foreign Direct Investment Regulations which were adopted in early 1968 and which are administered by the Office of Foreign Direct Investments of the U.S. Department of Commerce. These Regulations are extremely complex, and must be carefully studied before the regulatory "scheme" can be understood. However, in any case in which the proceeds of a foreign borrowing are being loaned back to the United States, there should be no difficulty in complying with the Regulations. Subpart N of the Regulations sets forth a standard procedure for reporting and filing a certificate with respect to such foreign borrowings. Nevertheless, there are other reporting requirements and limitations on "liquid foreign balances" which should be examined and which will certainly be brought into play by the foreign borrowing transaction.

Securities Regulations. If the debt is convertible into stock of the U.S. parent, on conversion, the issuance of stock of the parent is not a problem for the U.S. Securities Exchange Commission. The certificates, as a rule, must have a legend stating that they cannot be sold to persons or residents of the United States or within the United States. However, no 1933 Securities Act registration statement need be filed.

The President's Task Force on balance of payments problems recommended steps prior to 1964 to encourage foreign investment in the United States; one such step was to make it easier for foreigners to buy securities in a U.S. corporation. To do that, it was thought to be desirable to make it easier for U.S. corporations to issue shares to foreigners. Following the Task Force report, the SEC in a Joint Securities Act and Securities Exchange Act Release stated that it would not treat convertible stock offerings as public offerings for purposes of registration in the United States if they were made to foreign citizens who were not residents of the United States and who would not sell those shares within the United States. Shares which have that legend on conversion will save the U.S. corporation the cost of full registration.

The SEC has also issued "no action" letters with respect to compliance with the 1939 Trust Indenture Act and has indicated that it is not concerned about compliance with the Investment Company Act of 1940 in transactions of this kind. It may be prudent to request such no action letters in connection with this type of borrowing, nevertheless.

The securities laws of foreign jurisdictions are far from uniform, and indeed are in the process of very rapid growth. Serious suggestions have been made for establishing a uniform set of rules, outside of the United States, to govern transactions in the Eurodollar market. It is too early to say whether these suggestions will produce the desired results. Until they do, U.S. corporations which are involved in a Eurodollar borrowing will want to make sure that local securities laws are checked and that their requirements are met before any offering is made in each particular jurisdiction. For this reason, it is prudent to rely on foreign underwriters and foreign counsel for guidance.

The Interest Equalization Tax, a 1963 addition to the U.S. Internal Revenue Code, will apply to any acquisition by a U.S. person of those debt securities issued by the foreign subsidiary. This constrains the foreign borrowers not to sell their debentures within the United States. The tax currently runs up to 11.25%, depending on the terms of the debt.

Extraordinarily complex problems are presented, under the United States Internal Revenue Code, by the exercise of a conversion privilege contained in the debt securities. The consequences depend (a) in part on whether the stock issued upon conversion is issued directly by the U.S. parent corporation upon presentation to it of the debt obligations issued by the subsidiary, or (b) whether the parent's stock is instead issued by the foreign subsidiary (which presumably, in turn, has received the stock as a contribution to its capital from the U.S. parent corporation) directly. Additional difficult questions are raised by repurchase of outstanding debt securities, prior to maturity, by the issuing corporation or its U.S. parent or by their affiliated corporations. Such repurchase has in fact become desirable on occasion when the market value of the debentures has fallen substantially below their face amount.

The complexities of these problems are far beyond the scope of this paper, and the answers—to the extent that any clear answers can be given—depend on many variables, including questions involving income from forgiveness of indebtedness, the existence or absence of a consolidated return group, and so forth.

Foreign Use of Funds

When the borrowed proceeds may be used abroad to finance foreign ventures of your own corporation, the pattern of the transaction may be different. Once again, we run into a familiar problem: the interest paid by the borrowing subsidiary to the foreign lenders must be free of withholding tax. Normally, interest paid by a U.S. corporation *would* be subject to withholding, and thus (as discussed earlier) foreign subsidiaries are used. However, if the borrowing subsidiary in turn derives all (or almost all) of its income from foreign entities, the withholding tax may be eliminated.

When a U.S. domestic corporation pays interest abroad, it is not subject to withholding tax on that payment if it meets one important condition, known as the "80-20" test. For the past three years, or for any less period of time that it has been in existence, the U.S. domestic subsidiary must have derived less than 20% of its gross income from U.S. sources. The subsidiary will meet this test if it loans or invests all of its money outside the United States, because its income will then be derived from abroad in the form of interest or dividends paid to it by foreign entities. Therefore, although it is a U.S. corporation, it will not be subject to U.S. withholding tax on its interest payments.

Thus, generally, if the U.S. parent plans to use the proceeds outside the United States, it can use a domestic subsidiary company as the borrowing entity. If it is borrowing for use inside the United States, then it must use a foreign subsidiary company as the borrowing entity.

If a domestic subsidiary company is available, it is probably much more flexible in various ways than the foreign subsidiary. For example, there is no need to obtain a Section 367 ruling as a condition to capitalizing a domestic subsidiary with property (e.g., stock, securities) rather than money. This probably makes the 5 to 1 ratio less costly to meet and maintain.

Furthermore, domestic subsidiaries can elect to file a consolidated return with the U.S. parent for income tax purposes, whereas foreign subsidiaries can not be included in such a return. The IRS will nevertheless rule that the debt obligations of the domestic subsidiary are subject to interest equalization tax if acquired by a U.S. person, which is a most desirable result. Given such a ruling, a no action letter can also be obtained from the SEC indicating that no registration statement is required to be filed under the 1933 Securities Act with respect to the debt issued by the domestic subsidiary corporation. A no action letter can also be obtained with respect to the 1939 Trust Indenture Act and (under a special rule adopted specifically for this purpose) the Investment Company Act of 1940.

When investing abroad, the U.S. corporate manager runs smack into the Foreign Direct Investment Regulations. Since January 1, 1968, if the U.S. corporation has a substantial history of investing abroad, it has a so-called "base period allowable." Alternatively, the Regulations give the manager a standard "allowable" of $1 million per year into the various schedules (or $5 million for the underdeveloped countries) and the world is divided, for this purpose, into three parts. A third allowable based on earnings is also alternatively available. The U.S. parent can not invest in its foreign subsidiaries more than the limits of these "allowables" in any year, and earnings of its foreign subsidiaries count as investment for this purpose.

The important thing is that proceeds of long-term foreign borrowings are a deduction against the U.S. corporation's foreign investment for Foreign Direct Investment Regulation purposes. For example, if the U.S. manager wanted to invest $5 million abroad and had no allowable investment for it, he just could not do it; it would be unlawful. But if he borrowed $5 million abroad under appropriate terms, he could invest that.

In order to make the borrowing work so that the U.S. corporation can not only guaranty the payment, but can also pay up on the guaranty (if necessary) when it comes due, as a practical matter the borrowing must be for a term of at least seven years. The U.S. manager must also file a required certificate at the Office of Foreign Direct Investments as prescribed in the Regulations.

Also, the debt obligations of the borrowing corporation—that is, the domestic subsidiary—must be subject to the Interest Equalization Tax. The Foreign Direct Investment Regulations usually require that, and the Securities and Exchange Commission's staff will not issue a no action letter unless it applies; and the Interest Equalization Tax rules oblige (as mentioned earlier) in Section 4912 (b) (3) by stating that securities of a domestic corporation which is principally used to acquire stock or debt of a foreign corporation will be subject to this tax. And that, of course, is exactly what this domestic finance subsidiary is doing.

Historical Perspective

At this point, let us turn our attention to some of the borrowings in the Eurodollar market, which since 1960 has increased 20 or 30 fold. It really began to boom after the adoption of the Foreign Direct Investment Regulations in 1968. For a period of time, many convertible debt issues were offered, because the foreign investors were willing to settle for a relatively low interest yield in order to have the opportunity of making a profit if the parent's stock increased in value on the stock exchanges in the United States.

Following the market reverses of 1969 and 1970, convertible issues became substantially less attractive and, since other reputable financial institutions, including banks, were paying very high interest rates, the interest cost on foreign straight debt issues became quite high. Most recently, as liquidity problems eased slightly around the world, straight debt issues have come back into popularity and the interest rates have declined somewhat. There are still very few convertible issues being offered currently.

There have been some interesting straight debt issues in nondollar currencies. In particular, Deutsche marks and Swiss francs are often used and, for those who like the esoteric side of foreign finance, a so-called "unit of account" offering has also been used. Unit of account is a concept set up by the Bank for International Settlements as a certain measure of gold approximately equal to one U.S. dollar and to a number of other amounts in other currencies. By purchasing and selling in units of account, the U.S. manager assures himself the right of picking out any one of those currencies which he happens to want at the time he cashes in his units of account. Although it can be used for borrowing, only a few managers actually do so.

Floor Discussion

Question: How does Delaware fit into Eurodollar borrowings?

Dale: Delaware has quite often been used as a place of incorporation for a domestic financing subsidiary, when the proceeds are for investment outside the United States.

Question: Does the Antilles or Luxembourg treaty offer a "loophole" in the law, or is it a purposeful thing set up for some background reason?

Dale: There are a number of treaties that contain the same benefits, and the U.S. Treasury Department is well aware of them and in many ways needs them. While the Treasury *has* tried to close up certain "loopholes" in the operation of these treaties, it has not objected to the general benefits that I've discussed.

Question: In the "80-20" test, was that "three years or"?

Dale: Yes, "three years *or*," that's a good question. It's three years *or* such shorter period of time that the subsidiary has been in existence for the 80-20 test.

Question: In borrowing for off-shore use of proceeds, are foreign subsidiaries ever used?

Dale: Generally, not. It is easier for a number of reasons to form a domestic corporation. Where the proceeds are going to be used abroad, domestic borrowers have no disadvantage and many advantages.

Question: Does the subsidiary have to be capitalized in that case?

Dale: Yes. In order to assure yourself that the interest deduction is available for interest paid to that corporation, it can't be so "thin" as to be disregarded.

Question: Could you tell us a little bit about the market for Eurobond offerings for smaller companies?

Dale: The Europeans have at the moment a number of opportunities to look at; thus they are not searching for investments. In part because the Foreign Direct Investment Regulations have forced substantial U.S. companies to go to that market in order to expand abroad, there are more issues planned than the market will take. Smaller companies may find it hard to borrow abroad, unless they get excellent underwriting sponsorship.

Question: Is the deductibility of the interest that the parent makes to a foreign subsidiary treated any differently than interest paid on its own convertible bonds?

Dale: For purposes of deduction to the parent, the two are treated alike.

Question: Would it be your opinion that to raise Eurodollars a U.S. company would need to have a New York Stock Exchange listing?

Dale: No, but it would help, unless you are for some other reason well-known in European circles. It's possible that you could raise money elsewhere if your investment banker is aggressive enough. There have been private placements, I might add, for companies that are traded over the counter, depending on who their supporters or bankers are.

Question: Is the Office of Foreign Direct Investments aggressive in policing the Regulations?

Dale: Yes. However, in my experience that's been one of the most delightful agencies of government to work with. They are most cooperative, bright, and energetic. I think they don't want to prolong the program any longer than necessary politically, and they are going forward with their program, rewriting their general bulletins and interpretive regulations.

Question: You don't see any elimination of the Regulations?

Dale: In 1968, the maximum allowable for companies without history was $100 thousand; today, it is $1 million. There has been a substantial growth, and the Regulations may someday be relaxed again. However, it would be very difficult for the United States at the moment to abandon them.

If the Regulations were abandoned, the U.S. companies with good credit lines in the United States might replace their foreign borrowings by paying them off and reborrowing instead in the United States at a lower interest cost.

That would create a balance of payments outflow, because the net effect would be to flow U.S. dollars out of the United States. The U.S. government has been trying with some success to keep its official settlements, as well as its liquidity payments, in surplus, and the overhang would be difficult indeed. I don't think it's in the cards that the Foreign Direct Investments program will soon be cancelled outright, but I do think that the Regulations might be relaxed.

Question: I have a little difficulty following your approach to borrowing Eurodollars for use for foreign purposes. Are you suggesting that the U.S. financing subsidiary corporation borrow, and lend or invest the funds in a foreign subsidiary?

Dale: Right.

Question: Instead of borrowing Eurodollars, why not borrow Deutsche marks? Is there a difference, say, like the Japanese yen to the Eurodollar?

Dale: The Japanese yen is subject to exchange control and it is not convertible. There aren't too many Eurocurrency borrowings in nonconvertible currencies. There could be foreign bond borrowings in nonconvertible currencies, because you would then be borrowing in the currency of a country presumably for use in that country. If you wanted sterling and you were going to use it in Britain, you would not care too much about convertibility.

But for purposes of Eurobond borrowings, you would want to get a currency that is convertible. As a result, most of the borrowings have been in U.S. dollars, Deutsche marks, Swiss francs, and some units of account. For example, in 1968, of the total International Bond Issues outside the United States, 2.5 billion were denominated in U.S. dollars; 1.5 billion in Deutsche marks; and about .5 billion in other currencies.

Question: Which is used the most in the Antilles, Curacao or another particular island?

Dale: For our purposes it doesn't matter, because you are not going to have any people down there, I assume. Any one of the islands of the Antilles will do as a domicile. For U.S. purposes, if you are formed under the law of the country, then it doesn't matter which particular island you happen to be located on; you are entitled to the benefits of that treaty. You will find that the finance subsidiaries that are incorporated in Netherlands Antilles are not usually very heavily staffed.

Question: Are the terms of Eurodollar debentures relatively standard by comparison with U.S. borrowings?

Dale: I haven't observed that debentures *are* "standard" for U.S. borrowings, but perhaps that's because I spend too much of my time drafting them. There are formats that have been used with success and some that are now accepted customarily by European banking sources, and that is helpful. Of course, the specific terms of the issue will vary in any event from issue to issue, and there will be modifications. In this, you will probably be most guided by your legal counsel and investment banker.

Chapter 16

THE ENVIRONMENT FOR MERGERS IN THE 1970's

John Westergaard

A very exciting area for investment is to be found in identifying those managements which have demonstrated an understanding of the fact that we are in a changing corporate, economic, social environment and which have also demonstrated an ability to deal with that change.

This does not necessarily mean that it has to be done through mergers and acquisitions but, for most companies whose opportunities in their fields of initial endeavor might be somewhat limited, the merger-acquisition route does become fairly important.

Mr. Westergaard is President of Equity Research Associates, Inc., a leading financial research and consulting firm. He specializes in business combinations, reorganizations, and investment research.

I am not taking the position here that acquisitions are an end-all. They are in fact merely an extension of a management philosophy which says, "Here we are, we're a company, and we have this environment. What are we doing now to face up to our challenge and problems of the years ahead as corporate managers?"

Nevertheless, I do believe that acquisitions are an important and basic ingredient to the market of our economic system. Recognizing this fact, I shall first deal with the question: What is the rationale for merging companies together—this is, making larger entities out of smaller entities?

Then, in the second part of this chapter, I shall discuss the political outlook for the multi-industry corporation in the near term.

The Rationale for Merging

Certain basic points are important to keep in mind in girding to meet the corporate challenge. These basics include, for example, the fluidity of capital. Capital should move and be diverted into areas of need, areas of challenge, and areas of growth in the economy. In fact, this is what businessmen like the Textron people have done. They have gone through an evolution whereby they moved their entire capital base out of their relatively unattractive area in textiles and into more attractive sections of the economy.

Building a Balanced Configuration

As rationale for this discussion, I am suggesting a fuller utilization of corporate resources. Companies in many industries have little opportunity to deploy further assets in their respective areas of involvement; thus it becomes necessary or desirable for them to deploy their capital into other areas.

A prime example of this is United Fruit, which has done an outstanding job of springing back from the brink of disaster. Some years ago, United Fruit was a company in real trouble, but

—through a process of internal reorganizing and restructuring of its product, marketing, and raw material base—the company has come back to a level of high profitability and a supreme position in the marketplace. At the same time, however, the managers showed that they were quite unable to deploy their assets, which remained very substantial, into new areas of growth in other sections of the economy.

In other words, those managers were great in the fruit business, but they showed little ability and creativity to move beyond that specialized business. Here was a company with some $100 million in excess cash, and with probably $200 to $300 million more in borrowing power that was not being utilized— very attractive to people such as AMK, who subsequently took United Fruit over and created what is now United Brands.

Regardless of how good your business is and what industry you are in, there is in almost every case a great appeal in attempting to balance your configuration with other areas of the economy being represented. Thus, if you do experience a downtrend in whatever sector you are involved in, you still can look to the possibility of balancing it off in other sectors.

An example of this is International Silver Company, which back in 1958 was having difficulty. At that time, its stock was selling below book value, it had a poor outlook for its major markets, family formation trends were not going its way, and it faced rising competitive pressure from imports of stainless steel from the Japanese market. But International Silver's managers knew what to do to survive; they diversified. They built up their base in other areas for a period of about five years, at which point their basic business began coming back strong.

From their forecasts, they knew that family formations were going to increase again in the early 1960's, but they could not afford to sit back and wait that long. They had to make diversification moves in the interim to build up their earnings, their capital base, and their stock to discourage any potential take-over attempts.

Gaining Economies of Scale

The broader-based or multi-industry company gains a much greater awareness of what is going on in the economy. In turn, presumably from a top management point of view, this awareness gives it better facility to take advantage of the various factors in the economy, or at least to meet whatever challenges face it.

Of course, the multi-industry company normally has an increased professionalization of management. One of the questions that I hear frequently is: "What is it about the managers of the multi-industry corporation that enables them to be so smart in managing all these different businesses?"

That is the wrong emphasis. Usually, I turn the question around, and ask: "How can the managers of a small or medium-sized company learn to deal intelligently with all the problems they face as their company grows to a larger size and a broader scope?"

To illustrate my point, look at the case of a company started by two brothers in the 1930's. It has grown to a size of $40 million, and is now publicly owned. The managers have to worry about things like labor problems, new technologies, stockholder relations, adequate financing, and so on. Perhaps now they have to move away from, say, their local Connecticut bank and start establishing some New York bank ties. Or perhaps they have to consider whether they should have direct representation in Washington for a company of their size and capability. What do they do then?

Generally, it is at this point that a multi-industry corporate executive says to them, "Look, merge into our corporation. We'll take many of these problems off your shoulders. We'll bring them up to our corporate staff level. We'll take over your shareholder relations. We'll arrange for your bank lines, and other financing. We'll analyze where you should be going in terms of the DOD budget or other areas of government spending to take full advantage of your capabilities. We'll take over those problems, and you concentrate on what you really know the best, which is to deal with your specific market and to build your product lines."

The idea that management can only be so smart is a two-way street. I think that in many cases a multi-industry corporation takes off the hands of operating managers those problems which are generic to all companies, as opposed to specific product areas and specific markets. I also think that there are other benefits to size, including the international posture of these corporations. How important it is for corporations to build an international posture today, both in terms of meeting competition from abroad and in taking advantage of markets abroad.

Developing such skills as described above is not something that is done easily or lightly; it is basic to the future of our country and our industrial economy. I suggest that most small companies really do not have such capability and that again, by moving into the environment of a broader-based multi-industry corporation, they can gain access to this kind of capability.

In brief, the foregoing discussion offers some of the rationale for my conviction that acquisitions are an important and basic ingredient to the working of the U.S. economic system.

The Political Outlook

Let us now look at the present situation. There is, of course, a tremendous reaction under way on the part of the so-called establishment sectors of the economy. I think we saw a prime example of this in the B.F. Goodrich-Northwest Industries fight. As an old-line establishment company—one without a particularly outstanding record of accomplishment within its industry—B.F. Goodrich was vulnerable to take-over. However, when the attack came, the Goodrich managers handled the fight very aggressively in their use of economic and political pressures.

Another way in which they reacted was to change their charter substantially to institute staggered election of directors, cumulative voting, and a number of other elements that make it very difficult for any outsider to take over B.F. Goodrich.

A logical reason for this is that the people at B.F. Goodrich and similar companies want to keep their jobs. If they were to be merged, there is the danger that they might lose them.

I also think that there is a reasonable concern in terms of the communities involved. This is another area in which I can see the forces at work. For example, I spoke with Congressman Emanual Celler (D.-N.Y.) about this project in June 1969. He viewed the community issues in political terms, and said the first thing he is concerned about when a company is acquired is: Are the company's executives still interested in contributing to the local Community Chest? Are they, in fact, even going to be in the local community any longer? Or will they have to relocate in some other area of the country?

These are quite real considerations, however opinions vary in similar circumstances. In talking with Congressman Gerald Ford (R.-Mich.) in August 1969, I asked how he feels about conglomerates. He replied, "All I can tell you is that the conglomerates have made a real contribution to my district." I asked what he meant, and he said, "Well, Gulf & Western started in my district with the acquisition of a small company, and has brought that company up to where it is today an important employer in the community. Then Ling-Temco moved in and took over a Wilson sporting goods manufacturing facility. The result of that merger was a substantial increase in the capital investment in that plant and an increase of employment in my district."

I think that Congressman Celler's concern about community relations has been heightened by what has happened in the City of Pittsburgh. Within the last several years, some twelve major corporations, each of whose home base was in Pittsburgh, lost their identity as independent corporations. Rockwell Manufacturing, now North American Rockwell, is one that comes to mind.

The central point here is that business can be political, and a business manager should know which Congressmen represent the various districts in which his company has plants. In addition, he has to know whether he has good representation in Washington, for example through a law firm, lobby or trade association.

What is the position of Equity Research Associates on merger and acquisition? To a certain extent, we are sympathetic. Basically, we believe in the multi-industry corporation. We believe that a corporation has to be able to survive and grow if the United States is to have a viable, dynamic economy. The only way that this can happen today is to permit the corporation to direct its assets in the most promising sectors possible.

However, I can envision certain essential limitations, for example, on size. Once a company is among the 200 largest, perhaps there should be definite restrictions on its ability to make acquisitions. Or perhaps, rather than among the 200 largest, the constraints should enter in on, say, $1 billion in sales or $500 million in assets, or some other restrictive formula. But I see no need to be concerned about the very fact of size. For example, it is one thing to say that a certain sized company cannot make acquisitions; however, it is something else to say that if XYZ Corporation, given its size today, wants to acquire another company, it first has to get rid of some other unit.

I see as one problem that companies have been too unwilling to divest themselves of operations. I am all for a restructuring within the corporate environment in the years ahead, but it has to be a two-way street. Thus I am not opposed to some of the thinking projected by the Justice Department and Federal Trade Commission with respect to the use of size as a present consideration. However, I do disagree with the approach of the Justice Department which favors an extension of the Clayton Act rather than new legislation. Why not present this issue to Congress?

Finally more than anything else, I am concerned about what seems to be a lack of understanding in Washington of the overall function of a corporation. For example, people in the

Justice Department take the position that one of the great dangers of a conglomerate is that in acquiring XYZ Company, it may make mistakes, may not understand that business properly, and may run it poorly. In other words, they express concern that the conglomerate may drive the acquired company out of business.

To be sure, that may happen, but the management presently running the company might also do that. To use this line of argument as a legal justification or to weave into a legal basis of discussion, I find difficult to accept. I was really quite shocked some while back to hear a leading spokesman for the Justice Department present this line of reasoning as the one great danger of a conglomerate. If someone wants to argue that a marriage might be bad because the young man who marries a daughter may murder her tomorrow, then of course it is a potential danger; however, in business, as in anything else, we have to assume a certain rationality in the functions and actions of people.

In addition to finding a heavy political orientation, as I have described from talking with Congressmen and government officials, I also think that we should be concerned about what is going to happen to corporate democracy. I think that there is a trend in a large number of corporations to seriously cut down the ability of the stockholders to influence the fundamental course of business.

Thus, in the 1970's, I think the environment for mergers is not very clear. Moreover, as long as the Republicans are in power, I think this is something to be conscious of. I would venture to say that if the Democrats were restored to power in 1972, the rules of the game might change somewhat. I am making no predictions, but this is something to watch very closely. Again, the message here is simply: let us watch the politics—they are important.

In terms of the environment, we are dealing with the fundamental question of the survival of the American corporation. What I call establishment reaction could well boomerang against some of the establishment companies in this country. None of them can afford to be complacent and self-satisfied about the businesses they are in.

In 1969, my company issued a stock of the combination of Reynolds Tobacco, an old-time company, with McLain Industries, a dynamic new force on the industrial scene. McLain had not only led the entire race toward the creation of containerization as a component of the transportation industry in this country, but it had gone beyond that to restore the United States as a merchant marine power in the North Atlantic, which we were not five years previous.

These kinds of transactions are significant. We talk about such matters as balance of payments problems and where our country is going. If we can be restored as a world merchant marine power in one important segment of the market, the North Atlantic trade, this is something to recognize and to get excited about.

The point is that McLain needed what Reynolds had to offer, and I think that we must keep the structure of our economy such that the creation of new enterprises like Reynolds Industries can be effected in the future. Reynolds Tobacco and McLain Industries are not fly-by-night companies. Nor are they the new conglomerates like Gulf & Western and Ling-Temco, but Reynolds is doing much the same thing; it is talking the same language.

Thus I think that any of the establishment companies should be careful how far they go in fighting the acquisition environment of the 1960's. My conviction is that if we close off the merger route in the 1970's, we are going to create severe economic problems and limitations for ourselves in an overall context.

Floor Discussion

Question: How do you reconcile the fact that the largest 200 companies may be precluded from mergers unless they get rid of some other part of their business versus the need for old-line companies to shape up and make better use of their assets?

Westergaard: I don't really subscribe to the 200 theory. What I was really trying to get across is that I'm not opposed to the idea that there might have to be some guidelines drawn as to which companies can and cannot make acquisitions. I do think that the guidelines might be somewhat different for large companies when they get to be a certain size. It's a combination of using some sound judgment and being flexible. We might also consider separate guidelines for regressive industries that would apply to a company like Anaconda, which is having its copper mines taken away from it, or a company like Reynolds, which is having its markets circumscribed for health reasons.

Question: What's your reaction to the number of highly critical statements about the manner of accounting of per-share earnings of the conglomerates?

Westergaard: There have been a number of critical articles and comments on accounting procedures by conglomerate companies.

My attitude is that accounting is a matter of great concern and something in which the accounting profession should take a much more active role. I am 100% for sound, honest accounting, and to the degree that some conglomerates have been using unsound, manipulative accounting, I think it's not only very unfortunate, but that it's also something the accounting profession has to face up to and deal with.

Question: Do you think that the dispute on poolings of interest fits into an evaluation of the environment? I mean, does the government's criticism of pooling of interest accounting have an adverse effect?

Westergaard: I certainly think it does. In the stock market, these accounting questions that have been raised consistently over the past year or so have had a negative impact as far as the specific companies are concerned. Certainly, if pooling of interest accounting were outlawed, it would severely circumscribe the acquisition-merger trend, although I have a feeling that the accountants would come up with some new approach to it. People seem to be very imaginative when they want to do something.

Question: I have heard it said that the conglomerates haven't proved or cannot prove their ability to manage. Would you care to comment on that?

Westergaard: I think that if you look at the record of management of companies like Boise Cascade, Textron, and so on right down the line, these people have been much more than financial molecule manipulators over the years. They've done a good job in the companies that they have acquired over the years of introducing more aggressive and more imaginative management. The record is clear. Now, this doesn't mean to say that every conglomerate is well managed, or that some of them which have been well managed might not stub their toes at some point. But to say that they haven't proved their capabilities is absolutely absurd.

Question: Do you have some views on accounting for goodwill?

Westergaard: Goodwill is a very debatable question, and the accountants have been arguing about it for a long time. In my own company, we made an acquisition at one point in which we acquired goodwill. We carry goodwill on our books as an item that we paid for. It's basic to our business.

Perhaps we should amortize it. If so, goodwill should in fact be amortized over a long period of time, say, 20, 30, or 40 years. If it is worth anything at all, it will at least have value over that length of time unless, at some stage, it no longer is considered goodwill.

Chapter 17

PACKAGING
A MERGER
OR ACQUISITION

John K. Castle

It is not at all unusual for a company that has perhaps $50 or $100 million of equity to make an acquisition of a company of equal size through the use of common stock or some other kind of paper security. I think it is fair to state that one of the most important financial determinations that many corporations make is to merge or acquire, particularly when compared with decisions to buy capital equipment, or to go into new product lines or other areas of corporate development.

In this chapter, I will discuss the financing of the merger and acquisition transaction and the structuring of the package.

Mr. Castle is a Vice President of Donaldson, Lufkin & Jenrette, Inc. He specializes in merger and acquisition activities for this leading asset management firm.

In my experience, there are really three packages with which you are confronted when transacting a merger or acquisition:

One, is the business synergy package. This is everything about the transaction which makes it attractive from an operating business point of view to join the two companies together.

Two, is the management package. This includes not only what the acquired managers are going to be paid in the form of salaries, bonuses, and/or stock incentives, but it also includes the contractual and working relationships these managers are to have in your company in terms of their control, their titles, and their responsibilities.

Three, is the financial package. After all, a merger is a capital investment that requires a determination of value. Once he has arrived at that value, the buyer has to decide how he is going to give it to the seller.

Perhaps surprisingly, in most cases I consider that the business synergy package and the management package are considerably more important than the financial package in consummating a merger or an acquisition.

On the other hand, once the point is reached in a transaction where management is trying to lay out a package to offer another company, the financial package can have a profound effect on completing the transaction. As I indicated at the start, management could be paying $100 million for a company, and that could be substantial in comparison with its net worth.

Determining the Guidelines

I would like, first of all, to discuss certain aspects of mergers and acquisitions that I have found particularly helpful and useful in structuring a three-in-one package.

The problem is that, as with all cases, guidelines are never universally applicable. But they are good concepts and can be used to refine management's thinking a little bit. Ultimately, some of the guidelines are violated in almost every merger.

Nevertheless, they do provide a good starting point in thinking about how to proceed with a merger or acquisition.

The Seller's Goals

Perhaps the first and most basic step in a merger transaction is trying to determine the goals of the selling company. In thinking about this, usually the buyer finds that there are just a few seller's goals which are basic to almost every transaction:

- The stockholders, of course, want to maximize their selling price. They want to get the best deal possible.
- They frequently want to have a tax-free transaction. (In other instances, it may either be a tax deferred or a taxable transaction.)
- The selling stockholders may want a certain income level which can be either in the form of dividends or interest payments.
- They may want liquidity. Of course, the best liquidity is simply cash. But usually, when they say liquidity, they mean they want your company to have a listing on the New York Stock Exchange, or to have some large volume of stock turnover so that with relative ease they can feed out the securities into the open market.
- They want to have downside protection. By this, I mean they want some guarantee that if they are to get $50 a share for their package it is going to continue to be worth at least $50 a share. Hopefully, they would like it to be a lot more than that. One way they can sometimes be given guaranties is through dividend protection; at other times, it is through some special kind of offer to give additional stock or cash if your corporate securities decline in value.
- They may want a certain proportion of the total final corporation in order to have voting control. At least, this is true in a merger situation when companies of relatively similar size are joining together, or in an instance

where there is a substantial number of stockholders in either one of the companies.

I have noticed in many situations that it is most difficult for sellers to formulate their real goals. I have found this to be particularly true with entrepreneurial people who may be very excited and emotional. What they really want, they often cannot articulate.

I have frequently found, though, that on occasions when a seller cannot decide what he really wants, he may have no desire to sell. It is easy to agree on the benefits of business synergy and to agree on the fact that the seller is going to have a handsome salary plus stock options in the combined company. But when it comes down to the basis he is going to sell on, this is the one place where it is easy for him to beg out and say, "Well, that really isn't enough. I want even greater value."

The Buyer's Objectives

There are also some very specific goals in the mind of the buyer. They are really the key elements in how he is going to finance his corporate growth. Thus:

- In most instances, he wants to maximize his per-share earnings, whether on a near-term basis, on an immediate basis, or on a long-term basis.
- The buyer may also want a taxable or tax-free transaction. If he is buying a property at substantially over its book price, and he has to write up the values in a given transaction, he may find that the seller has a lot of depreciation or depletion. There may also be financial reasons why the buyer wants a tax-free transaction.
- He is probably concerned about the accounting treatment. In a merger or acquisition transaction, it is not what one does; it is what it looks as if one has done that is really important. For bankers, it is frequently most important to give the proper kind of appearance, and the right

kind of accounting may give that desired appearance. Part of this is what the final balance sheet is going to look like, such as whether there is going to be a large amount of equity, debt, or good will in the balance sheet.

Another problem within that whole structure—and the problem which confronts a buyer with goals—is the cash he is going to be paying for dividends. How hard is it going to be to support a structure of debt on preferred stock that he may be assuming?

I think that in doing acquisitions properly, the buyer could either load his company up heavily with debt, which today may be an appropriate thing to do if he wants to avoid a tender offer; or, on the other hand, if he has an opportunity to create a lot of equity that would not otherwise be there.

Assuming that the buyer is able to acquire a company with very little debt, he may be able to greatly improve his balance sheet without going to the public market. That is, without having an underwriting, dilution, or all the other things about which his stockholders may complain.

Structuring the Transaction

Usually, the first big issue in financing a merger is the question: Is it going to be taxable, or is it going to be tax free?

Once that decision is made, the buyer must determine the route that is the key in terms of how the whole transaction will end.

If the decision is that it should be tax free, it means that he is essentially limited to extending or offering securities to give an equity interest and a voting interest, in his company. In a merger transaction where the buyer has to give an equity interest, he is limited to using common stock, preferred stock, or convertible preferred stock.

In some instances, an additional benefit of a tax-free transaction is that usually those criteria will also permit the buyer to formulate a transaction on a pooling-of-interest basis. In acquiring a company at substantially over its book value, he does not have a write-up of good will, which destroys some of the balance sheet appearances.

On the other hand, suppose both the seller and the buyer make the decision that they really want to have a taxable transaction. In that case, you probably do not want to use common, preferred, or convertible preferred stock because their dividends are not tax deductible. Rather, you probably want to use debt instruments whose interest is tax deductible for computing your per-share earnings and shielding your income.

Examples of forms of payment in a taxable transaction would be cash, straight debt, seller's notes, convertible debentures, debt with warrants, and straight warrants which were quite popular a year or two ago in many tender-offer packages. However, a taxable transaction has certain disadvantages to the selling company in that its stockholders have to pay a tax either immediately or within a year after the transaction has been completed.

Within that extreme, there are a few transactions that are partly taxable and partly nontaxable, but a consideration of those is beyond the scope of this chapter. Suffice it to say, I will discuss those situations where some stockholders get cash, which is taxable, and where others get stock, which is nontaxable.

Cost of Capital

Once the buyer has made this basic decision, which is a key one in terms of financing mergers and acquisitions, the next step is to rank the kinds of paper that he is going to use, primarily according to cost-of-capital analysis. The essential ingredient here is that he probably wants to use the cheapest kind of capital possible when acquiring someone else—that is, cheapest in terms of what it costs his company.

We determine cost of capital by using the percentage equivalent of a price/earnings ratio. Thus, in the case of common stock, we use the price/earnings ratio itself; for debentures or debt, we use the price or the value of a $1,000 debenture, if you will, divided by the after-tax cost of carrying that debenture.

In other words, if it were an 8% debenture, it would be approximately 4% after tax, or a price/earnings multiple of about 25 times earnings.

The buyer can go through all the alternative pieces of paper that he has available to use in a merger. For instance, he may have straight preferreds. On an after-tax basis, a straight preferred with a yield of approximately 6% in early 1970, would have a multiple of about 17 times.

The whole name of the game, at least in the immediate future, is to use those pieces of paper that have the maximum multiple. Thus, if the buyer is doing a taxable transaction, he should use straight debentures (after using his cash), because straight debentures can sell for 25 to perhaps 30 times earnings. As a result, he is probably using the least expensive paper.

I say probably because I am making one important assumption here, which is that the buyer has a current price/earnings ratio of under 25, and his common stock is also selling for under 25. Naturally, the game changes if he has a high price/earnings ratio of, say, 50 times.

Let us talk, first of all, about a price/earnings ratio of 15 to 20 times. Under these circumstances, debentures would be immediately less expensive than common stock.

Then, perhaps, the next level would be debentures with some warrants, where the buyer would be putting in just a little bit of an equity kicker, but he would not have to give very much common stock to do the transaction.

A third level of expense would be convertible debentures, a situation that requires less common stock than in the case of straight common stock because usually it can be sold for a little premium over its conversion value.

In the case of tax-free transactions, probably straight preferred would be cheapest and common stock the most expensive form of equity to give in the transaction.

As I indicated before, the game is different if the buyer has a high multiple on his common stock of, say, 30, 40 or 50 times, because under those circumstances his price/earnings ratio is greater for both convertible and straight debentures.

As a rule, you are probably projecting levels of earnings' growth which mean that three or four years from now your price/earnings ratio of the common stock at that point is less than 25 times earnings.

If such were the actual case, then you could argue that on an immediate basis it would help your per-share earnings more to use common stock in doing an acquisition. But, if you were to project out for five years, it would probably help your earnings more to use some other kind of paper.

In most instances, if your balance sheet can carry it, paper is cheaper to use than equity. I guess it is clear at this point that I usually prefer debt to equity.

Other Alternatives. The buyer can use a contingent payout, which may be an inexpensive way of doing a transaction, where he makes a minimal down payment, and additional payments for the earnings growth of the selling company. This is a special sort of circumstance, and the cost of that capital is a little harder to determine.

Obviously, in some instances, it is desirable to have an arrangement in which payments are minimized until the buyer has seen the performance. This can of course create problems in some companies, such as limiting control over the activities of the acquired company. But it is probably the cheapest of all payment forms, because the buyer is certain about the earnings before he has to pay any money.

In summary, once the buyer has decided on a taxable or tax-free transaction, and has therefore limited himself to certain kinds of paper, he is now in a position to decide what is the cheapest kind of capital. In a taxable transaction, he would normally use as much debt as possible. Then, he would use the next more expensive form of equity financing, and rank it in much the same way he would if he were deciding on various methods to raise capital for a piece of equipment.

Impact of Dividends. Frequently, sellers want a certain dividend level. In the case of tax-free transactions, the convertible preferred, or preferred in some form, must be structured to provide adequate dividends in the event that common does not have a high enough dividend level to meet the dividend levels of the company to be acquired.

In a taxable transaction, enough debentures, or convertible debentures, have to be used to achieve the necessary dividend level before turning to warrants or other "funny" pieces of paper which have a lower cost of capital but which do not provide the seller with any dividend participation.

Finally, the buyer needs to take care of those people who are concerned about downside protection. This is something that he can usually do with dividends. If he provides, say, a 6% yield, then most of his investors are willing to believe that their downside risk is reasonably nominal.

In other instances, he may go to specific guarantees to the seller. For example, he may say that if the seller achieves certain earnings of, say, $400,000 a year after tax, he will guarantee him that the value of his securities will be worth 20 times that or $8 million by a certain fixed date.

There are probably limitations on how many shares the buyer will actually give the seller in that guarantee, as well as limitations on how high the earnings can be.

In short, there are two ways to guarantee the transaction: one is through dividends, and the other is making additional payments in the event your securities depreciate.

Three Case Examples

You might be interested in some of the ways in which mergers and acquisitions that my firm has been closely affiliated with have been put together to illustrate the basic points I have been discussing.

1. Tax-Free Exchange

This is the case of a tax-free transaction in which the seller's objective was to make a tax-free deal for his company for about 17 times earnings. Consider:

I. **Transaction Characteristics**
  1. Seller Goals—
     a) *17 × EPS*
     b) *Tax free*
     c) *No particular dividend goals*
     d) *Registration rights*
  2. Buyer Goals—
     a) *Maximization of EPS increase (Buyer multiple, 30x)*
     b) *Pooling-of-interest accounting*

II. **Solution**
  Stock for stock exchange with rights of registration as long as the registration did not violate pooling-of-interest accounting.

Since the company was owned by one individual, there was no particular dividend objective, although he did want to have the right to register his shares at some future time.

Because of the fact that the seller wanted a tax-free transaction, and the buyer wanted a pooling-of-interest accounting, it was necessary to use equity securities in consummating the transaction. This was a relatively simple thing to achieve. Since the seller had no dividend goals, there was no particular need to use any kind of special security to obtain dividends.

Given the seller's desire for registration rights and presumably a certain amount of liquidity, it made good sense to use the purchasing company's common stock.

Thus this transaction was simply consummated by the exchange of common stock with the guarantee of a registration rights offering.

The leverage is simple in this example in that the buyer has a multiple of 30 times earnings. Therefore, capital is very cheap. The seller has an objective of 17 times. In this particular case, both companies should grow at about the same rate, perhaps 15% a year.

As a result, the buyer is gaining immediate and rather substantial leverage—perhaps 10% in his per-share earnings—because he is using a higher multiple to acquire this company. In addition, because his company and the company he is purchasing are growing at about the same rate, I would expect that he would over time continue to achieve a certain amount of leverage in his per-share earnings.

The balance sheet impact of a transaction like this is rather nominal. Both companies have reasonably clean balance sheets. Therefore, when you join on a pooling-of-interest basis two relatively clean balance sheets, you end up with a balance sheet that looks decent, something that we shall be unable to say about our second example.

2. A Tender Offer

This example pinpoints a number of other problems that are associated with financing a transaction, particularly, a tender offer. To illustrate:

I. Transaction Characteristics
1. Seller Goals—
   a) *Maximum price (23x)*
   b) *Selection of the purchasing party*
2. Buyer Goals—
   a) *Gain control of United Fruit*
   b) *Maximize EPS gains (common stock 35x)* (*Taxable transaction and purchase accounting*)

II. Solution
Purchase Package—
$38.00 of 5½% convertible debentures

0.55 share of common stock
1.50 warrants to purchase stock at $46.00

In this particular case, we are discussing the United Fruit-AMK transaction. Ultimately, after AMK acquired a substantial block of stock in United Fruit, there were a number of parties who made tender offers. Textron agreed on a tax-free transaction, which was subsequently cancelled.

Eventually, after AMK had bought an original 9½% of United Fruit, the two management groups worked out an arrangement whereby AMK was tendering for United Fruit, and the transaction was being done on a friendly basis.

As I interpret the seller's goals—and here I am going to hedge a bit because you may have your own hypothesis about what the goals were—my feeling is that the first goal of the seller was to get a maximal price in his transaction. He ultimately sold for about 23 times earnings.

Second—and this was most important, I suspect, to the managers of United Fruit—they wanted to choose the people with whom they were going to be joining, the purchasing party; they were going on the auction block, and they wanted to select their own master.

On the other hand, the buyer's goals in this kind of transaction were, first, to gain control of the company and, second, to maximize the per-share earnings by doing the transaction.

Now, according to the prospectus, the buyer's multiple was about 35 times. I say "according to the prospectus," because there were such a lot of nonrecurring items.

There are a number of reasons why this was a taxable transaction. Generally speaking, except for strategy reasons, I do not think a nontaxable transaction should be used in a tender offer set of circumstances.

Even if you should use common stock or convertible preferred in a tender offer, you have to get at least 80% of the shares tendered to you within a certain time period in order to make it a nontaxable transaction. It is extremely unlikely that this will ever happen.

Although I have heard of instances where managers have called up the principals of a company they wanted to acquire and said, "Gentlemen, we are going to offer to your shareholders a tax-free securities exchange," as a rule this is a ploy—a kind of strategy which the seller offers even though it is unlikely that he can deliver. It is highly unlikely that they can make the transaction tax-free under normal circumstances, unless it is a friendly thing, which these deals usually are not, as you know.

Both convertible debentures and warrants are normally used only in taxable transactions. It so happened in this case that a little over half a share of common stock was also used, not because it was cheap but principally because it was needed to make the balance sheet reasonable.

In other words, the seller reached the point where he used as much debt and as many warrants as were possible. He had to turn to using some equity to make the balance sheet sensible in this particular circumstance.

The convertible debentures, of course, had the benefit of giving a substantial dividend to the United Fruit stockholders. Further, these had the leverage of selling at about a 15% premium over the common stock.

The warrants also had a certain leverage in that their exercise price was $46, since the premium varied in relationship with the common. (At the time of this transaction, AMK's common was approximately $50 per share.)

All of these factors then made sense in terms of meeting the goals of United Fruit's shareholders by providing a good dividend, a taxable transaction, and a shelter for which the company management had been looking.

3. Sale of a Subsidiary

This example is particularly interesting because it is a terribly complex transaction. In this day and age where high-technology companies have often sold at extraordinarily high multiples of

50 to 100 times earnings, this was the case of a company that desired to sell one of its high-technology divisions which was barely breaking even. Thus we see:

I. Transaction Characteristics

1. Seller Goals and Problems—

   a) *How to maintain stock price with the sale of its most glamorous technical subsidiary. (Stock 50x multiple apparently due to subsidiary which constituted 20% of revenues but none of earnings.)*

   b) *Liquid securities or cash*

2. Buyer Goals—

   a) *Mimimize dilution. (Purchaser stock 18x. The purchaser is many times the size of the subsidiary so earnings dilution can effectively be buried within the buyer operations.)*

   b) *Avoid good will. (i.e., pay book or get a pooling of interest.)*

II. Solution

????

Despite its lack of contribution to profits, the very fact that the division to be sold was a high-technology operation—and thus was highly exciting in the eyes of outsider investors—boosted the entire company's image to the point where, despite other mundane activities, its multiple was selling at 50 times earnings.

Subsequently, the company managers had discussions with a prospective buyer—one of the really large U.S. corporations —that was selling at 18 times earnings. The corporation was willing to pay $100 million for the division and could easily absorb the merger in terms of practically no earnings dilution.

However, the selling company managers figured that if they sold the division for the $100 million offered, they might be losing out on an extraordinary multiple of perhaps $200 million worth of capitalization of their company because of this one division. In a sense, they would be justified in selling it since they were otherwise limited in what they could do with it. In another sense, though, they would lose the glamorous price/earnings ratio which it brought to the rest of their company.

At best, the company managers felt that the market was irrational. Thus they were frustrated as to what their proper solution should be. This is the reason why you see all those question marks down at the "solution" line in this example; the selling managers never could reach agreement on the proper course of action to take.

There probably are solutions to this problem, but my associates and I never found them. Therefore, I think this third example illustrates that no matter how clever you are at packaging mergers or acquisitions, sometimes there is just nothing that you can seem to do to close the transaction.

Concluding Note

I really think that in a merger and acquisition transaction the important element is to determine the goals of both parties. Once you determine those goals, you can isolate some key criteria: (1) whether it is to be a tax-free or taxable transaction; (2) the dividend levels; and (3) whether it is to be a pooling or purchase accounting.

You can provide for the downside risk of the seller.

Most importantly, you can look at the impact of this transaction on your entire balance sheet, and pick the optimal paper in terms of those securities that will meet these criteria and yet have the least cost of capital.

Then, you add a little bit of luck, and I suspect a spark of genius, and hopefully you are able to package a merger or acquisition transaction that can be most meaningful for your company.

Floor Discussion

Question: On the United Fruit-AMK tender offer, what was the market price of the stock at the time of the transaction?

Castle: I believe the initial 9½% of the stock was purchased at approximately $56. Prior to that point in time, the stock had been trading around $50. The price of the ultimate transaction is also subject to great debate, but it took place in about the $85 to $90 a share range.

Question: In a simple tax-free transaction, under your solution, what is the problem of the right to register beyond what that is?

Castle: A registration limits a company as far as doing a lot of kinds of transactions because, as you know, there are many disclosure problems. Although not the most important, registration rights is usually a negotiable item.

Question: For your first example, were the companies fairly close in size, or was one much larger than the other one?

Castle: The companies would be a factor of one to ten.

Question: So the multiple would not be dragged down?

Castle: No, not at all. The buyer was ten times the size of the seller.

Question: In United Fruit, what was deemed to be the business synergy there?

Castle: Very nominal. At that point in time, United Fruit was probably looking for a savior, not synergy.

Question: Is it mainly financial in this case?

Castle: Yes.

Question: What was the final solution of your Example 3?

Castle: As I said, that is one of those things that we cry about a little bit. The transaction just didn't go. There is always a possibility it will be resurrected again.

Chapter 18

THE ROLE OF
A THIRD PARTY
IN ACQUISITIONS

Charles Zabriskie, Jr.

We at Peat, Marwick believe we know something about the acquisition business and I think it might be helpful if I share with you some of my experiences in acting as a third party for nearly a decade.

I think of you, the reader, as really a third party. In an acquiring company, if you are the officer in charge of acquisitions and mergers, you are really charged with the responsibility of finding, analyzing, and bringing together situations. In addition, you must sell your board of directors and your chief executive officer on the fact that a given situation is the right one for your company.

Mr. Zabriskie is a Principal of Peat, Marwick, Mitchell & Co., serving as the accounting firm's coordinator for all acquisition activities on a national basis.

On the other hand, you are the third party in talking with the principals of a company that you want to acquire, because you in essence are the middle man. If a man is to be called a real third party, in my judgment, he must represent the buyer. Incidentally, my firm normally represents only the buyer in acquisition and merger negotiations.

The third party—whether it is you, me, or an investment banker—basically is an individual (or a firm) that attempts to locate or find acquisitions that meet a particular plan. He then attempts to bring the individuals together. He analyzes the rudiments of the situation, assists in negotiations, and helps to set the yardsticks for the value, means, and terms of the proposed exchange.

One thing I have learned is that the primary contribution a third party can make is in what I call the people area. A third party must be mindful of the rationale and objectives of the individuals involved. He does not have to be a fantastic analyst—that is, he does not have to be a Houdini with numbers.

Rather, he must know where the individuals have been, where they are going, and how they are going to get there. And this means, of course, what they are trying to acquire.

A company with a large staff of junior analysts does not necessarily make the company any better at the acquisition business. Often, large companies which have one or two persons in their acquisition departments are the most effective. Even if a company has a top flight acquisition man or department, the participation of the chief executive officer is absolutely a must. Without his sincere and deep involvement, I do not think a company can ever be a good acquirer.

Important Considerations

As your company's intermediary in the role of, say, vice president of acquisitions and mergers, director of corporate growth, or whatever your title, there are a number of points you should keep in mind as you proceed in any given acquisition project.

For one thing, you should shoot with a rifle, not a shotgun. In other words, you have only a limited number of hours in a week and too many of those are spent in airplanes. Thus you have to zero in on your targets. For another thing, any deal worth pursuing should be well documented and personally known to the third party.

Does a 'Fit' Exist?

Of prime importance, a third party should first meet with the principal owners and officers of the seller and know their desires about such things as price, type of exchange, product lines, marketing and distribution techniques, and so forth.

Quite often, you have to work with people who do not seem to have a fix on the price; but, a price should be worked out very quickly, say on the first or second meeting. Price is tantamount to a deal, although price is often considered somewhat sacred and left behind.

In my opinion, you should get to the heart of this matter. If the price is not reasonable, then it is time to look at the next deal. Frankly, there are more deals available than you might imagine; actually, there are hundreds and hundreds of them. The question is: "Which one is for you?"

The type of exchange is important. Is there a heavy dividend requirement? Are the principals talking about preferred stock or common stock? Sometimes growth-minded companies do not have a high yielding common stock; therefore, they do not have any intention of declaring cash dividends.

The product lines must be considered. What are the product lines? What percentage does each line comprise of the whole picture? Is one 26%? Another 59%? Still another 15%? How much of the volume is military business? Will current business be retained? And what is the replacement market?

How does the company market its products or services? Does it use outside sales representatives? Are those reps properly directed? Or does the company use its own sales force?

Does it have branch offices? And so on. I know of a company in Cleveland that has no interest in any outside agent or "rep" situation because it has its own force of over 800 salesmen. Thus whatever new product lines it acquires, it markets through its own sales force. The principals feel that this is one of their corporate strengths.

What about distribution? Is it direct? Does the company do its own warehousing? Is it interested in selling large quantities to a few customers? Or is it a company that sells small quantities to many?

What is the depth of management? This, second only to price, should be the most important consideration.

The size of the contemplated transaction, along with the intended number of acquisitions, should be seriously considered.

On the one hand, I have never been involved in a deal for less than $700,000, and I consider this rather small. In fact, an acquisition of $700,000, unless it is a specific fit, will probably give you too many problems. The contribution to earnings of a deal of this size is probably not worth the effort and expense necessary to consummate the transaction and to manage the subsequent situation.

On the other hand, I do not think consummating, say, 20 deals a year makes you a great acquisition company. The important goal is to make the right acquisitions—ones that fit and become a part of the total corporate pie. Even though you can buy a company for part down today and part tomorrow, it still had better be a good fit. If you "get married," you have to live with them regardless of whether or not they achieve their ultimate payout.

Of course, patterns in distribution of ownership are important. Quite often, when you are talking to the president of a company, you are not talking to the owner; even when you are talking to the board of directors, you may not be talking to the principal owners.

Who holds the key to making a deal with a company you

wish to acquire? It may be a fund in Chicago; it may be a lawyer in Toledo; it may be the president; or it may be a little old lady. The individual motivations and desires of the key officers, the directors, and stockholders are important. I recall the case of a company that was growing like a weed. The chief executive officer's annual salary was $55,000. None of the other officers made over $30,000. They were all 45 to 55 years of age and there were no stock options available. They loved to run the company on a conference or group basis.

So the easiest way to do that deal was to get everybody in —especially the hungry ones—and to talk about stock options, increased salaries, and profit-sharing. The next thing you know, that company president had more fires to put out than he could handle.

There is some technique that works in every transaction. Everybody you deal with in an acquisition is motivated in one way or another. Before a profitable meeting of key executives of both companies is arranged, this homework should be done. Armed with a proper background in this important area, the third party can shape a deal for the buyer.

What Motivates the Parties?

Basically, after we have determined that a "fit" exists, our modus operandi is to make sure that we have met with both the buyer and seller before the executives meet. We insist on this so that we can understand what each party is seeking, what makes them desirous of making a deal, and what motivates them. This assures that first meeting will likely be much more effective. If the first meeting is not successful, it may take months to get them back on the track.

Timing is also important. I remember one situation that started out as approximately an $8 million ticket. Through procrastination and poor timing, the deal was finally closed nine months later for $28 million.

In another situation on the West Coast, I spotted an available company in the aerospace parts industry. I brought the situation to the attention of a major company in the Midwest. We were talking about $10 per share, but the major company did not want the West Coast company. The owners were afraid of too much dependence on military output.

The unfortunate reality is that 70% of the business was commercial, going into intercontinental long-range passenger aircraft. Within three years, that aerospace company's stock soared to over $100 a share.

I cannot begin to count up the number of times I have seen a deal that had its price go up substantially over the next six months. As the third party, you have to be in a position to act quickly—to look at a situation, to see if there is a fit, and to determine if the price is right.

An intermediary can help nudge a deal along by possessing a strong knowledge of the purchaser's securities, corporate history, and growth potential. With such knowledge, he may be in a position to indicate the expected market reaction should the transaction be culminated. This can be invaluable, because if you know your buyer and what the earnings input per share will be, you should have a good feel for what the stock will probably do in a favorable market.

At Peat, Marwick, Mitchell & Co., we try to weigh equally the motives, needs, and desires of both the purchaser and the seller. This unique position permits us, as a consultant, to render advice in negotiations, keeping in mind the demands of each party, thus creating the true role of a third party.

A Note of Caution

I feel very strongly that a good negotiator or third party should never put himself in a position of being a self-styled expert in highly technical areas such as taxation, SEC practice, and state or corporate law. He should not attempt to establish the value of an unusual asset or earnings pattern without profound knowledge and expertise in the necessary field. There are two principal reasons for my cautioning you about this:

1. If you qualify yourself as an expert and you are wrong, you weaken your stature in future negotiations. You may no longer be able to keep negotiations on the track.

2. It is all but impossible for you to be technically capable in all of these specialized areas. A true adviser's role is lost in deciding important issues without consulting with each of the companies' staffs.

Often, the best way to massage a deal is to work with key officials—such as the vice president of finance, the controller, and the general counsel of the respective companies—relative to the problems and positions of each party.

Every once in a while somebody asks me what I consider to be the most important contribution made by a third party. My answer is always, "Just plain people." Often, when I look at an aborted deal, the failure to interpret the seller's motivations, desires, and personal problems is revealed as the most important factor responsible. It is in this area that a third party can be of the greatest assistance.

Four Essentials

Another question I hear quite often is: What are the most important factors that lead to a truly successful acquisition program? After personally having initiated over 60 successful acquisition transactions since 1964, I have concluded that there are four significant considerations:

First, the chief executive officer should be actively involved in the implementation of the acquisition program and he must respond promptly to opportunities. The chief executive officer can get on a plane and, within hours, meet anywhere in the world with the seller. In my opinion, it is a necessity for him to participate in negotiations. He is neither going, say, to a board meeting to discuss the corporate pension fund, nor on a vacation. But he is going to discuss a tremendously important deal.

Second, and I touched on this earlier, in your role as third party you should pinpoint objectives in developing a plan for acquisitions. You have to know what you are looking for, you have to know where you have been, and you have to know where you are going.

Third, you must seek a good fit. I once read an article in a leading business magazine which stated that one out of every three acquisitions becomes a problem. Obviously, if there is not a proper fit, problems are likely to arise.

I recall one I was involved in. This was a situation in which a rug-cleaning equipment manufacturer acquired a garden equipment company. The problem was that rug-cleaning equipment and garden equipment cannot be successfully marketed by the same techniques. This was tried to the misfortune of the companies, and the deal quickly turned sour.

Fourth, consider the personalities involved and gear the negotiation approach to these personalities.

I remember going into New England with the chief executive officer of a large listed company to visit with the president of a small "available" company. Having done our homework, we decided that we were going to make an offer. We listened to the president describe his business, its history, and its finances. Then, at that point, the chief executive officer of the buying company took an envelope out of his pocket, pushed a couple of figures around, and announced that he would pay the president $15 million for his company. The seller was quite perplexed and upset; he did not want to end his business career on the back of an envelope.

The deal was finally made about nine months later. But

even then, we had to bypass the chief executive officer and bring in other key officials from the buying company who were more compatible with the seller's personality.

I recall another situation. I had been staying at the Fairmont Hotel in San Francisco on a project for a giant corporation. From there, I flew to the Midwest for another client, rented a car, and drove about 120 miles to a small country town. I checked into my hotel—$4 per day, no TV, no phone, and no alarm clock. For dinner, I went to the only restaurant open— a combination diner and gas station on the corner. The best meal it had was for $1. Having just left the Fairmont, this was some change.

Nevertheless, the next day I visited the company, and it was a real beauty. It had $4.5 million in sales, $450,000 in profits after taxes, and $1.7 million net worth. It was an industry leader and several top-flight companies were chasing it.

I sat down with the attorney-secretary of the company, and shortly thereafter in waltzed a man with a buttoned sweater and no shirt. To say the least, he was quite casual. After a moment or two of discussion and no introduction having been made, I turned to the informally dressed gentleman and asked, "Are you the sales manager?" He said, "No, I am the president."

I certainly had not put my best foot forward. After three meetings, I had made very little progress in trying to arrange for this acquisition for my client. Sensing a personality clash, I took one of my associates out for a further meeting. My associate was from Brooklyn and had never been to that part of the country. He said that he had never seen so much land and scenic beauty. Furthermore, he had never been fishing.

Well, it just so happened that the president had a summer home in the mountains, and he liked to disappear now and then from the factory to go fishing. To make a beautiful story, my associate fished with the president, went to baseball games with him, and so on. Within a week, the deal that I could not move was completed.

The lesson to learn here is that (and I have seen it so often) when a deal slows up, be careful that it is not because of the personalities of the people involved.

In summary, to be a good third party does not involve a great deal of analysis. You must know the basic financial information relating to the company, the personalities involved, anticipated price requirements, and the manner in which the potential buyer might meet these objectives.

With this understanding, third parties can be a key factor in bringing about many successful mergers and acquisitions that would otherwise never be consummated.

Chapter 19

WARRANTS— AN OLD TOOL WITH NEW USES

John S. R. Shad

A warrant is a security that entitles the holder to purchase another security (usually a common stock) at a stated price until a stated expiration date. When originally issued, warrants usually have a life of five or more years. Some corporations have perpetual warrants outstanding which never expire.

The "exercise value" of a warrant is determined by subtracting the warrant exercise price from the stock price. There-

Mr. Shad is Executive Vice President of E. F. Hutton & Company. As the head of the Corporate Finance Division, he has been instrumental in consummating numerous corporate financings. He is also the author of "The Financial Realities of Mergers," *Harvard Business Review,* November-December 1969, p. 133.

fore, if a stock is trading at $100 and the warrant entitles the holder to purchase the stock at $100, the warrant has an exercise value of zero. However, the market will generally pay a premium over the exercise value of a warrant in return for the long-term call on the stock at a fixed price.

In the example I just mentioned, it would not be unusual for the warrant to trade at $40. Thus the "option premium" would be $40, or 40% of the price of the stock. If the stock was trading at $200 and the warrant at $140, the option premium would still be $40, but it would be referred to as a 20% premium, since the premium would equal 20% of the price of the stock.

Historical Pattern

Warrants have been in use for over a hundred years. They were commonly used in the corporate reorganizations that came out of the Great Depression, when the common stocks of many companies were wiped out by the claims of creditors.

During the post World War II period, increasing use has been made of warrants as "equity kickers." For example, debentures with warrants are more commonly used than convertible debentures in private placements with institutional lenders. While such lenders prefer debentures with warrants, corporations favor convertible debentures, since the holders have to make a decision as to whether to take cash or convert their debt into equity securities.

During periods of tight money, institutional lenders sometimes insist that their warrants be exercisable either through payment of cash or the tender of an equivalent principal amount of the debentures. Thus they have all the advantages of a convertible security and none of the disadvantages.

The important point to bear in mind is that when a warrant is used as an "equity kicker," it enables the corporation to obtain funds at a lower interest rate, but the company rarely receives the "fair value" of such warrants.

Major Breakthrough

Even though warrants are "old tools," they have been one of the most difficult securities to value, due to the fact that their value is in part—but only in part—a function of the value of the underlying common stock. It was not until mid-1967, when Dr. Jack Sheldon at UCLA reported the results of a multiple regression computer analysis of warrants, that a reasonably reliable valuation technique was evolved[1]. I shall briefly describe Sheldon's formula, which is quite complicated, and then provide some simple rules of thumb for the valuation of warrants.

Sheldon's Formula. His objective was not to develop a theory as to what warrants "should be" worth, but rather to refine the variables which determine the prices at which they actually sell in the market place. From past studies, it was known that the maximum prices at which warrants sell are 75% of the price of the underlying stock. The minimum prices at which they sell are their exercise value, which is determined by subtracting the warrant exercise price from the price of the stock.

For example, if a stock is trading at $100 and the warrant entitles the holder to purchase the stock for $90, the minimum value of the warrant is $10. If a warrant does not at least sell at its exercise value, arbitrageurs will simultaneously sell the stock short, purchase and exercise the warrant, and deliver the stock thus obtained to cover the short.

Sheldon's objective was to determine the price between the maximum and minimum value at which warrants normally sell. He evolved the accompanying formula which is remarkably accurate. You subtract the minimum from the maximum value, multiply the remainder by $\sqrt[4]{\frac{M}{72}}$ (.47 - 4.25 Y + .17 L), and add the product to the minimum value.

M = the number of months before the warrant expires.

Y = the yield on the underlying stock.

1. See "The Relation of the Price of a Warrant to the Price of Its Associated Stock," *Financial Analysts Journal*, May-June 1967 and July-August 1967.

L = a factor that is added if the stock is listed on an exchange.

I shall briefly explain the significance of these factors.

The longer the life of a warrant, the greater its value. The market will obviously pay a higher price for a five-year warrant to purchase a stock at a fixed price, than for a one-year warrant to purchase the stock at the same price. However, it should be noted that the market will not pay a significantly higher price for a ten-year than for a five-year warrant. The premium begins to decline sharply about three years before the warrant expiration date. On the day before a warrant expires, it is of course only worth its exercise value. On the day after a warrant expires, it is of no value.

The investor has the opportunity to either purchase the stock or the warrant. When he purchases the warrant, he gives up the right to receive any dividends. Therefore, the lower the yield on a stock, the greater the value of the warrant.

Warrants that are traded on a national exchange generally sell at a higher price than comparable warrants which are traded over-the-counter, because listed warrants are generally more marketable and can be purchased on margin.

Rules of Thumb

A five-year listed warrant to purchase a nondividend paying stock at its current market price will typically sell at a price equal to approximately 50% of the price of the stock. Such a warrant purchased at such a premium involves no greater downside risk and offers twice as great appreciation potentiality as the underlying common stock.

One should never purchase a warrant unless he believes the underlying common stock offers favorable appreciation potentialities; however, Sheldon's analysis demonstrated that the premiums that the market will pay for warrants are not a function of the attractiveness of the stock, its volatility, or the price level of the warrant itself. Prior to Sheldon's analysis, these and a host of other factors were thought to be of significance in valuing warrants.

Nondilutionary Financing

Unsophisticated critics are quick to point out that warrants represent potential dilution for corporate issuers. Which is better, actual dilution through the sale of common stock, or potential dilution through the sale of warrants? In fact, many recent warrant offerings have been *nondilutionary*.

Superficial observers often fail to take into account the funds a company receives on the sale of warrants and the additional funds received on the exercise of such warrants. The employment of such funds can of course generate more per-share earnings on the additional shares to be issued on exercise of the warrants, than the company is currently or expected to earn on its existing shares.

A Case Illustration. The 250,000 unit offering which we underwrote for Kaufman and Broad, the nation's second largest homebuilders, provides a case in point. We are investment bankers for Kaufman and Broad, and I am a director of the company. The offering consisted of 250,000 shares of common stock with warrants to purchase 500,000 shares of common stock. Thus each unit consisted of one share of common stock plus two warrants.

The day before the offering, KB closed at 32½ and the offering was made at $65 per unit. Thus the purchasers paid $32.50 for one share of common stock and $16.25 for each of the five-year warrants to purchase the common stock at $32.50. As in the rule of thumb above, the investors paid a 50% premium for the five-year call on KB common stock at its current market price.

The net proceeds to the company amounted to $15,312,500. For the past several years, KB has been earning approximately 30% before taxes on its equity capital; however, if it is assumed KB merely uses the $15.3 million to retire bank loans at the 8% prime rate, the annual interest saving would amount to

$1,224,000 and the after-tax interest saving would amount to $612,000 or $2.45 per share on the additional 250,000 shares to be outstanding following the offering. This compares with the $.83 KB earned during the 12 months preceding the offering and the $1 KB expects to earn during the year following the offering.

Thus the per-share earnings on the additional shares to be outstanding (even if it is assumed that the proceeds of the offering will only be used to retire bank loans at the prime rate) will be three times as great as KB's per-share earnings during the year prior to the offering, and two and a half times as great as the expected per-share earnings during the year following the offering. If it is assumed KB will earn the same rate of return on this new equity capital as it has earned on its equity capital for the past several years, the per-share earnings on the additional shares to be outstanding will amount to an extraordinary $9.00 per share!

In addition, *if* the warrants are exercised five years hence, KB will receive an additional $16,250,000 (i.e., 500,000 shares X $32.50 = $16,250,000). If these additional funds are employed at the same rate that KB has earned on its equity over the past several years, the per-share earnings on the additional 500,000 shares to be outstanding will amount to $4.87. While KB's future prospects are excellent, no one expects the company's earnings to increase better than fivefold over the next five years.

Thus this financing is clearly not dilutionary at the outset and there is every reason to believe that it will not be dilutionary when and *if* the warrants are exercised five years hence. To the contrary, this financing will clearly contribute significantly to the company's per-share earnings.

Further, the KB warrants contain a relatively new feature, which can be employed to the advantage of both the company and the warrant holders, to in effect force exercise of the warrants at any time over the next five years. The Warrant Agreement provides that KB may, on 15 days notice, at any time and from time to time, voluntarily reduce the $32.50 exercise price by as much as 33.3% for 21 to 45 days. Thus KB could drop the warrant exercise price to as low as $21.68 for a brief period of time.

In the absence of extraordinary circumstances, it will clearly be in the interest of the warrant holders to exercise if the company significantly reduces the warrant exercise price in this fashion. The company will of course only avail itself of this option if it believes it can effectively employ the additional funds to be received on exercise of the options.

As is conventional, the KB warrant exercise price will be adjusted downward and the number of shares increased in the event of subsequent stock dividends or splits.

I believe it can be concluded that such a warrant financing is highly advantageous to both the issuing corporation and the investing public. As previously mentioned, the warrants involve no greater downside risk and offer twice as great appreciation potentialities as the common stock. In addition, the financing is clearly not dilutionary at the outset and there appears to be every reason to believe it will also not be dilutionary when and if the warrants are exercised.

Corporate Acquisitions

Now I would like to briefly describe some of the possible uses of warrants in corporate acquisitions.

Since warrant holders have no dividend or voting rights, they are not stockholders and warrants do not qualify as "voting equity securities." Under the Internal Revenue Code, mergers and consolidations effected through the use of other than voting equity securities are taxable transactions. There are various limited qualifications of this generalization, but the use of warrants along with voting equity securities can "taint" the entire transaction for tax purposes.

Although it is sailing close to the wind, some mergers have been effected through the use of voting convertible preferreds (which qualify as voting equity securities) that incorporate an additional warrant feature. Such preferreds are convertible into the common stock for a period of years on the payment of a specified sum. Since they typically pay a modest dividend, they derive a significant element of their value from their warrant feature. If they derive over half of their fair market value from the warrant feature, they clearly do not qualify as "voting equity securities," and the entire transaction may be taxable.

However, there are circumstances in which it may be in the interest of the parties for the transaction to be taxable. For example, if the selling company's shareholders have a higher tax basis for their shares than the present value of the company, it may be to their advantage to effect a tax loss on the transaction which can be used to offset other taxable gains.

Another situation would be one in which a company is being acquired for less than its net worth. By treating the transaction as a taxable purchase of assets, the selling company may be able to establish a tax loss which can be carried back three years and result in a substantial cash tax refund, which adds to the selling shareholders' net realization from the transaction.

It is also sometimes in the interest of the parties for the acquiring company to in effect pay the potential capital gains tax to be incurred by the selling company's shareholders by increasing the price accordingly.

When it is the desire of the parties to effect a transaction on a taxable basis, warrants often offer unique advantages. They add to the issuing company's equity base, and thus enable additional borrowing on better terms than would otherwise have been available. No dividends (or interest) are paid on warrants and they provide the issuing company with a source of future funds, when and if they are exercised.

Residual Securities

Warrants are residual securities if, at the time they are issued, the market value of the stock is 125% or more than the warrant exercise price. For example, if a stock is trading at $50 and warrants are issued which are exercisable at $40, the warrants would be residual securities on the date of issuance and the company would have to report its per-share earnings as if the warrants had been exercised.

In addition, outstanding warrants may become residual securities if the stock sells at 150% or more than the warrant exercise price for a six-month period. For example, if the warrant was exercisable at $100 per share, and the stock sold at $150 for six months, the warrants would become residual securities.

Warrants become nonresidual securities if the stock sells at less than the warrant exercise price for a six-month period. For example, if the warrant was exercisable at $100 and the stock sells at $99 or less for six months, the warrants may then be treated as nonresidual securities.

If a warrant is treated as a residual security, the issuing company assumes that the warrant is exercised and that the proceeds are used to reduce the company's bank loans. Thus the company increases the number of its outstanding shares and also its net income by the after-tax interest saving. If a company does not have any bank or term loans, it can assume that the proceeds were used to purchase government securities or commercial paper.

Floor Discussion

Question: Do you see any possibility of issuing warrants that are not attached to other securities?

Shad: Yes, as warrants become better understood by the investing public, I believe there is a good possibility that a number of companies will do public offerings of warrant issues that are not packaged with other securities. In addition, companies which have warrant issues outstanding that are actively trading on an exchange, could use them just as readily as other securities to effect acquisitions. Their market value would be readily ascertainable, and as previously indicated, under certain circumstances, warrants in fact offer a more attractive risk reward ratio than the underlying common stock.

Question: Are you indicating that it is always cheaper to issue warrants than common stock? I recently read about a company that was issuing $1.5 million of warrants and only had $2.5 million of common stock outstanding. Would you care to comment on this?

Shad: While the proportions you mention sound quite unusual, I would need additional facts in order to express an opinion as to whether the company was merely flooding the market with "Chinese currency," or if the financing appeared to make sense from both the issuing company's and the investing public's point of view. The market value of the common stock, the offering price, exercise price and life of the warrants, and the intended use of the proceeds from the financing are all material considerations.

Question: Do you think that if a company has more warrants than common outstanding, the warrants will hold a premium?

Shad: In the case of the Kaufman and Broad offering I mentioned, the company had 3.6 million common shares outstanding prior to the offering. The 250,000 shares sold on the offering brought it up to 3.85 million shares. Thus the 500,000 warrants sold on the offering amount to less than 12% of the 4.35 million shares to be outstanding on exercise of the warrants.

There is of course the point at which the warrants would not command a premium if they represented a disproportionate amount of a company's capitalization. However, in order to pinpoint this level, it would be necessary to determine the point at which the initial sale of the warrants or their subsequent exercise would be dilutionary.

A company which has a disproportionate amount of warrants outstanding, might, for instance, have a difficult time effectively employing the proceeds when the warrants are exercised, if for example those proceeds were to double its equity capital overnight.

Companies should do their level best to maintain a consistent compound annual growth in their per-share earnings. If a company went overboard on the size of a warrant issue, which prevented it from maintaining a consistent compound annual growth in its per-share earnings, it is not likely to be in the company's long-term best interest.

Question: Can you explain in a little more detail how you can force exercise of warrants?

Shad: Yes. The issuer can force the exercise of warrants by dropping the exercise price. This does not truly force the exercise of warrants, in the sense that a company can force the conversion of convertible debentures by calling them, for if they are not converted, they will be retired for cash at a lower price than the holder could have obtained by converting the debentures and selling the stock. However, under certain circumstances, if the exercise price of a warrant is reduced for a short period of time, it can be clearly in the holders' interest to exercise and thus obtain the stock at a much lower price per share than the original exercise price of the warrants.

For example, assume a company had warrants outstanding to purchase its stock at $50 per share, the stock was trading at $50 per share, the warrants only had a two-year life and were therefore trading around $10 per share, and because the company had an immediate use for the funds, it dropped the exercise price 33.3% to $33.50.

Given those conditions, it would be in the warrant holders' interest to exercise their warrants, even if they turned right around and sold the stock, for they might in this fashion realize $16.50, or $6.50 more than the probable market value of the warrants within a few weeks when the warrant exercise price reverted back to $50 per share.

The company might be induced to drop the exercise price, because it had an immediate need for the additional funds which it could employ on a nondilutionary basis. Such funds might also represent a company's cheapest source of equity capital, for no underwriting or other costs are incurred when warrants are exercised.

Chapter 20

CONVERTIBLES—
THE TWO-WAY PLAY

Jerome S. Katzin

Corporate growth can be financed in three ways:

- From the internal generation of funds.
- From outside capital introduced into the business.
- Through acquisitions and mergers.

Convertible securities are an important means of financing in the last two categories. They are a basic medium for enlisting new capital for an enterprise, whether the company is in the early stages of its development or a mature company. More-

---

Mr. Katzin is a Partner of Kuhn, Loeb & Company. A member of the bar, he specializes as a financial adviser to a number of public utilities and regulated industries.

over, they are an important medium of exchange in the ever-popular atmosphere of corporate mergers and acquisitions.

What Is a Convertible?

A convertible security is one which by its terms is exchangeable at the option of the holder, and under specified conditions, into another security. Generally, but not always, the exchange is into an inferior ranking security of the same company.

Different Types

There are various convertible securities. Their range is limited only by the ingenuity of their creators and the willingness of investors to accept them. The most common type is one that is convertible into a junior security, such as a debenture into common stock, or a preferred stock into common stock.

It may also be convertible into the same class of security but with different rights; for example, a nonvoting common, or a limited-dividend common, into ordinary common shares of the same company. This situation occurs most often in a company that goes public for the first time and where a substantial ownership is retained by the original owners. A company may want to forego dividends on their stock (because they do not need the income) and to conserve cash in the company, while at the same time provide the public with some return on its investment. Or they may want to assure voting control, while having less than 50% ownership of the company. Thus they classify the common stock in order to retain or assure these benefits. But they retain the right to convert that classified common stock into ordinary common should they ever want to sell out a part of their holdings. The special reason for the classification then disappears.

A third type of convertible provides for conversion into a portfolio holding of the issuer or into securities of another company, which may be the parent or an affiliated company of the issuer. For example, in 1969 my firm marketed a $60 million issue of convertible debentures for Burmah Oil Company. These debentures are convertible into common shares of Shell Trading & Transport, which is a portfolio holding of Burmah.

The large and growing market in Eurodollar convertible securities is similar in that convertible debentures of a specially formed subsidiary, either in Luxembourg or Delaware, are marketed in Europe primarily to raise dollars for foreign investment. They are guaranteed as to principal and interest by the American parent company, and they are convertible into the common stock of the parent. However, it is not uncommon to raise money abroad and deposit the proceeds in a foreign branch of an American bank, thereby enhancing one's credit back in the United States where conditions might be too tight to get a loan. Essentially, Eurodollars convertible securities are used to invest abroad and, under the limitations on foreign investment, they are what more and more American companies have enlisted to raise the needed capital for expansion abroad.

There is a fourth and rare type of convertible which provides for conversion into a higher ranking security of the same company. For example, this may arise in a merger as a device to give added value to a security in the event that certain contingencies such as, say, a given rate of earnings do not occur. A man may be willing to accept your common stock in exchange for his company, but if you do not perform, then he may want to convert into an outright senior position.

Special Advantages

Let us consider some of the characteristics of convertible securities. A Swiss banker described them as "God's gift to mankind." I do not go completely along with that, but it is easy to understand why they are considered so favorably as a method of investment.

Essentially, convertible securities, whether in the form of a debenture or preferred stock, have the advantage of a two-way play.

They represent a senior security with a fixed income return

and a claim on assets ahead of the underlying common shares. This gives them an apparent measure of safety and assured income that can be a defense against declines in common stock prices or falloffs in earnings which might reduce or eliminate common dividend payouts.

Moreover, if the market value of the residual security into which the debenture or preferred is convertible appreciates, the option or call on a common stock provides a springboard to participate in higher common stock prices. Thus there is the opportunity to benefit from a rise in stock prices from the comparative safety of a debt or senior stock position. This is particularly appealing when there is a period of inflation coupled with an active and rising stock market.

There are institutional investors whose ability by law to purchase equity securities is limited. A convertible debenture provides the permissible way to participate in the equity market.

Another advantage to investors of convertible debentures is in their cost: the brokerage commission is less than that of stock, and the margin requirements are less strigent. Whereas the margin on stock is 80%, on convertible debentures it is only 60%.

Potential Disadvantages

There are some disadvantages to convertible securities.

The protective character of these issues from the investor's point of view is sometimes illusory. When the price of the underlying stock falls below the conversion price, so that there is no immediate significant market value to the conversion right, the debentures will increasingly sell on a yield basis.

Moreover, as the stock price continues to decline, the convertible issue will go to a discount. Since the interest rate in the case of the debenture was imposed from the outset usually less than the credit standing of the issuer required, and since the debenture is usually a subordinated security to other classes of debt, the discount can grow very large, particularly when there is little expectation of recovery in the stock price to the conversion level. It is not unusual to see convertible securities of important companies selling at 68¢ or 70¢ on the dollar.

What Is the Issuer's Position?

There are many considerations involved in a convertible issue from the issuer's point of view.

As indicated earlier, the interest rate on a convertible debenture, or the dividend rate on a convertible preferred, is almost always lower than if the company were issuing the securities without the conversion feature. Thus the carrying cost is less.

Because these securities are always subordinate to other long-term debt, they provide a type of underpinning in the capital structure without going so far as issuing common stock and diluting the equity. In all likelihood, they will eventually be converted into permanent equity capital. Analysts tend to view these convertible securities in the capital structure in this dual position.

An argument is frequently made that the convertibles are essentially equity in the capital base since it is most unlikely that they will be taken out by redemption. Rather, they will be converted into common stock.

The issuance of a convertible delays, and then reduces, the dilution to the common stock which would have occurred had common been issued in the first place. This reduction occurs because public issue conversion prices are usually set between 10% and 20% above the market price of the common at the time of the offering. When the conversion does take place, if indeed it does, the company will have issued 10% to 20% fewer common shares than if it had originally raised the funds directly through a sale of common shares.

The reduction in dilution may even be greater because announcement of a forthcoming common stock issue frequently causes some decline in the price of the outstanding common shares. Thus, if the offering is large in relation to the number of shares outstanding, the new shares may have to be priced at some discount from the market, particularly if the common is offered on rights.

On the other hand, announcement of a convertible debenture issue rarely depresses the price of a stock. Its conversion price is at a premium rather than a discount, and selling costs are less. Moreover, in buoyant markets, when demand for convertibles is strong, announcement of a convertible issue on rights may actually cause some rise in the price of the common stock because of the anticipated value of the subscription rights.

Reporting Earnings

Changes in accounting practice are eliminating what was once considered an important benefit from convertible debentures in that per-share earnings used to be reported on the basis of actual shares outstanding during the period, including any which may have resulted from conversion. Net income was then computed after deduction of interest on the convertible debentures outstanding. Since interest payments were a deductible expense for federal corporate income taxes, the government was in effect absorbing half the carrying costs, and common share earnings were higher as a result.

For the past several years the accounting profession has had this subject under scrutiny and as a result of recent opinions of the Accounting Principles Board (Numbers 9 and 15), the requirement is that per-share earnings must be reported on two bases:

    1. Earnings applicable to each share of common stock, or other residual security outstanding.

    2. On a pro forma basis, assuming conversion of all outstanding convertible securities and exercise of any outstanding warrants and options.

Note the words "residual security." A residual security is defined as one which clearly derives the major portion of its value from its conversion rights or from its common stock characteristics. The concept of a residual security stems from the realization that regardless of how a particular security may be denominated, its character derives from its rights and market status. Thus a convertible debenture selling at a substantial premium in the market, convertible at the option of the holder —and even under certain circumstances callable by the issuer to force conversion—is for all practical purposes an equity security which the company at any time may be required to convert to be reclassified.

Changes in accounting treatment have in no way diminished the use of debentures. Particularly for new money purposes, the convertible debenture remains a preferred type of issue. In fact, under certain market conditions (rising levels of interest rates and a shortage of investment funds for fixed income securities) a company might be able to raise funds on reasonable terms only through convertible debentures.

The convertible preferred, on the other hand, is very rarely used for new money purposes. Its greatest appeal is in acquisitions. Convertible preferred terms are flexible and can be tailored to the situation. The exchange is tax free. In addition, the market price provides a premium which improves the value of the consideration at no cost to the issuer. And, finally, it is possible to limit voting powers so as to preserve the pre-existing balance of control.

What Are the Security's Provisions?

Most conversion issues are convertible on the same terms over their life. Some provide for a diminishing conversion ratio; in other words, they step up in price, either at stated intervals or on a graduated percentage basis. This is a mechanism for encouraging conversion. As each change date approaches, the investor must decide whether to exercise his option and convert his holding, or to remain with his protected senior position and see some erosion in the value of his call.

The exchange ratio can be stated in two different ways:

1. *Convertible at a stated price per share.*

For example, convertible into common at $25 a share. Thus each $1,000 debenture can be exchanged into 40 shares of common stock. This is the usual formula for convertible debentures since they have a face value, and it would be the same formula for a preferred stock with a par value, which is generally required for public utility companies.

2. *Convertible into a stated number of shares.*

For example, each share of preferred is convertible into half a share of common. This is the usual formula for convertible preferred shares which either have no par value, or have a par value without significance.

Conversion Privileges

When a company wants to delay conversion indefinitely, provision is made for an ascending number of common shares into which the preferred is convertible. Thus the preferred continues not only to act in the market in harness with the common, but it also becomes more valuable each year. These are known as accelerating or accumulating preferred issues.

For example, the accumulating convertible stock of Ling-Temco-Vought, which was convertible into three quarters of a share of common stock during 1967, rises incrementally for 12 years to 1.5 shares in 1980 and thereafter. The shares receive no cash dividends, but they do receive a 3% annual stock dividend. Strangely enough, this particular issue does not appear to have any preference rights. It is not denominated as either a preference or common stock. It is simply called accumulating convertible stock.

Debentures are normally convertible from issuance until

maturity. It is not uncommon to delay the commencement of the right of conversion for a few days in the case of a public issue in order to let the market settle down, or for a period of up to a full year in special circumstances. Eurodollar convertibles are generally not convertible for the first year. This is to keep the common stock from coming back into the U.S. market and counting against the investment credit that the corporation has.

These delayed conversion rights also occur in merger situations when the exchange is based in part on a projection of improved per-share earnings, or when the ownership is concentrated and the management of the acquirer wants to restrain conversion into full voting rights.

Occasionally, the conversion privilege will terminate before the maturity of the debenture; in the case of preferreds, it will operate for a fixed term of years. The main purpose of this feature is to set off a mechanism to force conversion and to prevent the threat of dilution from being a permanent overhang on the market.

Convertible securities are callable at the option of the issuer on due notice, and usually with payment of a call premium equal to the interest or the fixed dividend rate. In the case of debentures, this conversion premium may be scaled down annually or semiannually to maturity. There may also be a nonrefunding provision, at least in a tight money market, for the early years.

There is usually a provision that the holder can exercise the conversion after the call has been published, and before it becomes effective, since the main purpose of the call in most cases is to force conversion rather than to repay the debt.

The issuer may send out a call for a variety of reasons: (a) in connection with a new financing plan to simplify the capitalization; (b) to clear up a small amount of the issue that is still not converted and remains as an overhang on the market; (c) in a merger or acquisition transaction where it may just be too complicated to carry over the conversion rights into the new combined company; (d) to remove particular covenants; (e) to effect ownership control; and (f) in a situation where the earnings have reached the point that the dilution effect is so small it is desirable to eliminate these securities from the capital structure.

Protective Provisions

Convertibles have very few of the protections normally associated with debt securities or quality preferreds. The debentures are generally subordinated to any amount of senior debt which might be issued in the future and permit unlimited additional issues of subordinated debt of the same class.

There are usually no working capital requirements or coverage tests. However, there is usually a restriction on accumulated surplus limiting dividend payout. In addition, preferreds sometimes carry a modest sinking fund which has the effect of maintaining the price in the market.

Generally, the life of a debenture runs 15 to 20 years, but increasingly toward the longer end, and occasionally up to a 25-year convertible debenture. Here, a sinking fund will usually retire about two thirds of the issue prior to maturity.

About the only event of default in convertibles is failure to pay the interest, meet the sinking fund payments, or pay the principal at maturity. Additional series of the same class can be issued with different maturity, different conversion rights, different call features, and different sinking fund features.

One of the most complicated provisions in any convertible agreement has to do with antidilution protection. Inasmuch as the conversion formula is established at the time of issuance with reference to the junior issues outstanding at the time and constitutes, in effect, a call on a fixed percentage of the total equity of the company, provision must be made for adjustment of that formula should there be a change in the number of outstanding junior shares. In other words, the purpose is to protect the exchange ratio.

Thus there is an automatic pro rata adjustment of the conversion rate to cover stock splits and stock dividends, but not for ordinary cash dividends. Where small or fractional stock dividends occur, the fractions may simply be allowed to accumulate to a predetermined figure before the formula conversion adjustment takes place.

A problem is created when additional common shares are issued for consideration which may be more or less than the conversion formula price. Hence a number of different provisions have come into use to deal with this situation. Some provide for the adjustment of the conversion price in any case where new stock is issued at less than the conversion price. In other words, an effort is made to reduce the conversion rate to the new price at which the additional common stock is issued. There are a number of approaches in use.

How Is the Issue Priced?

Whether for public offering or for use in connection with a merger, the issuer of a convertible debenture has four factors to take into account:

    1. The interest rate.

    2. The premium of conversion price above the current price of the common stock.

    3. The underwriting discount or spread.

    4. The issue price, whether at par, at premium, or at a discount.

A larger selling allowance in the spread encourages more aggressive dealer interest in the security. This is important when there is a heavy calendar of new issues and real competition for dealer and investor interest.

In setting terms, the issuer, of course, seeks the lowest possible interest rate and the highest reasonable conversion premium. The underwriter attempts to arrive at the optimum combination.

The state of the equity markets has more of an effect on

pricing than does the level of interest rates. In a rising market, the premium is generally higher; when market receptivity is doubtful, the premium narrows; and there are instances, particularly in private placements, when the conversion price is fixed at or below the market price of the common.

Publicly offered convertible debentures are usually priced to the public at par, with the underwriting spread subtracted from that price in the net proceeds paid over to the issuer. The objective is to sensitively adjust the various factors so that the issue is received well by investors, and goes to a slight premium in the secondary market. Some cushion is needed to absorb the resales by investors who change their minds.

Somewhat different considerations come into play when fixing the terms of the convertible preferred issue for use in a merger, but all can be tailored to meet the needs of the situation:

- The dividend rate is usually related to the return which has been paid on the common stock being acquired.
- The preferred rarely has a par value. But this can be fixed at any level, as can the liquidation preference.
- The call price can be a third factor and put at any level.

The Premium Question

The largest area of discussion in negotiations usually occurs over the question of what premium over the underlying common the new preferred will command in the market.

On the one hand, the acquirer naturally believes in the maximum premium. He has great pride in the stock and in where his company is going. He also seeks to convince the other side that there will be a maximum premium, because that will reduce the number of common shares he will eventually have to issue. On the other hand, the company to be acquired is generally not so sanguine about the value of the option.

Attempts to adjust for this difference of opinion create give and take in the dividend rate, in the liquidation preference, and in the call price.

That is also the reason why the companies that are engaged in an active acquisition program endeavor to have at least one convertible preferred issue actively traded in the market; it is easier to get a fix on the value of the consideration to be used in subsequent acquisitions.

One way of getting such an issue into the market is to offer it in an exchange to your own shareholders for a common stock, thereby shrinking the common stock capitalization, increasing the leverage, and creating a medium for exchange.

Floor Discussion

Question: How would you compare a debenture with warrants, say, with a convertible security?

Katzin: There is a considerable difference in two respects.

First, at some point, the warrants separate from the debenture, either initially or at some later date. When the warrants separate, the debenture has to stand on its own. It has lost the residual call that a convertible has. Therefore, a debenture with warrants generally carries an interest rate pretty close to what that company's credit requires in the market. The warrant is a sweetener which makes that straight debt salable.

On the other hand, the conversion right, except in limited situations, goes for the life of that debenture. The market values both the interest claim and the conversion right. Therefore, the interest rate will be lower than the straight credit requires.

Second, the warrants usually represent a call on fewer shares than a convertible does. The debentures are fully convertible into shares. Warrants can be flexible as to number of shares.

Question: In a situation where you have two classes of common stock, which one is issued to the public?

Katzin: Usually, the shares with restricted voting and ordinary dividend rights are issued to the public. However, if you want to list the shares, they must be voting.

Let's say you are going to sell half the company to the public, yet you want to keep two thirds of the voting power. You set a value on the stock that you retain so that, in effect, you get two votes per share of the equivalent of what the public is getting.

But you convert those two shares into one public share when you dispose of your holdings.

Question: What are the considerations from the acquirer's point of view and the seller's standpoint as to the registration of a convertible preferred issue?

Katzin: Ordinarily, if the stock that you are acquiring was publicly traded, the stock given in exchange is free stock. If it is a publicly held issue, you go through the proxy statement requirements of the SEC in order to affect the exchange.

The stock that comes out is of the same character as went in. In other words, the public stockholders have no restrictions. If you happen to be a controlling stockholder of the company being acquired, then the stock you get is similarly restrained. But ordinarily, you then are part of a larger enterprise, and you may find that you can dispose of your stock under the 1% rule over a period of time without the registration.

Obviously, it is of value to be in a listed company that has certain liquidity attributes, and it is of great value to have free stock. If the stock was not free stock going in, a special agreement would have to be obtained to assure that it can be registered on demand.

Question: Will you explain that 1% rule a little more clearly?

Katzin: There is an exemption under the SEC rules which permits a controlling stockholder, a director, or a group to sell up to 1% of the outstanding stock in unsolicited brokerage orders, or the equivalent of one week's trading on a listed stock, whichever is the greater number. Those shares can be sold without registration, even though the stock is ordinarily restricted.

This does not apply to stock that is taken under an investment letter. That cannot be traded under the 1% rule.

But there is this safety valve which permits a director, an officer, or a controlling stockholder to sell a little of his stock without registration. It is the so-called 1% rule.

Question: What is the frequency period?

Katzin: Each year. It gets very complicated if two directors try to sell, whether they are acting independently or together.

Question: Are the restrictive covenants in debenture issues easier than on straight debenture issues?

Katzin: Yes, they are much less restricted. A debenture issued with warrants is designed to sell on a yield basis in the open market without the warrant. Therefore, an attempt is made to build some quality into it by inserting some protective restrictions.

Chapter 21

HOW WALL ST. REACTS TO CORPORATE FINANCIAL DECISIONS

Martin Zausner

You have probably heard the comment, or perhaps made it yourself, "We don't worry about the price of our stock. We just concentrate on running a good company and let the stock market take care of itself."

Fortunately, most people who make this kind of statement do not really mean it. If they did, they would be doing a substantial disservice to their stockholders and violating a stockholder

Mr. Zausner is Chairman of the Board of Arthur Schmidt & Associates, Inc., a leading financial public relations firm. He is often cited for his work on tender offers, acquisitions, and corporate financial policy. He also is the author of *Corporate Policy and the Investment Community* (New York, Ronald Press Company 1968), and consulting editor, *The Stock Market Handbook* (New York, Dow-Jones-Erwin 1970).

This chapter is adapted from material copyrighted by the author and used here by special arrangement.

trust to develop the most realistically evaluated equity possible.

Per-share earnings are the most important single determinant of how Wall Street, collectively, prices a stock. But there are so many other factors, many of them intangible, that influence a stock's price. Not being aware of them can easily create a situation—unknowingly—that can drastically alter the price/earnings multiple the stock market assigns to a company.

Differing Corporate Policies

What I am referring to are the company's internal policies and their implementation. Most of these policies are financial—or financially related ones.

Whether or not a company realizes it, or even accepts the fact, the investment community scrutinizes its actions, regardless of what pertinence or importance you ascribe to them. To ignore the influential Wall Street factor is to do so at your own risk. Those on the Street comprise a generally astute group; they have long memories and keep careful records.

A Case Example

Let me give you an actual illustration of how two companies handled a similar situation in opposite ways—and came out with opposite results. Both situations occurred within the last half of the 1960's. The companies involved were considered to be glamour companies and each was making an acquisition that would increase its earnings by about 50%. Both were listed on the New York Stock Exchange, had good records, bright futures, and highly regarded managements.

To use fictitious names, Alpha Company was selling at 50 times earnings, while Beta Company was selling at 35 times earnings. Both Alpha and Beta reached out into nonglamour fields unrelated to their own operations to acquire companies which traditionally sold at 12 to 14 times earnings.

The head of each of the companies to be acquired was to

become president but not chief executive officer of the surviving company. On the surface, there seemed little fit between the acquiring company and the company to be acquired.

At the crucial point of explaining the acquisition, the methods of the two parent companies differed. Alpha made it clear in every announcement that it would be the dominant company, that its chief executive officer would continue in that role, and that its management philosophy would dominate the organization. Beta made its merger seem a combination of two equals, and never indicated who would be chief executive officer or how the company was going to be run.

Alpha widely explained the logic of the acquisition to the investment community, made it palatable by reviewing the dynamics of the situation, and convinced Wall Street to accept the fit as management saw it. Beta did not bother to explain its acquisition other than in general terms that were virtually meaningless. Security analysts just could not figure out the logic of Beta's acquisition on their own, and Beta's management gave them little help. The results of these different approaches to a similar situation show a remarkable difference in how Wall Street reacted to them.

Alpha retained its 50 price/earnings multiple with no difficulty. Beta saw its multiple start a sharp slide the second day after the merger was reported. Six months after its merger was first announced, Beta's multiple had dropped from 35 times earnings to less than 17. The stock of Beta after the acquisition —which was transacted through an exchange of stock—had a total value in the stock market of less than what Beta's was before the merger. Its stockholders saw the total market value of their equity drop by over $150 million in less than six months.

Important Indexes

The results of differing internal policies usually are not so obvious, immediately reflected, and easy to calculate. Nevertheless, they can be significant. The financial ratio, for example, should be an item of corporate concern. Wall Street uses it as a guide to determine whether a company is a leader in its industry, and leaders traditionally enjoy high multiples on their stock.

Examine your return on equity. If most companies in your industry earn 10% after taxes and your company earns 7%, you are going to be regarded as a marginal company in your field. That may be a true representation. If so, there is nothing you can do about it other than to improve your operations. But if your balance sheet is filled with nonproductive assets that should have been written off long ago, by doing so now you can prove you are as efficient as the others in your industry.

A low return on sales brings similar reaction from Wall Street. Again, if this occurs because you are a marginal producer, there is little you can do about it. But if you are a low-profit margin from a unique product that results from a unique product mix—which is often the case—break down your sales into various areas to help show how you compete effectively and efficiently against your competitors in each product category.

What is your attitude toward allocation of capital funds? Is it the same as Wall Street's, which decrees that capital should flow to operations where the best return can be obtained? If you are in an industry with a traditionally poor return on equity, are your retained earnings, borrowings, and capital going into the same industry? Or are you finding more effective ways to use them?

Wall Street no longer accepts as rational the position that just because you are in a specific industry, additional funds—other than for maintenance and efficiency—should be funneled into the same industry. If you continue to pour additional money into low-return industries, you cannot expect Wall Street to value your company highly.

Acquisitions & Other Considerations

Virtually every company boasts that it is on an acquisition program, but few actually know how to make acquisitions of any consequence. You have to prove to Wall Street, first, that you know how to make acquisitions and, second, that you know how to manage acquired companies.

The day is past when all you had to do was announce you were embarking on an acquisition campaign to watch the price of your stock run up. And even if you make acquisitions, you have to do more than obtain an immediate increase in per-share earnings. Now Wall Street wants to know the underlying strength of the acquired companies and whether earnings can be increased in the acquired company after it comes under your management.

How you pay for acquisitions is another factor that affects Wall Street's opinion. Are you merely trading stock and achieving no earnings increment? Or are you using cash, leverage, or high-priced stock to make acquisitions? Each will affect Wall Street's reaction.

Another aspect to look for in making an acquisition is: What will it do to the past year's results, if they must be restated? Will it make your earnings record look better or worse? Be cautious about changing a rapid growth record into a static one. It may be easy to explain how the true earnings picture should look, but you may not get a chance to explain it. Many investors are put off from learning more about your company if a quick glance at the revised earnings seems to indicate that your company is going nowhere.

Examine your methods of raising capital. Are you a company that points with pride to how strong financially you are—that you have no debt? If so, Wall Street will not appreciate you nearly as much as if you had gone into debt and put the money to work efficiently; or, had at least taken your excess cash to repurchase your own stock and shrink your capitalization to a point where you make the most productive use of it.

Even supposedly unimportant items like a company's name can affect Wall Street's reaction. If your company is named XYZ Steel Company when XYZ Electronics would be much more descriptive, you are going to find it difficult to get people to accept the fact that you are really an electronics company which deserves a high electronic multiple rather than a low steel multiple, despite a good earnings record.

Handling Earnings. In another area, think of the many ways of handling per-share earnings. One of the most important things Wall Street is seeking is growth—and by growth the financial community means continuous growth. All other things being equal, if two companies showed a five-year earnings progression from, say, $1.50 to $2.75 a share, but one company accomplished it by increasing its earnings in each of the five years while the other experienced an earnings decline in one of these five years, the odds are that Wall Street would evaluate them differently.

Consecutive annual earnings usually mean a growth stock to Wall Street; hence, a high price/earnings multiple. Fluctuations in annual earnings often signify cyclical situations, resulting in a low multiple. The difference between the low and high multiple accorded to such situations can be significant—the growth stock often being evaluated at double or more than that of a cyclical stock.

Suppose your company is having a disappointing year. What can you do about it? Usually, nothing. A bad year is a bad year, and you have to take your lumps. But suppose it is only slightly bad. Then you may have some discretion to determine whether the year will be a declining one or an increasing one.

There are many adjustments made toward the end of the year that affect earnings—depreciation, special writeoffs, charitable and profit-sharing contributions, bonuses, and a host of other factors—that can legitimately be handled in one way or another. Consider:

▼ If your company earned $2.25 per share last year, the difference between $2.27 and $2.23 is important in terms of the investment community's evaluation of your company. True, the immediate reactions of Wall Street will probably be negative in either case. But, in subsequent years, it can make quite a difference. The main point that will stand out years later will be whether you had an unbroken string of annual increases in earnings, not how small the increase was in just one year in the series.

▲ Conversely, if your earnings are going to show a substantial jump in any one year, conservative handling of discretionary items gives a lower target to shoot at the following year and also "saves" some earnings to help that year.

However, if earnings are going to be really off, you might just as well get all the bad news out of the way at once. Write off everything you can and start the next year with a clean slate.

Dividend & Reporting Procedures

Another internal action that establishes the company's character in the mind of the investment community is dividend policy. The impact of dividend policy is usually evidence of the type of investors who are attracted as stockholders and the price action of the company's stock. It is not my intention to discuss how large or how small the cash dividend of a company should be. Earnings growth, current cash situation, cash flow, future cash requirements, and the nature of a business are the primary determinants of the size of the dividend. After these factors are taken into consideration, a great deal of flexibility is still possible.

If a company elects to pay a cash dividend, then consistency and continuity are important. The reputation of a company that cuts or eliminates its dividends suffers drastically. Therefore, a dividend rate should be set so that payments can be maintained despite typical earnings fluctuations.

Even a token dividend paid during the year can prove important since it may enable a company to report—some years later—that it has paid annual dividends without interruption for, say, 25 years.

However, if a dividend must be cut, it should be done as quickly as possible and all at once. It is far better to have one large dividend cut—and to get it out of the way—than to reduce the dividend in several agonizing stages.

Making Announcements. How a company reports its

financial information clearly affects Wall Street's reaction. This is true in terms of when it is reported and what is reported.

Let us look at when it is reported. Poor timing can result in needless problems. Naturally, every company would like to inform its stockholders at the same time it makes announcements to the financial press, and many a company holds its announcements until the printed report is mailed. If doing so means delaying an earnings announcement for several days after it is ready, the delay can have harmful consequences.

When earnings are on target with general expectations, little harm is done. When they differ—being either higher or lower—the stock often reflects the earnings report by moving up or down before the announcement is actually made. This causes both antagonism and distrust.

Virtually every company I have spoken to which does not issue its earnings as soon as they become available justifies such action on the basis that the information is confidential; only two or three executives know the results, and they can be trusted. This sounds good, but I doubt if it is ever the case.

We once made a postmortem tracking operation to determine how many people knew of a "confidential" earnings report that somehow got out. After we counted up the few top executives who knew about it, the internal accounting people, the auditing, legal, and public relations staffs, the printers, and the secretaries involved with each of these groups, we came to almost 50 people who were aware of the supposedly closely guarded secret.

Looked at realistically, when more than one person knows, you have to assume that the news is going to leak out. You should eliminate this danger by making immediate announcements. This is true not only of earnings, but of acquisitions and other major corporate developments. You should never expose your company to the danger of having its stock move up or down just before important news is announced. When this happens, suspicions are aroused—and rightly so—that certain individuals learn of events before they become generally known in Wall Street. This is one way to steer investors away from your stock.

In terms of what is reported, make sure you give full, truthful explanations. Vague statements lead to conjecture which is often incorrect; misleading statements and projections will rapidly develop distrust. Give true answers, even though the news may be unfavorable. If you do not, rumors will start which can make a situation seem worse than it actually is. Correct misleading statements and impressions, whether made by the company or by outsiders, as quickly as possible.

Try not to withhold facts from Wall Street under the guise of protecting your competitive position, when the information you are concealing is already known to your competitors—which is a typical situation. To an important degree, how closely your company will be followed by Wall Street will be tied to the amount of or lack of information you are willing to provide.

Concluding Note

I have touched on only a few of the many financial and financially related policies that are sure to get a reaction from Wall Street. Virtually every action in this area will be one of the bits that contribute to determining how Wall Street will assess your company.

No matter how sound your internal financial procedures are in terms of courting favorable reaction, they are not good enough if Wall Street does not know about them. Internal procedures have to be developed to let Wall Street know about company activities. A well-developed and well-executed financial relations program must be conducted with specific executives and special counsel assigned to the task. A company must accept its obligation to keep Wall Street informed, rather than assume that it is Wall Street's responsibility to find out about the company.

Keep in mind that every time you make a decision on specific aspects of financing, you are influencing the way Wall

Street evaluates the price of your stock. This should in no way be the sole determinant of your decision, but you should certainly be aware of the consequences of any such action before the final decision is reached.

Floor Discussion

Question: You made the point that Wall Street looks to the nature of the acquisitions, whether it is for cash or some sort of debentures or stock or what, but you didn't give us any indication as to how Wall Street regards these different forms of acquisition. Would you care to comment on this?

Zausner: All other things being equal, Wall Street is looking for leverage which will give the greatest immediate impact on earnings growth. Therefore, any form of acquisition which will do the reverse of diluting earnings will be best. Obviously, cash will increase earnings per share greater than any other means.

Borrowed cash is best because it means you are working with the greatest amount of leverage. Thus, if you examine it from the viewpoint: Will my form of making the acquisition give the greatest impact to earnings?—it will be what Wall Street is looking for.

Question: How does Wall Street look at conglomerates making acquisitions, and what sorts of acquisitions should you, in effect, be making?

Zausner: Today, you want to avoid the conglomerate taint. There is no question about it. You are better off making acquisitions either that have obvious fits to your company or are going to enable you to invade a new area. Now this doesn't mean you are going to invade ten new areas, because if you invade ten new areas you are going to end up being a conglomerate.

But, let's say, you are a drug company and you want to make an obvious acquisition that is not directly related. Cosmetics would be one example, and water pollution would be another, that fit into this type of activity. Both would make sense, yet be different. But if you acquired a steel mill, you are likely going to have trouble.

Question: Who should do the communicating with Wall Street? And how often should a company communicate with the Street?

Zausner: I think if the president could spend all of his time talking with Wall Street, that would be fine and there would be no need for anyone else to do it. But obviously, he has other functions. And the same is true of the chief financial officer.

When you get into the area of financial public relations, you have to be extremely careful. Who is doing the talking about your company from the financial public relations counsel you have retained? Similarly, you should be just as careful who internally is talking about your company. I think a clear rule should be that only the president, chief financial officer, or a financial spokesman from your financial relations firm should be talking about your company.

Now, in terms of how often you should be talking to Wall Street, there are both written and oral communications. When you count up the number of obvious times, and add in quarterly, dividend, and annual reports, and preliminary and profit statements, you are talking to Wall Street a minimum of eleven times by written communications.

Add to this special announcements on acquisitions, capital expenditure programs, new product development—things of that nature—and it can run way up. I think you should be careful, though, to try and hold this to a minimum. Send to Wall Street only what is pertinent. Say to yourself, "Does the analyst really want to know about this? Does he want to file it for future reference?" If the answers are "Yes," send it to him. If it is just another mailing to keep him informed about routine things, don't send it to him.

Now the other aspect is oral communications. How often should you be talking to a security analyst? I think it is a good idea to have small luncheon meetings of 10 or 12 analysts and to do this on a routine basis of, say, every six or eight weeks.

Zero in on the people you specifically want to reach. Not only in New York City. It just might be Boston, Los Angeles, San Francisco, Dallas, Chicago, Atlanta, and so on depending on your own particular interests.

If you are a company that doesn't have wide-spread public ownership and you should have more exposure on the West Coast because of facilities or sales there, you should have more meetings on the West Coast.

Your own company interest will determine where, and how often, you are going to be talking. But it should be routine, it should be frequent, and it should be with small groups of interested people.

Question: How do you reconcile these intimate meetings in various cities around the country with the view that if you are going to tell anybody anything you have to tell everybody everything at the same time?

Zausner: Obviously, everybody wants news but that is not the analysts' collective purpose in attending. You don't arrange for a small meeting of 10 or 12 people in order to announce that "We earned—" (and then give them the quarterly figures) or to tell them that "We are going to make an acquisition which we are going to announce next week."

What you want to discuss with these people attending the meetings are such things as the background of your company, your operating philosophy, where your direction is, and so forth. You want to give them an understanding of your company. You do not give them news; even if you had some news item to give out that day, you would not tell that particular audience.

Then there is no conflict. Unfortunately, many attorneys don't understand this. They have never attended such meetings and assume that the company spokesmen are giving out all sorts of corporate secrets to a select group of 10 to 12 people.

We have run into this problem with attorneys who said, "You can't do this." And we said, "Come to the meetings. Find out what we tell people." And when they did, they learned for themselves no inside information was divulged, and yet a lot was accomplished at the meeting. Thus there is no reason to be concerned about holding small group meetings.

Question: In your opinion, who are we writing the annual reports for? And also what do you consider the principal weaknesses in them from the analyst's point of view?

Zausner: The two most important audiences will always be your stockholders and security analysts. Now with stockholders you have a problem; they don't readily understand financial language. For example, "return on equity" is a meaningless phrase to most stockholders.

Or perhaps the report mentions something about investment tax credit, and they don't even know what the words mean, much less understand how you carry it on your books. So you have to handle the annual report in a way that will get across the basic facts of your company to your stockholders, without talking down to the security analysts.

Now the other part of the question was in regard to what the security analysts look for in your annual report. They look for several things, such as the sales and earnings mix, who you sell to, how you buy, and other factors that affect your company. You have to provide analysts with sufficient information so that they can understand not only what happened last year, but also what makes your company tick.

Index

(NOTE: page numbers in **Bold Face** indicate exhibits)

Donaldson, Gordon, 87, 92
Dow Jones Industrial Average, 57, 58

E

Earnings
    conglomerate, reporting, 41-42
    measurement of, 12-13
    per-share. *See* Per-share earnings
    retained, 12
Earnings before interest and taxes, 119
Economy
    effect of federal policy to dampen, 62, 64-67, **65**
    future assumptions about the, 138-145
    government management of the, 59-67
    slowing the, 61-67, **63**
Ellis, Charles D., 85-102
Entrepreneurs, sources of venture capital for, 1-10
Equities
    preference of professional investors for, 70
    underlying, valuing, 46-47
Equity financing
    expense of, 73-74
    public, 69-84
Equity offerings, pricing, 78-79
Equity securities, combinations of debt and, 85-102
Eurodollar financing, 197-211
Expansion, public equity financing for, 69-84
Extraordinary nonrecurring expense, 52

F

Factoring, 175-176
Federal, Reserve credit, money supply and, 62, 63
Finance companies, commercial
    developments affecting nature of business of, 180-183
    services and techniques provided by, 175-180

Financial analysis, long-term capital structure and, 118-133
Financial decisions, coporate, reaction of Wall Street to, 275-287
Financial Executives Institute, 41
Financial ratios, common, 120-124
Financial reporting procedure, Wall Street's reaction to, 281-284
Financing
    accounts receivable, 176-178
    cash flow forecasts and, 147-158
    choosing right type of, 76-77
    commitment to, 18-19
    debt and equity, 136-137
    equity, 69-84
        expense of, 73-74
        for expansion, 69-84
    Eurodollar, 197-211
    impact of recent accounting developments on, 36-55
    industrial time sales, 179-180
    intermediate, 134-146
        sources of, 135
    inventory, 178
    long-term, 134-146
    managing, choosing an investment banker for, 75-76
    methods of, 109-114
    mistakes made by management, 19-24
    nondilutionary, 253
    off-balance sheet, 14
    secured, 174-184
    segmental, 159-173
        definition of, 159
        financial leverage and, 162-164
        sale of a minority interest in a division, 161-162, 167-168
        sale of a total division, 165-173
    venture, 1-10
Fiscal policy, government, 61-67
Flink, Salomon J., 147-158
Ford, Gerald, 217

◼ W ◼

◼ Z ◼